❧ Custody

Books by Elizabeth Morgan, M.D.

The Making of a Woman Surgeon
Solo Practice: A Woman Surgeon's Story
Custody: A True Story

Custody

➤ A TRUE STORY

Elizabeth Morgan, M.D.

LITTLE, BROWN AND COMPANY

Boston   Toronto

FIRST EDITION

Some of the material in this book appeared previously in *Self*
magazine.

Library of Congress Cataloging-in-Publication Data

Morgan, Elizabeth, 1947–
Custody: a true story.

1. Morgan, Elizabeth, 1947–   . 2. Divorced mothers—
United States—Biography. 3. Women surgeons—United
States—Biography. 4. Custody of children—United States.
I. Title.
HQ834.M67   1986   306.8′9   85–16041
ISBN 0-316-58294-8

FG

Designed by Patricia Dunbar

Published simultaneously in Canada
by Little, Brown & Company (Canada) Limited

PRINTED IN THE UNITED STATES OF AMERICA

To Lucy

author's note

ALTHOUGH THIS IS an autobiographical work, I have not used actual names for any of the individuals mentioned except for certain members of my family, my secretaries, and their families. None of the other names in this book are intended to refer to actual people; any resemblance between such fictional names and actual persons is entirely coincidental. For the purpose of conveying my subjective perceptions of the story, some figures in the book (including Ms. Jones and Nadine Hoskins) are fictional composites. Neither the events described nor the attributes of those characters refer to an actual individual.

acknowledgments

MY FAMILY and friends helped Lucy and me; Molly Friedrich, my agent, encouraged me; Genevieve Young, my editor, criticized what I wrote; Beverly Smith, Elaine Gordon, and Nancy Williamson transformed my illegible scribble to the printed word. There would be no book without their help. To everyone, all I can say is, "Thank you, I am very grateful."

ᴥ Custody

⇒ *one*

*M*Y MARRIAGE, like a hemorrhaging patient with a gun-
shot wound in the chest, was rapidly dying. I had my
hands folded on my pregnant stomach, and inside me, under
my dress, I felt Lucy's feet kick a violent tattoo. She would be
born any day. It was less than a week from my "due date" for
delivery and I was exhausted. Today, a Friday, had been my last
full day in the office, but I would be seeing patients part-time
during the coming week. I was already too tired to move. The
past nine months had used up all my energy — not only my
pregnancy, but my futile struggle to save the life of a hopeless
marriage. I had to find more energy somewhere, to cope with
its death.

It was nine o'clock at night and it had just turned dark. The
damp August heat was oppressive indoors, even with the air-
conditioning on. I could hear, outside, the cicadas screeching
loudly and the occasional burp of a tree frog and howl of a dog.
I sat slumped on the sofa, listening to my husband. Pregnancy
had made me a physical wreck; my brief marriage had made me
an emotional one.

"You what?" I heaved myself up at last from the depths of
the sofa and turned to stare at him, feeling betrayed, attacked,
dismayed. "You what?" I almost shouted. I could feel my eyes
start to flash and my hands itched to grab something and smash
it, but I knew the old fire was gone. I was miserable. I felt defeated more than angry. There was nothing within my reach

except July's plastic-surgery journal. I couldn't destroy it — I hadn't read it yet. As a plastic surgeon, I needed my journals, especially if I was destined to be a surgeon and a single mother as well.

And after all, what was the use of fighting the obvious? It was time to admit defeat. My impetuous, romantic marriage was a complete and total failure. My husband — intelligent, gifted, and, in courtship, charming — was a man I could not live with. Looking back, I now could see that we had been doomed from the start, but I had been too much in love then. I was still deeply in love. He possessed me. I had sworn never to leave my husband. Now, glaring at him, I knew I still loved him but that my love was of no use. With a shock, I saw that the man I had married, my dream-come-true, was an illusion.

I wanted to stay. I wanted this not to be true, but I had to leave him now or never. I would not subject my child, my unborn daughter, to a home of strife. It would destroy her. I did not have my mother's strength. She had an indestructible cheerfulness that had brought her and her children through upheaval and chaos. If I stayed with my husband now, Lucy would be trapped forever by our jangled emotions. It had taken me thirty years to untangle my feelings toward my own father. I had to protect Lucy from what I had suffered. She would have her problems. I didn't want her to inherit mine as well.

My surgical training had taught me to be decisive and practical in the face of disaster. Sleepless, wrenching nights during my seven years of surgical residency had trained me well. This catastrophe, somehow, I would survive. I hoisted myself gracelessly to my feet.

"It's over," I told him flatly. "Our marriage is over. I'm leaving." I turned to make my dramatic exit and lumbered like a wounded buffalo from the living room.

I had worked, pregnant, sick, and with a breaking heart, for nine months. At least I had found time to have an amniocentesis done. The test results had been normal and, incidentally, showed that my baby would be a girl. "Thank God it's a girl," I said to myself as I lurched from the living room in tears. "I don't think I would have the strength to raise a boy single-handed." She would be Lucy Domenica — Lucy was my husband's choice; her middle name, Domenica, was mine. It is my mother's name, and my mother and I are very close. "I'll keep the damned name. It's one less thing to think about." I leaned against the wall in the hallway and started to sob, but it seemed wrong: I was too desperately miserable to cry.

I waddled into the bathroom and pulled a large plastic bag out from under the sink. Most of life's problems can be solved by a large plastic bag. I glanced up at the mirror. Once upon a time I had been pretty. Now, tears were streaming down my face, which was puffy and blotched with pregnancy. My long, brown hair straggled limply. Whatever else might happen, my looks were gone. I averted my gaze and grabbed the soap dish. It clattered into the plastic bag. My brush followed. Comb. Deodorant. Curlers. Lipstick.

"What is going on, Elizabeth?" It was my mother. She had lived with me for two years when I was single. Just before that, she had been extremely ill. She had almost died. Her illness had been followed by a separation from my father, and she had lived with us since our marriage. During my pregnancy, my mother had driven me to work when I was too sick to drive but had had to go in. She had looked after me. She had been a housekeeper for us and a peacemaker, and it had tired her.

In her bathrobe, she looked in from the hallway; her silver hair was brushed back from her face, her gray eyes anxious. She clutched an open jar of cold cream. I had a horrible fear that the fiasco of my marriage would make her ill again and would kill her. It couldn't happen. I love my mother very much. She is a quiet person, whose feelings run very deep. She would suffer with me. Somehow I had to protect her, but still I needed her. Lucy needed her.

"I'm leaving, Mother. It's over. I'm throwing in the towel,"

I choked, turning my face away. I threw my towels and washcloth into the plastic bag.

"It's a big decision, Elizabeth. Are you sure?" She spoke dispassionately, as though we were talking about tomatoes in a grocery store. It stopped me short.

"I'm positive." I turned to face her, one hand on my hips, the other clutching the plastic bag. "Look at my face. The happy, expectant mother? Who am I kidding? I'm being destroyed by this. Why do I have to love him? This marriage is hopeless. Haven't you known? For months? From the start?" Toothpaste, vitamins, plastic cup skittered into the plastic bag with a furious clatter. She didn't answer at first. My mother is British and has a British reluctance to interfere with anything, especially her children's lives.

"I've seen no hope at all for a long time, Elizabeth," she said at last, "but it was not for me to say anything. It's your marriage. Are you sure now is the time? Why not after the baby? Wouldn't it be easier?" she asked gently.

"For him?" I snarled bitterly. "Less embarrassing?"

"I'm not thinking of him," my mother snapped. She only snaps when she is upset. "Easier for you."

I leaned on the sink, to get the ache out of my back. "I've been a dope. I've been a fool, but I'm a surgeon. There's one thing you can say for surgeons: they can make a damned decision. Putting it off for a week or a month serves no purpose. It makes it worse. For everyone. If Lucy is born on time — God willing — I have exactly one month before I go back to work. Five weeks before I start to operate. I am exhausted, Mother. Totally exhausted." I yanked a Kleenex out of the box on the sink and blew my nose. "My practice is busier than it ever has been. I've been awake every night for weeks. I can't go on like this. If I'm going to leave, I have to do it now. Mother, I can't move out and cope with a baby and be a surgeon too," I wailed in panic. It woke Lucy up. She kicked furiously inside me, her feet making a frantic journey across my abdomen.

"May I come too?" my mother inquired. She is so practical. I looked at her and started to laugh. "As long as you don't mind my methods of packing," I said, dragging the bag along the floor into the master bedroom. I yanked out a drawer and shook my underwear into the plastic bag. "I'll come back tomorrow with Jim and get the rest of our clothes." Jim, my older brother, is a commodities broker. Whenever I get in a jam, he rallies around to help me out. He has always ended up helping me move, even though he hates moving as much as I do.

I surveyed the top of the dresser grimly, then I lined my makeup and perfume along the edge. "Bombs away." With a scoop of my arm, bottles and brushes hurtled into the plastic bag. It made me feel better. I needed action — anything to block out the pain. Twenty minutes and six plastic bags later, my mother and I had hoisted the last bulging bag into the trunk of the car. My husband, his arms folded rigidly across his chest, followed us out to watch. I climbed, ungainly, behind the wheel and turned the key in the ignition. Nothing happened. I turned to my mother.

"I'm going to sleep on the grass if this car won't start. I'm not going back inside," I said defiantly.

"You're in reverse, dear," replied my mother. With the car in neutral, the engine roared alive, drowning out the cicadas. Gravel shot out from under the tires. We lurched out of the driveway into the blackness of the country road.

"Do you know where we're going?" inquired my mother when I braked violently at the crossroad.

"Home. Thank God I have a place to go," I said. Pregnancy had left me too tired to sell or rent out my tiny townhouse, my home when I was single. "Do you want me to drop you off with Daddy?"

"Good heavens, no." My mother sounded shocked. My parents had remained polite after they started living apart, but nothing more. Though I am very close to my mother, my relationship with my father is different. I am fond of my father because he is my father. He is a man of many talents, but he likes to be in charge and he demands much of other people. When I was growing up, I always felt that no success of mine was enough to satisfy him. He had been a spy, a guerrilla fighter, and a war hero in World War II, and had never been happier. He was a psychologist by profession, as my mother had been. She retired after her illness. He never fully retired. My mother helped patients by listening and advising. My father helped his by inspiring them to fight against their problems and conquer them. He did a great deal of good. In some ways Rob, my younger brother — a sky diver, a Green Beret, a boxer — takes after my father, but I feel close to my brothers. To me, my father is always hard to understand.

"This will upset your father terribly. There's no need for him to know about tonight," my mother said hastily. "Don't get him involved." I nodded. We needed peace and quiet. I thought I had found it when I married.

I thought of my husband and stamped on the accelerator as though it were he. I had been blinded by his charm and his intelligence. Or had I deceived myself? He was not what I had thought. Was that his fault, or mine? Had he loved me? I had loved him as I had loved no other man. I had stored up my affection for eleven years during medical school and my surgical training. I had only myself to blame. I married him. No one made me do it.

The car shot ahead. If there was one thing I was determined Lucy would have, it was what I had never had: a peaceful, happy home — a port in the stormy seas of life.

"I'll say this for you, Elizabeth. Once you make a decision, you don't let the grass grow under your feet," said my mother. Looming, black trees rushed past in the darkness. "We'll get there just as well if you drive the speed limit."

I slowed down, swerving to avoid an opossum taking a nap

in the middle of the road. "Mine is going to be the first divorce in the family, ever," I said.

"No one will be surprised," said my mother. "Jim was never enthusiastic about your marriage." I smiled. Jim has a very expressive face. He had never said a word against my marriage. I was grateful for that. What gave him away was his face. When I mentioned my marriage, Jim's face closed like a door.

We passed a raccoon out for a walk in the ditch. A groundhog reared up from the underbrush to glare at the headlights. Another left turn and we were on the main road to home. "I never dreamed I would be a divorcée," I added plaintively. "I want to be a wife and mother."

"You don't always get what you want in life," said my mother gently, as though to a child. "Surgeons tend to be dogmatic. One should keep an open mind." She patted my shoulder in the dark.

"I tried so hard." I put my left hand over my mouth to force down the tears. I couldn't drive and cry at the same time.

"You were a good wife," said my mother loyally. "Marriage has been very good for you. And at least you have your child. You couldn't have known you weren't compatible." It wasn't true, I thought. I should have known. I had known. It was there to see, but I was swept away. "Life is full of the unexpected. Have you considered how you can stay in private practice and manage as a single mother?" continued my mother. It took my attention off my tears. I couldn't cry and be practical.

"I'll manage," I said firmly. The car rattled across some potholes. "At least my suffering about my marriage is behind me. I've done that." There was no reply. "Don't you think?" I asked.

"It's only just begun," said my mother. "Your father and I have been married for thirty-seven years. I will always love your father. I will never get over him. Never. Your marriage was mercifully brief but you will never be the same." My mother did not raise her voice, but she spoke with intense feeling and conviction. She was right. I had a faint grasp of what she had been through in the past few years. "By the way," she added, "that light was red."

"I can see it," I said, stepping on the brake.

"No, you can't see it," persisted my mother. "It's behind you. You drove right through it."

When we got to my house, we both flopped into bed, exhausted. I closed my eyes to sleep. I saw my husband. I heard his voice. I opened my eyes to avoid him. I couldn't escape. The heart does ache, physically. I lay awake all night, staring at the curtained window, aching. Nothing, it seemed, would ever take away the pain. Time, perhaps, but each minute was interminable, and as the hours marched on, I felt worse.

In the morning, I called Jim. He hates being called early on a Saturday morning. I waited until nine, but I couldn't wait any longer. My life was in turmoil. I had to keep doing things and moving out was what I had to do. Jim's phone was picked up on the third ring, dropped, and picked up noisily. There was a sleepy grunt.

"Jim?" I spoke hesitantly. "I walked out on him last night. Can I ask a big favor? Can you help us get our things?"

There was a silence, and then, "Oh sure, I'm sorry about that. I'll be right over." Enormous self-control and generosity lay behind that cheerful reply. He was half-awake. I knew he wanted to go back to sleep.

"Want me to deal with him?" offered Jim an hour later, driving me out in his car for the final move. "I know how to handle him." Jim is a big, dark man. He can look intimidating until he smiles. Then he betrays his sunny disposition. He is still the same gregarious boy that invited the neighborhood in to eat mother's fresh-baked cherry pie while she was out shopping.

"No, Jim, thank you. It's not like that. Really," I said in a flat voice. I had swung between shock and tears all morning.

"I have no personal need to kill the guy," Jim hastened to explain. "Live and let live, but hell, you're my sister." He looked over at me thoughtfully. "Listen, I know it's like the end of the world, but you have to cut your losses." He turned into the driveway. "Here we are. His car's gone. He probably figured I'd come out here looking for him with a baseball bat." Jim came around to open the car door for me and hauled me out.

"I'm here to help," I told Jim firmly.

"You sit where I put you, kid. I don't need pregnant women to help me carry suitcases," he said in disgust. "You stay here and I'll have you moved out in an hour." He parked me in the kitchen. "Sit, Fido." He patted me on the head. I settled down like a tired blimp. I looked around the kitchen. I wanted my husband to be there. I wanted him to want me. I wanted him to be the man I loved. I was dreaming like a child. Five hours later, Jim led me through the house, opening drawers and closets for my inspection.

"You've got everything, Jim. The rest is all his stuff," I said at last. We walked to the front door. On the way out, Jim picked up the white wicker bassinet that I had bought for Lucy, and a black umbrella.

"Yours or his?" Jim held up the umbrella.

"I don't know." Jim inspected it closely and grinned. "I think it's mine. Okay, kid. The party's over." He stuffed the umbrella in the bassinet, stuck the bassinet under his arm, and slammed the front door behind us. "Do me one favor. Don't go in labor till I get you back home and unpacked." He drove me home. I couldn't talk, so he turned on the radio. The rings on my hand seemed to mock me as they lay across my bulging stomach. Surreptitiously, I slipped them off and put them into my purse. There was no point in pretending anymore.

* * *

One week later, I went into labor. My obstetrician, Dr. Prescott, had told me to call him when I had contractions regularly every five minutes.

"Good timing, Elizabeth," said Dr. Prescott, when I called him at midnight on Friday. "Pack your toothbrush, dear. Have your husband bring you in." I didn't explain. I couldn't. My husband was precious to me still. I had to protect him as well as myself. My mother called Jim and the two of them took me to the hospital. Then I told them to go home and get some sleep. I asked my mother to call my husband once she got home. I didn't have the physical or the emotional strength to do it. I thought I would just start crying. Jim and my mother offered to stay with me. They had done too much for me already. I couldn't let them stay. They were both tired; my mother's face was white with fatigue. Besides, if I couldn't have my husband, I wanted to be alone. The labor room was gray and bare, the way I felt. There was a big window with the shade pulled down, a sink, a television, and gray walls all around me. I concentrated on a gray wall. I had plenty to think about, but I couldn't think coherently. My thoughts were like bouillabaisse — an occasional solid memory in a brown stew of reflection. My memories were of my marriage and they were not happy. I let them slip away from me while I studied the gray wall impassively. I felt empty, as though all my feelings had drained away.

"Nice, strong contractions," said the night nurse approvingly when she came in to turn on the monitor at my bedside. She put the Doppler probe on my stomach and turned up the sound to listen to Lucy's heartbeat. I heard it racing away. It sounded much too fast.

"What's the rate?" I asked quickly.

"One-forty, Dr. Morgan." The nurse smiled. "That's normal." She turned down the light and left me. I couldn't sleep. The contractions were not painful yet, only uncomfortable. The night nurse returned to check me again an hour later. She did a pelvic exam. "You're moving along quickly now," she said after examining my cervix. Peeling off her gloves and tossing them away, she glanced at the clock. "You started at two-forty with the cervix dilated to three centimeters. You're up to five now." The measurement refers to the width of the cervix as it relaxes to let the baby through. At about nine centimeters, the second stage of labor begins, because then the opening is wide enough for the baby's head to push through the cervix, into the vagina, and out into the world. At six AM, after six hours of labor, my cervix had fully dilated, and the second stage of labor began. With it, the contractions changed. In the first stage, there was discomfort. When the second stage began, my contractions advanced briskly from uncomfortable to painful to frank torture. I gritted my teeth, arched my back, and moaned with each contraction. I tried to remember the right way to breathe. The breathing routine was pure garbage. It was mildly distracting for pain — it did nothing for torture. The night nurse hustled in again on her rounds before the change of shifts.

"Eight to nine centimeters," she said triumphantly, after examining me. "You're having quite a bit of discomfort now, aren't you?"

"Yes, I am," I said through clenched teeth as a contraction hit me.

"You're not doing natural childbirth, are you?"

"Not now I'm not."

"I'm so glad. Why these girls do it, I don't know. Did you discuss anesthesia with your doctor?"

"Yes. I would like an epidural," I gasped.

"Good decision. I'll organize it right up."

Ten minutes later, she had me sitting on the edge of the bed, clutching a pillow to my stomach. A sleepy anesthesiologist in rumpled scrub clothes came in to stand beside me.

"Hi, Dr. Morgan. I'm Dr. Ridgeway. Ever had one of these before?"

"No." The pain from the contractions made me monosyllabic. Whoever he was, I wanted him to hurry up.

"Well, you'll feel cold soap on your back. Must be funny to be on the other side of medicine, being a patient for a change." I didn't see the humor in it at all.

"Now you'll feel a needle stick into your back," he continued. "This is to numb the skin. Don't jump. Try to relax."

I relaxed — not because he told me to, but because the contraction subsided.

"Now you'll feel pressure."

"Ouch."

"Is that sharp?"

"Yes."

"Sorry." There was a pause. "I'm giving you more Xylocaine." Another pause. "Now you'll feel pressure. Am I right?"

"Yes."

"I am about to enter the epidural space. It will feel as though you have been kicked in the back."

I felt a sickening thud in my lower back and groaned as the needle pierced the membrane around the nerves in my spinal canal.

"Do you feel all right?" Dr. Ridgeway asked anxiously.

"Yes." I felt horrible, but yes seemed as good an answer as any.

"Now you will feel electric shocks in your legs. I am injecting the Marcaine anesthetic." For the moment that he did so, I felt as though I was being electrocuted. I thought I was going to be sick. Then the electric shocks in my legs subsided. Dr. Ridgeway taped the long, thin plastic tubing coming out of my lower back over my shoulder. This tube was my lifeline for pain. If the labor pain returned, he could inject Marcaine through the tubing into the space around my pelvic nerves to make them numb.

"All done. Give it fifteen minutes to begin to work. Goodbye." He left with a cheerful smile. My nurse helped me lie back again. Almost immediately, the intolerable torture relented. I knew I wouldn't have to scream. In thirty minutes, I was blissfully numb from my toes to my hips and I fell asleep.

An hour later, at seven-thirty, I woke up to find sun coming in the window and a new nurse in my room. The day nurse, Roxanne, was putting on gloves to examine me again. She frowned afterward. "We've lost a little ground I think, dear. Can you feel the contractions?"

"No, I can't feel anything." My medical-school training in obstetrics had been brief, but I knew I was entirely too comfortable.

Roxanne shook her head and left me, closing the door. An hour after that, Dr. Prescott came in. He stood studying the uterine contractions on the fetal-heart monitor. "Elizabeth, you probably know all this, but let me explain what's going on. Dr. Ridgeway gave you one cc of point-two-five-percent Marcaine. That relieved the pain, but it worked almost too well for you. It didn't stop your contractions, but your cervix is no longer dilated. The baby can't get through."

"So we start over again?" I asked. I had thought that the past year had drained all my resources. Now I was surprised to find that from somewhere within me came unexpected reserves of strength to deliver Lucy. Fatigue, depression, even the threat of death — women still die in labor — were remote and unreal. Only one thing in life mattered at all, once labor began: delivering Lucy, alive and well.

"Yes, we start over, Elizabeth, but it's not that easy. We have to wait till the numbness wears off completely. Your pain will be worse this time. Bear with us. If it gets too bad, I'll give you something. I'd rather not. It will delay things and we want to get little Lucy into the world."

"Whatever you say." I was a plastic surgeon, not an obstetrician. I hadn't delivered a baby since medical school, eleven years ago. If Dr. Prescott didn't know what he was doing, we were out of luck, because I certainly didn't.

As each minute went by, the anesthetic wore off a little more. At first the pain was not bad. By nine o'clock, it was horrible. I lay there dreading the start of each contraction; each one was worse than the one before. At ten o'clock, the nurse, Roxanne, came in again. She had short, brown hair and a cheerful, round face with a turned-up nose. She settled herself cross-legged on a chair by my bed, like a track coach about to give a pep talk. She waited until the contraction passed before she spoke.

"You're going to need some help to get through this. Now I want you to do what I tell you, Dr. Morgan. You listen to me. I can see the monitor. I'll tell you when the contraction is coming and what to do. I want you to relax. You think you're relaxed, but you're not. That's better. Relax more. You'll feel the contraction start now. Now do the little slow breaths in and out. That's it. Keep it up. Relax more. Breathe. Don't hold your breath. Relax. Now the pain's on the down slope."

"Great," I gasped, drenched in sweat.

"Good girl. I'll watch the monitor and tell you when the contraction peaks so you'll know there's hope. Contractions always hurt much more after an epidural, but we've got to get you back to nine centimeters. Relax now. You've got one coming." She put a cold cloth on my forehead. "This will help, too."

At eleven, Dr. Prescott returned to examine me. "You're seven to eight centimeters, Elizabeth. How are you doing?"

"I'm still alive," I said limply. I remembered watching women in labor when I was in medical school. It wasn't a pretty sight.

"Keep up the good work. The water has burst. That sometimes speeds things up."

A contraction started and I tuned out Dr. Prescott before he finished speaking. I heard Roxanne's voice saying, "Relax, Dr. Morgan. I want you to start taking big, deep breaths now. Blow out slowly. Slowly," she repeated urgently. I closed my eyes to concentrate. Her voice was my salvation. As long as I could listen, she could talk me through.

Half an hour later, a man came in looking vaguely like Clark Gable. "I'm Dr. York," he told me. He paused considerately and waited until my contraction had subsided. "I'm the neonatologist. Dr. Prescott told me all about the problem with the meconium. I don't think you'll need me in the delivery room, but I'll be around in case I'm needed."

"Thank you." I had no idea what he was talking about. I tried to smile, but the next contraction had started. They were coming very close together — on top of one another — and relaxing and breathing didn't help at all. I wondered vaguely about meconium. I felt sure I could remember what it was if only the pain would stop so I could think, but it wouldn't stop. I couldn't think, but a vague memory told me that whatever meconium was, it was bad for the baby.

I couldn't listen to Roxanne now. I couldn't speak. At noon the pain changed from intolerable to savage torture. I dragged myself into a sitting position like a terrified animal and sat, my legs crossed, my head thrown back, and my body rigid. My body was alive with pain. It was a physical impossibility to relax. The word meant nothing anymore. I didn't know when I would start to scream, but it would be soon. I knew screaming wouldn't help, but I couldn't control my body any longer. My body had to scream.

Through a fog, I heard Roxanne saying in the hallway, "She's really uncomfortable now, Dr. Prescott."

"Have Dr. Ridgeway come and give her some Marcaine. I'll check her now." Dr. Prescott came into the room and examined me. "Good girl. Nine centimeters. That's a big baby you have. We're going to start the epidural again. Dr. Ridgeway is on his way."

I held on until Dr. Ridgeway arrived. He injected the Marcaine into the tubing in my back. Again, he told me it would take fifteen minutes to work, but in three minutes the torture of each contraction had subsided to mere pain, and I lay back thanking God that I was delivering a baby in an American hospital in 1982, not in England in 1945, where my mother went through nineteen hours of tortured labor without a doctor while she begged three useless nurses to help her. They would not call the doctor at night. Doctors did not come to the clinic until the afternoon. Those were the doctors' orders.

Roxanne tapped my arm. I opened my eyes and returned to the present. "Got your breath back?" she asked sympathetically.

"This is divine."

"Now comes the work. Your baby's head is coming through the cervix. You have to push it out. Can you feel any contractions?"

"Nothing. It's bliss."

"I'll watch the monitor and tell you when to push. I want you to bend your knees. Grip the soles of your feet with your hands. Put your chin on your chest and when I say push, push with everything you've got. Get ready. Here comes a contraction. Push. Harder." Her voice became urgent. "Harder! Push! Relax, the contraction's gone. Remember to hold your legs so you don't push with your legs. That does no good. Push with your chest and your abdomen. Okay, here comes a contraction. Push! More! More! That's it. Good. Excellent. Relax. Dr. Prescott will give you two hours for this. If you're doing well, he'll let you go a bit longer." So I had two hours ahead, pushing with all my might, to get Lucy out into the world, assuming that her heart rate remained normal on the fetal monitor. It was exhausting, but anything was better than that pain. An embarrassed young man with a beard pushed open the door to my room and looked in uncertainly.

"Dr. Morgan, I'm the OB medical student. I'm working with Dr. Prescott today."

"No problem." He obviously wanted permission to watch. As long as he didn't talk to me, I didn't care. I didn't want to talk. I had a job to do and I needed all my concentration.

"Is this your first baby?" the medical student asked me, closing the door behind him.

"Push," instructed Roxanne. "She can't talk now."

I pushed. "Yes, it's my first," I said when I could speak.

"Did you have any problems during pregnancy?" he inquired casually, sitting down for a friendly chat.

It wasn't his fault. He didn't know what it was like for me now. Someone had ordered him to take a history so he could learn.

"I had an *E. coli* urinary infection in the first trimester and a low-grade right pyelonephritis, treated with ampicillin, in the fourth month," I told him, all in one breath.

"Push," commanded Roxanne. I stopped talking and pushed.

"Do you have any medical problems?" the student asked me hopefully. I ignored him. I didn't speak for the next two hours. Every two minutes, I pushed for one minute with all my strength, and the next minute gathered my strength for the coming contraction. It was an enormous physical effort. I had been awake for over forty-eight hours since my false labor began on Thursday night. It was now Saturday afternoon. I felt like an animal, not a person, and I had a single purpose in my life: I had to get my baby born. There was nothing else in life. At one o'clock and again at one-thirty, Dr. Prescott returned to check me. At ten minutes before two, Roxanne said, "He'll probably let you go till two-thirty. You're doing great."

Eight minutes later, Roxanne looked at the monitor where Lucy's heartbeat blipped across the screen, then looked again, frowning. She jumped to her feet. "I'll get Dr. Prescott now," she said and turned the monitor so I couldn't see it. A corner of my worn-out but conscious mind told me very clearly why Roxanne was frowning. I didn't want to see the monitor. I was glad she had turned it away. Lucy's heart rate must suddenly have dropped, and if she wasn't born quickly now, she would die or be brain-damaged. There was nothing I could do. I had

· *19* ·

good doctors and good nurses. I needed good luck. Dr. Prescott strode in with Roxanne. Another nurse came in close behind, wheeling a stretcher.

"Elizabeth, we're going to get little Lucy born right away. I think you've had enough," he said calmly.

Roxanne pushed the stretcher up to the bed. "Can you scoot over?" she asked. I scooted awkwardly, like a giant panda lying on its back. My legs were numb, but somehow I moved.

"Good girl," said Roxanne, pushing the stretcher rapidly into the hall. There was no rush, but suddenly everything was done fast. I was wheeled into a green-tiled delivery room. Dr. York, the Clark Gable–look-alike neonatologist, smiled reassuringly at me as he tied a surgical mask over his face. He had said he would be there only if Lucy had a problem. She had a problem. I knew that already. I refused to think what it would be like if I had to watch her die. I wanted to scream in despair. I wanted someone to promise me she would be born alive.

"Move onto the table, Elizabeth," said Roxanne. I moved. "Down more. Good. We're putting your knees up on these steel supports. You know the operating-room routine. We're going to wash you with Betadine. The usual."

"Fine."

Dr. Prescott was scrubbing his hands at the sink outside and watching us through the broad glass window. Dr. York hooked up another monitor to check Lucy's heart rate. Dr. Ridgeway, the anesthesiologist, put my left arm out to one side on a padded metal arm board.

"Is the epidural wearing off?" he asked.

"Yes, I'm beginning to have some feeling."

He injected some more Marcaine into the epidural tube on my shoulder and then tapped the intravenous catheter in my left hand. "Does this hurt?"

"It's a little sore."

"It looks swollen." He moved around to look at my right hand.

I looked up at the intravenous solution. "It's pouring in. I think it's okay. I have unusually big veins."

"You do indeed. I don't think I'll start another one. Your pressure's good. Has the epidural worked?"

"Yes."

"Do you want some sedation?"

"Please, no," I said emphatically. "I'm fine." I wanted to be awake, whatever happened.

Dr. Prescott came in with the bearded medical student behind him. Roxanne handed them both gowns and gloves and Dr. Prescott sat down on a stool while Roxanne hurriedly tied his gown in the back. All I could see was the top of his surgical cap.

"Any pain, Elizabeth?"

"None."

"You will feel pressure. Don't push unless I tell you." Dr. York stood behind him, watching. "I'll have to use low forceps, Elizabeth."

"I know." I heard the harsh, metallic click of the Mayo scissors.

"Are you doing an episiotomy?" I asked.

"Yes. Can you feel it?"

"No. Yes, I can. I can bear it."

Dr. Prescott laughed shortly and then muttered inaudibly. "The position looks good," he said quietly. I felt pressure and pushing inside. The forceps were going around Lucy's head like great, steel sugar tongs.

"Push," said Roxanne, her voice breaking in crisply. "Push hard. Relax." She waited for a signal from Dr. Prescott. "Okay, Elizabeth, push with all you've got. Push!" I pushed so hard my head throbbed and I thought I'd explode. At last, "now relax," said Roxanne.

"Head's through," said Dr. Prescott. He wasn't talking to me. He was talking to himself. "Shoulder's stuck. Big shoulders." Broad shoulders are a Morgan hallmark. Lucy was going to be the fourth big-shouldered generation. I almost started to laugh out loud and I realized I was on the verge of hysteria.

I stopped when I saw Dr. York stare at the fetal-heart monitor. He looked back at Dr. Prescott and back again to the monitor. He shook his head. Inside I felt as though my body was being used for a tug-of-war. Suddenly, my abdomen deflated like a popped balloon and Dr. Prescott's hands placed an enormous, gray baby on top of my abdomen. Dr. York steadied the baby on top of me. Dr. Prescott's hands disappeared to clamp the umbilical cord.

"Two twenty-one," said Roxanne.

"She's huge," I said in astonishment, bending my head to look at her lying on my belly. I didn't like her color. Lucy opened her mouth to cry, but there was a high squeak and nothing followed. She wasn't breathing. Her gray color turned blue and then deep blue. She was on the verge of death. She had no oxygen to keep her alive. She couldn't die. She couldn't. I remembered a baby with leukemia. I had watched her die one night when I was a surgical intern, rotating on pediatrics. I had pronounced her dead. Her mother had been frozen with grief, watching helplessly. I felt the same way now. Dr. York carried Lucy to a table in a corner of the delivery room. By craning my head, I could watch him. He put a tube inside her mouth and suctioned it out. She turned a deeper blue, and then a blackish purple. He grabbed a tiny, L-shaped metal laryngoscope in order to examine the upper windpipe. He put it in gently and peered down. There was a horrible wheezing sound. Lucy's chest lifted convulsively and the purple faded to almost blue.

"Suction," said Dr. York. Roxanne handed him a soft, clean plastic tube. He threaded it past the laryngoscope into her lungs. "There's a chunk of meconium below the vocal cords." He said nothing after that, but he suctioned her lungs. Lucy turned from blue to gray to pink, as her chest heaved up and down. Dr. York removed the laryngoscope, and I watched him watch her. Suddenly there came the fearful squawl of an indignant newborn baby. Lucy was alive.

"Eight pounds, eight ounces, Elizabeth," he said, as Roxanne put her on the scale. "Twenty-one-and-a-half inches. Born at two twenty-one on the twenty-first. That's easy to remember."

"That's the placenta," said Dr. Prescott from below, and he dropped something squashy into the steel bucket at his foot. "You're going to be one sore mother. You have a whopping hemorrhoid."

"Internal or external?"

"External, my dear, but it won't be fun."

"I refuse to have a hemorrhoidectomy," I protested.

"Spoken like a true surgeon," said Dr. Prescott, laughing. "I wouldn't let anyone cut on me either."

"Do you want your baby now?" Roxanne asked me as I scooted, no longer pregnant but a mother, back onto the stretcher.

"Please." I held out my arms. I didn't want anyone else to have her.

She handed the little bundle to me, and I cuddled Lucy in the crook of my arm. She had a rosebud mouth; curly, brown lashes; and dark brown eyes. She looked at me and smiled. I smiled back, in adoration. Suddenly she burrowed frantically into my side in a search for milk. Labor was over. She was safe, and I remembered now what meconium was. It's the stool inside a baby's colon. Once the amniotic sac bursts at labor, the baby's colon may evacuate and if so, clumps of meconium can get into the baby's mouth and lungs, blocking the airflow. It can be fatal. I gazed at her, feeling peaceful, triumphant, and enormously clever. I was a mother. It was the most important achievement in my life. We were wheeled out together to the recovery room. My husband was there. I had never wanted him more. Having him there gave me a glimmer of hope that our marriage might work, if only for Lucy's sake.

Everyone in my family came to see me that evening. Lucy was the first grandchild. Rob and Janice, his wife, came together, with flowers. Jim, Mother, and Dad all came to congratulate me. Lucy was the star.

"It's an astonishing thing," said my father, taking his hat off and pulling up a chair. "I've been studying Lucy in the nursery. That child looks exactly like me." He beamed — round-faced and broad-shouldered; big, brown eyes; dimples and a smile. He was in a great mood. It occurred to me that Lucy might, somehow, be the force to make him resign himself to a contented retirement. It would be nice for everyone, especially my mother. My marriage was probably broken beyond repair, but I was still young. I could still hope for the future. For my mother, even separated, my father was the only man in her life. My father patted the sheet over my knee. "Congratulations." I took his hand. I was very happy to be a mother. I was happy to be a wife. I smiled at my husband. I held my hand out to him. Our problems could wait. Perhaps they could be solved.

They couldn't. He came back the next day to talk. That night I realized I was severely depressed, defeated, and confused. My marriage had failed. My life was in chaos. I was single. I had a baby. I wanted to run away from my life, but with Lucy I couldn't run. She needed me. I wanted to love and protect her. In four weeks I would be operating again. There were bills to pay. I had to work, more than ever before. I couldn't do it. I needed someone to lean on, someone to help me. He wasn't there.

It didn't help that my hospital roommate, my age and a lawyer, had just had her first baby too, and her adoring husband had been at her bedside all day. I didn't grudge her the happiness, but at eleven that night I covered my face with a pillow so my roommate wouldn't hear me crying. I knew I was very lucky to have Lucy. It didn't help. I was lucky to be healthy. I had a wonderful career. If my health didn't fail me, if I could force myself back to work, I would be able to support Lucy and to support her well. I had my family — Jim and my mother would do anything for me. Rob and Janice, busy with their own lives, would help too. I counted my blessings and kept on crying, feeling disgraced by my own ungratefulness for all I had. I had been taught all about this in medical school. My diagnosis was "reactive postpartum depression." I hated the hospital. The loneliness was unbearable. I felt myself teetering on the brink of a black void, all the strength of my personality gone. I couldn't think what to do except to sit up in bed and scream and keep on screaming from frustration, from disappointment, and from anguish. I didn't. It wouldn't help. I would simply be sedated and locked up on a psychiatric ward. I wasn't mad. What could a psychiatrist do to help? I needed to start a new life.

In the morning, Dr. Prescott made rounds and listened, somewhat puzzled, while I pleaded to be sent home. Reluctantly, he agreed to let me go. I assured him that I felt wonderful. I smiled cheerily. He studied my face and looked dissatisfied. If I had not been a doctor, he would not have discharged me. I told myself my private sorrow was none of his business. It was, actually. Had he known how tired and how depressed I felt, he would have insisted that I stay. I knew it and I was determined not to let him guess. I didn't want him to. I was beyond his help. I was beyond medical care. I had to go home and be with my baby and be a child again myself. I needed my mother.

"I think Rob would like to come with me," said my mother when I called her to say I would be discharged. I depended on her so much. "It's his turn and he wants to help. We'll be there in an hour to take you home." Rob has a watchful, kind, impartial face, like a benevolent judge's. He inspected Lucy as if she were a scientific specimen when the nurse wheeled her bassinet out into the corridor. I was waiting in a wheelchair.

"Isn't she very little?" Rob inquired politely of the nurse, as though a waiter had arrived with one four-ounce sirloin.

"Oh no," said the nurse. "This is a big baby."

"A big human baby," Rob corrected her. "Now if she were a baby elephant, she'd weigh a hundred pounds." He took Lucy and anxiously put her in my arms. "Don't drop her, Elizabeth." The procession began: Rob pushing me in the wheelchair, Lucy in my arms, my mother with the flowers, and the nurse with my overnight case. I emerged into the hot August sun — a surgeon, a mother, and a bewildered soul. It delighted me to look at Lucy. On the drive home, I couldn't take my eyes off her sweet, puckered, faintly yellow face. I knew vaguely that I needed a good night's sleep and that my new life would have to include a lawyer and a divorce. It never occurred to me that a struggle for custody of Lucy could arise. I was her mother. Naturally I would raise her. I couldn't imagine it any other way.

➔ *two*

*L*UCY SLEPT in my arms on the way home. The little side street where I lived was filled with the noise and fumes of commercial traffic. Trucks used it as a shortcut to the traffic circle. The trees gave no relief from the intense heat and glare of the August sun. We went into the house. It was dark and cool and welcoming compared to the hostility of the heat. It was a tiny house on two levels. Two bedrooms, a kitchen, a dining room, and a living room were squashed into six hundred square feet. It was big enough for one medium-sized adult. With Mother, Lucy, the baby-sitter, and me, it would be a crunch. The second bedroom was the size of a large closet and held only a bed and a small chest of drawers. This was my mother's room. My room held a bed and Lucy's bassinet, a chest of drawers and a small chair. Boxes of diapers were stacked in the tiny hall. There was no other place for them. It was a tiny, tiny house. Rob put Lucy in her bassinet, helped me upstairs to bed, and reluctantly left to go back to work. I was exhausted. My mother sat down on the chair in my bedroom.

"You can't raise a child here," she said in a whisper, so as not to disturb Lucy. I looked at my mother feeling irritated and despairing. How would I feel in her place? I knew how hard it was for her to see me floundering. I understood in a way that I never had before. I wanted to be nice. I wanted to be cheerful. I wanted to be kind and reasonable and loving. I didn't seem to have it in me anymore. Perhaps my love for my husband and my suffering for him had made me cold.

"Why can't I?" I asked. This was my home. Moving would be yet another insuperable hurdle, and I would not contemplate it.

"It's not safe. As soon as she's walking, she won't be safe outside. This is a very busy street."

"She won't be walking for a year, at least, Mother. Don't be silly." How could my mother bear me? I couldn't stand to listen to myself. I sounded so rejecting and ungrateful.

"It will come sooner than you think, Elizabeth. And there is nowhere for her to play. No playground. No other children. It's not the sort of place a baby-sitter will want to come. I wouldn't want to be in this little house all day. Would you?" She spoke gently, coaxing me.

I looked at Lucy, my precious bundle. I wanted to be good to her, if I could. I relaxed and smiled at my mother. She came over and sat down next to me, smoothing the hair away from my brow just as she used to do when I was a cranky, fussy three-year-old, waking up from my nap.

"Baby elephant," murmured my mother. It was the beginning of a lullaby she used to sing to me. My eyes welled up with tears. Remembering my childhood made me sad. It was all mixed up with love and marriage and babies and heartache and divorce. I reminded myself that I had Lucy. I wasn't making funeral arrangements for her. That had come frighteningly close.

"Let's talk," I said at last.

As we talked, our voices rose to a conversational level. I sat up and peeked at Lucy. She lay on her back as sunlight filtered onto her through the curtains. I wanted to hold her but she needed to sleep. I watched her, entranced. She was practicing making faces. She raised her eyebrows, frowned, smiled, winked, looked disapproving, surprised, cautious, bewildered, and startled. Her eyes closed and opened, closed again, and she fell asleep. My mother and I continued talking. She didn't stir.

A police car, its siren blaring, raced down the street. Two shrieking fire engines followed it. Lucy didn't budge. She was a trouper from the start.

I needed sleep but I couldn't get it. I wanted to breast-feed Lucy. She was a large, hungry baby and I didn't make enough milk. She nursed for hours that afternoon, looking up at me accusingly with big, brown eyes, crying with frustration and hunger. She nursed all night and still cried in hunger. I changed to formula. She didn't take kindly to that either. It gave her colic and she and I were awake all night, every night, for that first week. She alternately screamed for food and shrieked with pain. I rocked her all night in the living room, listening for the gurgle of gassy bubbles in her intestine that signaled the end of an attack of cramps. I wouldn't let my mother sit up with Lucy. I was Lucy's mother. I wanted to be with her. Besides, my mother needed sleep. It would be the end of everything if my mother got sick again. I couldn't cope with that as well. During the day, my mother looked after me. Laura, the baby-sitter, looked after Lucy. I had chosen Laura with great care, months before. She was young and divorced, but she seemed reliable and conscientious.

"It's not my work," Laura complained to me one morning when Lucy was a week old. Lucy hadn't slept at all that night, and I was beginning to wonder how long it would go on.

I turned to her. "What's not?"

Laura looked at me, grumpy and sullen. "Looking after the baby is not my work. When I had my baby, my mother took care of him."

I was speechless. I had hired Laura to look after Lucy and to keep the house clean. Yesterday Laura had announced to me that she didn't expect to do housework. These days everything I did seemed to turn out wrong. Laura couldn't let me down. If I didn't have Laura, I couldn't go back to work. I had to work. Lucy needed me to work.

Lucy began to cry and I picked her up. "Laura, didn't you just feed her?" Lucy shoved her little fist into her mouth and sucked passionately.

"Yes, yes. I fed her. I'll show you the empty bottle." Laura trotted downstairs to the kitchen and returned with an empty baby bottle. "She took eight ounces in fifteen minutes," said Laura defiantly. My mother came in behind her.

"A newborn baby can't drink eight ounces at one time," said my mother, "and certainly not in fifteen minutes."

Lucy continued to scream. We all trooped back downstairs to the kitchen. I warmed a bottle for Lucy. She attacked it greedily, a fist shoved into each cheek. She seemed starved. It was a pathetic sight.

"I fed her," repeated Laura, watching Lucy guzzle on the bottle. She looked censorious. "She eats too much." She stared at me, angry. She didn't like me. I didn't care. She didn't like Lucy, and it made me seethe inside.

Four ounces and twenty minutes later, Lucy hiccuped once and relaxed into sleep, like a drunk slipping under the table.

"Laura, you know you didn't feed her," I said fiercely. I knew now how peaceful women could kill to protect their young.

"I fed her. Eight ounces."

"No, Laura," I said.

Laura shrugged. "She wasn't hungry. Your baby won't eat." It was absurd. Lucy had flung herself on her bottle like a seal on a fish. She had needed to eat, and this woman had let her go hungry. I had hired Laura. I felt guilty. I had laughed at my mother's guilt feelings many times in the past. She had even felt guilty once because Rob's godfather gave him an all-day sucker at the zoo but didn't give me one. It didn't seem silly now. Anything that happened to Lucy was important to me, and not feeding her was unforgivable.

"No," I said harshly. Behind Laura, through the panes of the kitchen door, I saw a stray cat pacing like a miniature tiger on the patio. Lucy was my little kitten to be protected. I wanted to pounce on Laura like a cat. I restrained myself. "I do not think you are happy here. You should leave, Laura."

"Good." Laura smiled for the first time in days. "I will go now." Until Laura had come to work for me, her cousin had supported her for almost a year. Laura's mother took care of her child. The cousin would be supporting Laura again. She got her purse and left, swinging her bag merrily in her hand as she strolled down the tree-lined street in the bright sunlight. I watched her go. Then I rocked Lucy in my arms. I was glad to see Laura go. I wondered how I could ever have hired her, but I envied her too. She was so carefree. I had been like that when I first fell in love. I began to ache for my husband. I remembered little things — the way he ordered wine in a restaurant; his voice on the phone. I didn't want to love him anymore. I didn't want to remember. If I could only wash him out of my hair — but the little things came back to haunt me. Lucy fell asleep and I put her down in her bassinet. I needed sleep too. I hadn't slept in over a week. My brain felt fuzzy. I wanted to do things right. I didn't know how to begin.

I turned to my mother. "Mother, I can't go on," I began. My voice rose to a wail. "What sort of a mother am I going to be for Lucy anyhow? Maybe he was right. A failed wife. A failure as a mother. I mess everything up. I wish I were dead!"

I was hysterical. I felt trapped, and I wanted out. My mother cut me off curtly. "Get hold of yourself, Elizabeth." She was right. My husband had been moody. It was self-indulgent. I couldn't be like that. "You have a child now, and all you can think about is how sad life is for you! What about your family? I'm doing my best to help. What about your daughter? Lucy didn't ask to be born."

"I know." I stood in the middle of the living room, wringing my hands. "I can't take it anymore, Mother. I've reached the end. I still love him. I think about him all the time." I started to cry. A painter walked by carrying a ladder on his shoulder and looked in the front window curiously. I turned away, toward the patio, where there was only the cat to stare at me, and cried and cried. I couldn't stop. I was defeated. All the major decisions in my life had been wrong. I had married the wrong man. I had bought the wrong house. I had hired the wrong help. I had trained in the wrong career. My surgical practice seemed incompatible with motherhood, let alone with being a single mother. Nothing I did turned out right. I saw no light ahead. I felt like flotsam, washed up on the shore of life.

"My poor dear." With her arm around my shoulders, my mother rocked me back and forth. "My poor, poor dear. It's not what I wanted for you." I felt guilty letting her comfort me. My mother needed support too. Her life had been hard.

I sniffed and wiped the tears away with my hand, like a child. "I gave up seven years of my life to train in surgery and I'm paying for it now," I said at last. "And a lot of single mothers who made the same mistakes I have would love to have my career."

My mother went into the kitchen and returned with a glass of sherry. "True. Drink this. It helps. All the same, if I had known what surgical training would be like, I would have urged you not to do it."

"You couldn't stop me." I gulped down the sherry. "I was determined. I did it because they said a woman couldn't do it. I did it to prove myself, to me and to Daddy."

"The question now is," continued my mother, "what are you going to do?"

"Well, I want to go back. But that would be crazy. Our marriage didn't work. It was a disaster. I won't subject Lucy to that. She would have a miserable childhood. I want to see her happy." I heard my voice rise again. I took a breath and calmed down. Even thinking about my marriage made me agitated, but the marriage was over. My husband, like my father, would never change. I had to accept it and move on. I tried to see myself objectively. I worked hard. I was friendly. I had been romantic, to the point of folly. "Mother, I think part of the trouble is that surgery protected me from life. I finally did what I was destined to do — fall in love with the wrong man. Most girls do it at seventeen, and get over it and put it behind them in their twenties. I thought I was being the smart one, but I just waited longer to make my mistake. And I made a big one."

"I agree," said my mother after a while. "You wanted someone dashing and different. I wouldn't want to see you waste the next ten years of your life trying to make a hopeless marriage work." My mother spoke with feeling. "Now, to be practical. We have a very rough year ahead of us, Elizabeth. Lucy isn't going to be a good sleeper, and if you don't sleep you'll get sick. You should have a nurse come in until Lucy sleeps through the night."

"Mother, I can handle it. I don't know if I can afford a night nurse." I had started my practice four years earlier, but one of those years I had not worked. I took a full year off to take care of my mother during her almost fatal illness and her separation from my father. She lived with me now and I loved having her, but it had been slow getting my practice going again. Then, when I had paid off my debts, I had done what so many people do the moment they have a little money. I had invested badly. I bought gold and diamonds at the top, shortly before they crashed in value. My practice was doing well. I was earning money, but my savings were almost gone.

"You have to have a nurse come in at night, Elizabeth." My mother warded off my protests. "Now don't be stubborn. You can't be with Lucy day and night. If you're awake all night, you'll get sick, and that won't help Lucy, will it?"

I gave in to her. She was right, but it bothered me that I was better at spending money than in saving it. It was another item on my list of faults.

"As for your practice, Elizabeth, it is your livelihood. It must come first, at least now. And, even though you don't agree, you will find that you cannot raise Lucy in this house. Lucy will be hit by a car as soon as she walks." I shuddered. She patted my hand. "You grew up in a dark house on a main road, isolated, with no friends. Don't make the mistake I made."

I sighed. "I know. And you know as well as I do that this area is getting pretty weird. Lucy can't grow up here. We'll have to move." Should we rent or buy? I wondered. My husband and I had looked for places to live before we married. The rents were astronomical then. They were worse now. An apartment big enough for Lucy, Mother, and me in a nice neighborhood would cost as much each month as a mortgage, or more. We had to move. I would have to buy and I couldn't afford a mistake.

"And I think you might go to Haiti and get a quick divorce," suggested my mother. "You'll never be free until you're divorced. If you do it here, it will be at least a year. It makes no sense to buy a house and try to start over before things are resolved between the two of you. You want this whole unpleasant business behind you as soon as you can."

I poured myself another slug of sherry. Did I want a divorce? I couldn't think about it yet. I wanted my dream to come true, but I knew it wouldn't. I looked at my mother — her gray eyes, her silver hair, her autocratic nose, the alert expression, and the sweet smile. She was beautiful. She was easily hurt, but she was very strong. All during my childhood, no matter how difficult her children or her husband had been, she had never shown how it upset her. She smiled. She forgave. She kept on working. Her psychology patients adored her, with reason. I've never figured out how anyone grew up without my mother.

"Mother, I have never needed you so much. I am so grateful for your help."

She smiled, pleased. "I love my children. I enjoy helping you. Lucy is your baby, but you and Jim and Rob will always be mine." She stood up, full of energy. "Now you go and get some sleep. I'll call an agency and arrange for a night nurse."

Suddenly I leaned forward from where I was sitting. I could see my patio and my neighbor's patio and the fence that separated his patio from the alley. I didn't have my glasses on, but what looked like a hand and then a head had appeared over the fence. I got up and went to the patio door. A husky teenage boy in running shoes vaulted over the fence onto my neighbor's patio and another one followed. They didn't live around here. I opened the door briskly.

"Excuse me," I said severely. "Can I help you?"

They froze.

"Are you looking for someone?"

"Yeah," said the bigger of the two, approaching me with a swagger. "The guy that lives here."

"It's rude to come around to the back like this. You're much more likely to find him by knocking on the front door." I spoke primly, like an elderly spinster with wire-rimmed glasses. I was annoyed. The husky teenager stared at me. "Go around to the front. I'm sure he's in," I snapped.

"Right on." Still staring at me, he backed away, and they vaulted over the fence.

"Elizabeth, you are quite insane," said my mother as I closed the door. Her face had gone white. So had mine. "What if they had had a gun?" I nodded and called my neighbor. He was very alert. He had already seen the boys and called the police.

"I can't believe it," continued my mother. "The only reason they didn't assault you and rob this house was sheer shock. You told them to try the front door! They must think you are out of your mind."

I was shaken. "I do need sleep, Mother." She nodded and steered me up the stairs to bed. In my bedroom, I lingered over Lucy's bassinet. She stirred. She opened her eyes and grinned at me. Scientifically, I knew she couldn't see me yet. Irrational as it was, I felt the grin was meant for me. We both fell asleep, smiling.

My mother called the nursing agency and they sent us Brenda. She was a cheerful, middle-aged nurse with a motherly shape. She cooed happily over Lucy that night. It was Lucy's worst night for colic. As I climbed wearily into bed, I could hear her downstairs with Brenda, crying, and I imagined her little face screwed up in misery. I felt sure I would stay awake worrying. In a moment I fell asleep. It was my first night's sleep in over a week.

"What does her pediatrician say about her colic?" Brenda asked me in the morning. I evaded the question, feeling guilty again. Lucy had a pediatrician, but I hadn't called her. Odette was a close friend. She was gorgeous, a platinum blond who dressed in red and had a dramatic flair. I should have called her before, but Lucy hadn't seemed sick enough to need a doctor. I didn't see what Odette could do over the phone, but I called her.

"No problem," said Odette confidently when I had described Lucy's colic. "Lucy is allergic to the sucrose. All the infant formulas have sucrose. It's cheaper. But most natural food has glucose, which is 'real' sugar. You need Carnation milk. Real milk has lactose, not sucrose. Give it to her half-strength, and add two tablespoons of Karo syrup. The dark kind works best. Carnation is constipating and Karo will correct that. If she gets cramps with that, give her weak chamomile tea with a teaspoon of granulated sugar. The belladonna in the chamomile will stop cramps. So how is the husband helping?"

"About my marriage, Odette." I gave an embarrassed laugh. "It's over. I left the week before Lucy was born. It was hopeless."

"Men!" said Odette indignantly. "Men! What are they good for?"

"Not all men, Odette. My brothers are super," I pointed out. They were loyal to me. I wanted to be loyal to them.

"And so is my husband," said Odette, "but there are millions of others. What I see in my practice, you would not believe. You. At least you can pay the bills. What happened to one of my patients? Five children. The father is the head of a big corporation. Last week he eloped with his secretary. Not even a good-bye. They don't know where he is. She is trained for nothing. She is desperate. They don't have money for groceries! It makes me sick. So, call me anytime about Lucy. Who will look after her when you go back to work? Your mother?"

"Not my mother. She's not strong enough. She would do it if I asked, but I won't ask. I need to find someone. I just fired the one I had."

"Always happens," said Odette. "Don't feel bad. I'll keep my ears open."

I decided to ask my office manager, Beverly Smith, to help find a baby-sitter for Lucy. My choice of Laura hadn't worked out. Beverly would do better. Beverly had three teenage children. She had much more experience with babies than I did, and it was time I put the problem to her.

I fed Lucy, packed a bag for her, and dressed her for the expedition to see Beverly at the office and to buy Karo syrup and Carnation milk.

"Do you think she needs all that?" asked my mother when I brought Lucy down. I had put a sweater and a cap on her and had wrapped her in a pink quilt. "It's ninety-eight outside."

"Oh." I removed the cap and sweater, but brought the quilt. My mother looked amused. I knew it was silly but I was afraid Lucy would catch cold. She was so little that she sank to the bottom of the infant seat and promptly fell asleep. She woke up grinning when we arrived at the office. She was always ready for a party.

Beverly Smith had a wealth of talents. She was organized,

sensible, loved numbers, and had a brilliant memory. I had rapidly learned to appreciate her good judgment. She had come to work for me only a year ago. Clare Ring had been my secretary before then, from the day I opened my office. Clare had had to cut back to part-time work because of her back pain. Gentle, violet-eyed Clare had a back that had collapsed during the years she worked for me. I knew the cause and so did Clare. It was bone destruction from metastatic breast cancer. When she turned fifty, Clare had found a lump in her breast. Her doctor had assured her that the hard lump was normal. A year later, he referred her for a biopsy. It was cancer, of course, and by then it had spread. She had a mastectomy, too late. Clare, a widow and an orphan, had no children but many devoted friends. She accepted her disease cheerfully. She was determined to conquer it, but she was fighting a losing battle. When the cancer spread to the bones in her back, Clare could not sit long enough to work full-time. When I had hired her, I knew her chances of survival were less than 20 percent. The least I could do as a doctor to offset her negligent physician was to see that she had a job as long as she wanted, until the end. Very slowly, the end was coming. It had become hard for her to work for me, even part-time.

Two weeks after Clare cut back to part-time work, Beverly Smith took over my disorganized office. She looked at the printout from my computer accounting firm and called the manager. "We speak English in this office, Mr. Hoxie. I send accounts to you in English. Don't send them back to me in Chinese." She had the accounts in order that month and fired the computer.

Beverly could solve life's practical problems with ease. She could do comfortably many things that were difficult for me. I knew she could find the right baby-sitter.

I entered the office with diaper bags strung about me like a human yak. I carried Lucy in my arms. I felt proud and a little self-conscious bearing my prize possession.

"Oh, isn't she precious," said Beverly. Lucy opened her eyes, gave an enormous, toothless yawn, and grunted. "So who's going to look after her now that Laura's gone?"

"That's the problem," I said. I put Lucy down on the sofa with her pink quilt and tucked her in. She gave a characteristic wiggle and fell asleep.

"Well, you want someone who can take her early and keep her late, because of your schedule," said Beverly. "Does it have to be someone who comes to your house, or could it be someone near the office?"

"Anyone. Beverly, I just have to be able to work." I thought about my house. In a way, I couldn't blame Laura for wanting to leave. As my mother said, who would be content to stay shut in there all day? My mother, through an agency, had found a woman who would come to our house. She had arrived one day for an interview. I opened the front door. She was a stout woman in a blue uniform. She looked me over. "Won't you come in?" I asked. She took two steps back and studied the front of my tiny house.

"I don't think I will," she said at last. "This is not what I am used to. This is not what I was expecting." She turned on her heel and left.

Beverly didn't try to find someone to come to the house. She had too much common sense. She knew it wouldn't succeed. Besides, I had my husband to think of too. Whatever my feelings, Lucy had to be accessible to him. Wouldn't it be better for my husband if he didn't have to come to my home to see Lucy? It was awkward and painful enough for both of us.

Beverly had no trouble finding people to take Lucy in their home. In two days, she presented me with a selection to choose from. I settled on Nadine Hoskins, an experienced older woman who lived halfway between my office and my husband's. He could see Lucy anytime. I called to tell him. My hand was shaking when I called him. My voice was shaking when I spoke. I sat shaking in the chair after I hung up. I couldn't believe what marriage and love had done. Where was the me who was drilled in surgery, who was trained for crises? In my work, I controlled my emotions. In my life, my emotions controlled me, like wind battering a fallen leaf.

It seemed too short a time before I had to go back to work. I wanted to stay home and be with Lucy. I loved to hold her, and to see her tiny fingers curl over mine. I could watch her all day. I could hold her for hours while she slept. Even the way she sighed delighted me. I wanted to be with her. Besides, my body wasn't ready yet for the strain of work. There were too many things to do. Diapers and Carnation milk vanished in huge quantities. I had to buy strollers and rubber pants and more baby bottles. I studied the real-estate ads in a desultory manner, in search of the perfect home for Lucy.

Work was welcome, all the same. The moment my mind strayed from Lucy, it churned up the past, day and night. Even in my dreams, rest was impossible. I needed action to distract me.

My first day back to work began with Lucy and a box of baby food, clothes, and diapers. Lucy watched me get ready with her big, brown, unfocused eyes, kicking her legs with a smile. Our first stop was Nadine Hoskins, Beverly's discovery. Nadine was a teacher who had left her job to do baby-sitting at home. Her husband, a burly, cheerful man, was a government worker. Raucous barking greeted me when I drove up to the front of their white frame house, on the way to my office. Nadine opened the door. "Don't mind the barking," she called out. "That's China, our Chow. He lives outside."

Lucy was asleep. I took her in and tucked her in a little crib in the corner. This would be home for her, five days a week, from eight AM to six PM or longer. It had sounded like a good arrangement. Now I wondered. I hated to leave her. What I had done was good for my husband, but what about my Lucy? Should I have found a sitter nearer my home? She was only four weeks old and already she was a commuter. Lucy cared only about being warm and fed, but I didn't want to go.

"She's in good hands," Nadine reassured me. "I love babies. I'll take good care of her." Lucy didn't cry when I left. I felt happy that she was content, sad that she didn't miss me, and ridiculous, because she was too young to know who I was.

I drove off to work, feeling forlorn. Being a doctor, I had thought I could be calm and detached about motherhood. I was as foolish and adoring as any mother could be, and more so than most. I had lost my husband. I had no other children to help me keep Lucy in perspective. Lucy was everything. I walked up the steps to my office, a brick townhouse in an office development. Beverly waved to me from the bay window of the waiting room.

"Welcome back!" she called out when I came in. "I booked you a light day, but don't go into your office."

"Why not?"

"You'll die."

I went in all the same and staggered out again. Piles of charts, reports, and mail from the past month were stacked on my desk like the Himalayas.

"Beverly, can we torch the place, collect the insurance, and run?"

"They're on to that racket."

"I'll have to deal with this?"

"Looks like it."

"You're no help at all."

"I made some coffee. That'll get you started."

Despite my protests, I was happy to be back. This was something I could do well. Simply doing my paperwork reassured me that the world could be put in order. Compared to being a mother, plastic surgery was easy. Besides, the work had to be done and it let me put off facing personal problems.

My first patient was Fred Melford, an athletic, tanned young man with a red sweatband around his head. He had gone through the windshield of a friend's car six weeks before. His emergency surgery had been my last operation. Lucy's bulk had made it difficult for me to get close enough to the operating table. I had sent Fred home from Smith Center Hospital two days before I went into labor. He had been in a panic over whether I would go into labor before he was discharged. He was afraid of being left in hospital, forgotten, like a prisoner in the Bastille.

"Hey, Dr. Morgan, I notice your shape has changed since I saw you last." He pulled off the sweatband. "Why doesn't this heal?" His forehead had been a battlefield of glass, blood, and lacerations after the accident. Now he was healed except for a small lump of red, raw tissue protruding from the middle of his temple. Fred lay down on the exam table and I poked into the open wound with forceps.

"Does it hurt, Fred?"

"Nope."

"I think we have the problem right here." I poked around with the forceps and felt something hard. I pulled and extracted a sliver of white bone. "That is a remnant from the fracture of the outer table of your frontal bone." I showed it to him.

"Oh good," said Fred without enthusiasm. "Now what?"

"The rest is hypertrophic granulation tissue," I said. "A touch of silver nitrate should fix this." I rummaged in the cabinet for the nitrate sticks.

"What's that?" Fred turned around to keep me under close surveillance. I had been out of the office too long. Usually I explained things properly.

"That red area can't heal. It grew so high that your skin can't grow over it. If I cauterize the raw tissue with silver nitrate, the tissue will shrink and your skin can heal."

"If you say so." He didn't believe me.

I rolled a silver nitrate stick across the cherry-red nodule. It turned gray from the silver nitrate and shrank down, oozing clear fluid. I felt triumphant. It was another victory for wound healing.

"And in six months, you can operate on my scars?"

"Yes. It takes at least that long before your scars are soft enough to work with."

"Okay, Doctor. Thanks a lot." He carefully put on the sweatband. It made him look dashing, like a buccaneer. He strode away.

"I have a question for you," said Beverly when he had gone. "Do you know a Mrs. Jackson?"

"No."

"She wants a face-lift, but she doesn't want to spend any money on it, so she wants you to fill in a false insurance form saying she had jaw surgery instead. Insurance will pay for jaw surgery."

"No way. Tell her I don't do fraud."

Beverly held up her hand. "I promised her I'd ask you, and I haven't finished. I explained you wouldn't, so she said she knew a dentist who would write a letter saying she needed a face-lift for medical reasons. She heard you just had a baby and figured you'd be eager to make some money."

"How sweet of her to care," I said acidly. "That would give the insurance review committee a good laugh. She's wasting her time."

Beverly nodded. "Okay, her last question: Can you refer her to a plastic surgeon who would help her defraud her insurance company?"

"Of course not."

Beverly looked at me narrowly. "Jackson. That name doesn't ring a bell for you? She called us six months ago."

"For what?"

"The same thing."

"What did I say then?"

"The same thing."

We laughed. You have to credit some people for sheer determination. I returned to my desk and considered the mountain of mail in front of me. Microscopes! A Colorado firm wanted me to buy an operating microscope. Another had a laser for thirty thousand dollars. Ridiculous! I had a nice, solo plastic-surgery practice. I didn't need microscopes and lasers. I couldn't afford them, either. I wondered who did buy them. A big cardiology clinic in the area had recently gone bankrupt. They had bought so much equipment that they couldn't pay for it. Medicine had gone berserk over technology. Beverly buzzed me on the intercom.

"Elizabeth, a man just walked into the waiting room with a cut nose. He's bleeding all over the floor. Do you want to see him or should he go over to the emergency room?"

"Oh, no." I leapt to my feet. Action was better than micro-scopes. "I'll see him at once."

"Also, a lady called, all upset. She has a very painful breast and she thinks she has breast cancer. I explained that usually a general surgeon would take care of the cancer, and you would do the reconstruction. She still wanted to see you. You have a cancellation. What about it?"

"Absolutely." I straightened the sleeves of my white coat and went out to meet the bleeding nose. It belonged to Burton Prentice, a chunky, elderly gentleman in brown, blood-spattered work clothes who was holding a handkerchief to his face.

"Come on back to the examining room," I told him.

"Gosh, am I glad you're here, Doctor. I'd bleed to death be-fore I ever got to the emergency room," he said breathlessly, lying down on the examining table.

"You can't bleed to death from a cut on the nose," I said to calm him. "Let me take a look."

"Not bleed to death? I lost a lot of blood! You didn't see it," he said, outraged. "I must have bled a couple of pints."

"It sounds dreadful," I replied. Two teaspoons of blood at most, I thought to myself. If he was determined that this was a major hemorrhage, I wouldn't argue. He pulled away the handkerchief. The skin of the top of his nose was cut. It would heal better with a stitch or two.

"That's a nasty laceration," I told him. "It will need stitches."

"See! I was right. I knew it was bad," he said gleefully. "Go right ahead, Doctor. I'm in your hands."

"How did it happen?" I asked, opening the operating instruments.

"A hot-water furnace fell down," said Mr. Prentice.

"I beg your pardon?"

"A hot-water furnace."

"But how did it cut your nose?" I asked, opening a 6-0 nylon suture onto the operating stand.

"It fell on me."

"How did it fall on you? Were you trying to fix it?"

"Oh, no. I'm retired. I'm seventy years old last March."

"Congratulations," I said. "Were you trying to move your furnace?" I started to wash my hands.

"It's not my furnace."

"Whose is it?"

"My neighbor's."

"How did your neighbor's furnace fall on your nose?" I asked, putting on sterile gloves.

"It slipped."

I was utterly bewildered. "You know, Mr. Prentice, I don't think we're on the same wavelength. I assume this furnace is kept on the floor, not on a shelf."

"That's right."

"How did it slip and fall on your nose?"

"I was underneath it."

I gave up, and washed the blood off his face with sterile saline.

"I was carrying it downstairs on my back, of course, to do him a favor," Mr. Prentice said as an afterthought. "I felt it begin to slip, turned to try to catch it, and the darned thing fell on my nose. It must weigh a couple hundred pounds. Luckily, I was almost at the bottom and I caught it. No damage done."

"And you're seventy? You're lucky you aren't dead. You're going to feel a needle stick," I warned him. "I'll inject slowly, but the tip of the nose will hurt." I put a sterile gauze over the wound and injected. When the nose was numb, I put in three sutures.

"It must take a lot of stitches," Mr. Prentice said hopefully. His eyes were covered with gauze to protect them from the surgical light.

"Three."

"Is that all?" he asked. He sounded heartbroken.

"No. I'm wrong. Five stitches," I said hastily. "My mistake."

"Oh, yes. I thought three wouldn't be enough," he said smugly. To really healthy people, there is a glamour in being hurt.

I put in two extra stitches. It did no harm and made him happy. I bandaged his nose and Beverly gave him an appointment to have the stitches out. He gripped my hand fervently before he left.

"You're a pretty young thing, Mrs. Morgan, but I want you to know you saved my life today and I appreciate it. God bless you. And your husband, too."

"Thank you." An irrational urge made me want to tell him all about my problems. "Five stitches," he went on, oblivious to my inner turmoil. "Wait till I get home. My wife will never believe this happened. Fifty years of marriage and I've never had stitches. What a great day."

"He's cute," said Beverly when he left. "How did it happen?"

I grinned. "A hot-water furnace fell down."

"I beg your pardon?" said Beverly.

Mrs. Hastings, the lady who was sure she had breast cancer, was already waiting to see me. She was a glamorous woman in a yellow knit suit, with golden hair tumbling about her shoulders.

"I have a breast problem," she told me as soon as I had closed the examining-room door. She stopped talking.

"Yes?" I said to encourage her. Breast problems are embarrassing to talk about.

She started again with great determination. "It's taken me six months to get up the courage to see you," she said, sitting down on the examining table. "I know you'll tell me I need my breast cut off. When I hear the bad news, it will be easier for me, coming from a woman. At least you'll understand if I pass out. You must be used to that." She gave a nervous laugh. "I'm happily married and my husband won't hate me if I have one breast, but I'll hate myself. I refuse to go around lopsided for the rest of my life. A woman plastic surgeon can be more realistic about building a new breast. After all, you wear bras, too." She glanced at me. At the height of my pregnancy, I had still been flat. "I mean, I guess you do," she finished lamely.

I laughed. "Yes, I wear bras. Why are you so sure you have breast cancer?" I leaned one shoulder against the wall. It was fun being back at work.

I wondered how Lucy was doing on her first day at Nadine's. The day was half gone. I had meant to call Nadine to check on Lucy. I hadn't done it. I didn't know why. A surge of guilt intruded. I pushed the thought down. I was working. I couldn't think about Lucy now. It was too distracting. Somehow motherhood and surgery didn't mix. It made me feel uncomfortable. I could be a surgeon or a mother. I couldn't be both at the same time.

Mrs. Hastings was talking. "I had twins a year ago and I tried to breast-feed. Breast-feeding was a complete joke, by the way. I don't know if you've ever done it?" She looked at me.

"I tried and failed," I replied.

"So you know about that. My breasts made no milk and the babies were miserable, so we went to formula. Two months later, my left breast, almost overnight, hurt and got hard. I knew it was cancer, but I ignored it. Then I got a lump right here." She poked the upper part of her breast. "My husband felt that last night. He made me come to see you. If I have breast cancer, I won't live to raise my children." She clutched her hands tightly.

"Have you had any breast surgery?"

"No. After my first baby, I had cosmetic surgery to make my breasts bigger. Does that count?"

"Yes," I said. "Do you remember what kind of implant was used?" I asked, jotting notes on her chart.

She hesitated. "Something like about a hundred-ninety-cc silicone gel. Does that sound right?"

"Yes. I can almost tell you at this point that you don't have cancer, but let me examine you."

She lay down. Even under the sheet, the outline of her left breast jutted out, like a ball. It felt hard. The lump she was worried about was firm but squishy. It was silicone gel, not breast cancer.

"Can you find the lump?" Mrs. Hastings looked up at me anxiously. "If you don't find it, you'll think I'm imagining all this. I know it's there."

I smiled. "I can feel it. Is this it?"

She checked for herself. "Yes, that's it."

"Good. Now, sit up so we can talk." I pushed in the foot extension of the examining table, and she sat up with the sheet wrapped around her. "First of all, you don't have breast cancer. You have a hard scar around your silicone implant. That makes the whole breast feel hard. The lump is the silicone implant poking out through a hole in the scar," I explained. "Sometimes surgery is done to try to improve it —"

She waved to interrupt me. "With the children, I couldn't possibly afford it."

"That's fine, because surgery often doesn't work. A big advance came the day a professional football player hugged his girlfriend at a party. She had hard scars around her breasts from implants. During the bear hug, the breasts went pop."

"Oh, disgusting," wailed Mrs. Hastings.

"It is bizarre, but her breasts got soft. Anyhow, I can try to rupture the scar capsule in the office. If it works, your breast will become soft and stop hurting, but the scar will form again. You'll need to have the procedure repeated from time to time."

I discussed the risks — implant rupture, bleeding, failure of the scar to rupture.

"I'm ready," she said gamely, lying back. "I can't tell you how happy I am it's not cancer." She wiggled around to get settled. "Go ahead."

I put both hands around her right breast and squeezed hard. The capsule didn't budge. I repositioned my hands and squeezed harder. There was a crackle, like tearing paper. I felt the scar rip apart inside. I kept squeezing and the scar tore all around the breast implant. Her breast was soft again and the squishy lump had disappeared.

"Oh, bizarre!" said Mrs. Hastings. "I could actually hear the scar rupture." I helped her sit up. "Now that's incredible." She felt her breast. "It does feel soft. Now if it gets hard again, I just come back?"

"Certainly."

"You know, this may seem like a dumb question, but why did this happen? And why on only one breast?"

I shook my head. "It's one of medicine's mysteries."

"At least you can treat it. That's good enough for me. Are you married? Do you have children? You do? Do you have pictures? No?" She was shocked. I wondered if I hadn't photographed Lucy because I didn't love her enough. "I have to show you mine." I studied the twins in yellow jumpsuits and an older child in overalls and she breezed out of the office. I got out my office camera, folded it up, and tucked it into my briefcase. I was determined to photograph Lucy that night.

Being a mother was changing me. I didn't just love Lucy.

Every child struck a new note of sympathy in me. Lucy and the twins made a bond between Mrs. Hastings and me. My inevitable impending divorce was changing me, too. I had always been open about myself. Now I was wary. Divorce was so painful that I didn't want to name my status. To say I was married seemed a fraud. To say "separated" invited people to give me well-meant encouragement for a reconciliation when I knew there could be none. To say I was divorced was not true. I didn't mind Mrs. Hastings asking me if I had children. I was proud of Lucy, but I was upset when Mrs. Hastings asked me if I was married. I knew she meant well, but it was a struggle to keep my work and my personal life apart.

After Mrs. Hastings left, I took a break and headed for Beverly's room to chat until the next patient arrived. We collided.

"You're not going to like today's mail, Elizabeth," Beverly warned me, as we sorted ourselves out from the doorway. "Are you ready for a nasty shock?"

"How nasty?" I held out my hand for the letter.

"I don't know about you, but I'm astounded," said Beverly.

I saw the elegantly engraved envelope, the dark blue lettering on distinguished, cream-colored stationery. It was a bill from the law firm that had advised me on my practice in the past. I opened it and found a bill for their tax advice.

"Eight thousand dollars," I exclaimed. "Eight thousand dollars? For incorporating me? This is grotesque!"

"I warned you," said Beverly. The bill was a horrid shock. Life seemed to be a series of catastrophes of my own making. This was not the first time I had put myself in the hands of the wrong lawyers. I wondered what was wrong with me. Why couldn't I learn? I couldn't even choose the right law firm. Something over a thousand dollars had been their estimate a year ago. I felt like the eternal idiot child. Jim and my mother were more canny and more astute. I decided to call my younger brother, Rob, for advice. He was the lawyer. Rob and I are quite different. He was the liberal in college. I was the conservative. He likes boxing and books on political history. I like ballet and murder mysteries. Rob has admired things I have done, like being a surgeon. I have admired him for his courage in the war and for his dedication to law. I had helped Rob with medical problems in the past. I knew he would be willing to advise me now.

"Rob, if I babble," I said as soon as he answered, "tell me to stop, but I'm so upset, not to say totally bankrupt if I pay this bill, that I hardly know where to begin. I need your advice."

"You're babbling already, Elizabeth," Rob advised me solemnly. "Go ahead. I'm listening."

"Here is the problem. I went to this firm allegedly — I emphasize allegedly — because they are one of the best law firms in town. Ha! They're totally greedy cretins, that's what they are. They told me I should incorporate. They incorporated me, all right. They told me other firms would charge about a thousand dollars, but they were the best, so their bill would be a bit more."

"Oh, Elizabeth!" said Rob. "Right there you know they're going to sting you. Let's face it. A big law firm can be just as greedy as a little one. How much did you get stung?"

"Eight thousand dollars."

"Christ," said Rob. "They do have nerve. Most lawyers would only rob a big business on that scale. They usually don't bother with the small fry like you."

"Rob, they said they would send monthly bills. They never sent one until now, when the whole thing's over."

"You didn't ask, either. Your mistake. Keep talking."

"They did everything wrong. They had to file four times. They said it would take four months to do. It took a year!" I paused for breath. "And! And! They set it up wrong. Now I have to start all over and reincorporate in Virginia. Needless to say, I have a new lawyer."

"So they were incompetent," said Rob. "That's nothing new."

"And six weeks ago, one of their lawyers told me, with a jolly laugh, that they had never done an incorporation before and decided to learn, on my time, how it was done."

"What did you say to that?" asked Rob.

"Say? I was speechless."

"You ought to be grateful. They were incredibly stupid to tell you that. They'll cut your bill significantly if you squawk."

"What if I refuse to pay?"

"Waste of time. They'll take you to court and walk right over you. Lawyers know how to deal with uppity clients. Can I give you some advice, Elizabeth?" Rob asked politely. "I've told you this before. Big law firms have big reputations. They bill in the hundreds of thousands of dollars. If you're Coca-Cola or U.S. Steel, they may be worth it, but they don't know anything about legal problems for human beings. You need people tax advice. Anyhow, give them a hard time. They ought to give you some reduction for being a guinea pig.

"By the way, Janice is working late tonight, so I'm making dinner. Beef stroganoff. It should be delicious," he added with pride. Rob and Janice had been married for several years. I envied them their happy marriage.

"I didn't know you could cook, Rob."

"I'm a most resourceful man, Elizabeth. I've done my research and I've found that if you open the package labeled 'Beef Stroganoff' and put it in the microwave, you usually get beef stroganoff. It's worked so far." He cleared his throat. "Do you have a minute, so I could ask you something?"

"Of course."

"How do you find motherhood and a career working out?"

"Fantastic." I stopped. It was hell, so far. "I take that back. Rob, I'm miserable, but that's not Lucy. That's my marriage. Being a mother is fantastic. It seems to make my wasted marriage have some meaning. I love Lucy. I wouldn't trade her. I'd do it all again to have her. Lucy is a joy."

"Hmm. Can't have much personality at four weeks, can she? I didn't think the brain was that developed."

I felt ruffled and astounded. "Lucy has lots of personality. She's sweet-natured, and jolly and affectionate and cuddly —"

"Seriously," said Rob.

"I am serious. Wait till you're a father."

"Seriously," said Rob, "we've been thinking about it. Janice says we ought to move first, to a better house. It's hard to find the right house in the present market. Should we wait for the house? Maybe this wouldn't be the right time for a baby."

"If you ask me, Rob, there is never a right time. I had my life all planned and look what happened. You could still be waiting for the right house when you're a hundred. Babies now. Houses later."

"Well. We'll take that into consideration. Thanks a lot, Elizabeth," he said warmly.

I thanked him too and called the law firm.

"Elizabeth, how are you?" chirped Byron, the lawyer. "Cutting up a storm?"

"I got the bill, Byron."

"The bill? The bill? Oh yes, the bill. Is there a problem with the bill?"

"Eight thousand dollars is a big problem for me."

"I went over it carefully, Elizabeth. I gave you a significant reduction on it."

"That is a reduced bill?" I said in disbelief.

"Oh, significantly."

"Now wait a minute. It took you a year, three times longer than you said."

"These things happen, Elizabeth. The Virginia government held us up."

"Oh, no. You sent the wrong forms."

"There is that."

"And I was supposed to get a monthly bill."

"My fault," he chirped. "I apologize."

Apologies! I fumed. I tried to sound reasonable. "Last month you told me this was the first time your firm had done this. You said you were learning from my case. I don't mind being a guinea pig. I don't pay to be a guinea pig."

"Now don't get bitter, Elizabeth."

"I am bitter. If it takes an intern ten times longer to remove an appendix because he's never done one before, the patient doesn't expect to pay ten times as much." I heard the ring in my voice. I was more upset than I ought to be. My emotions were spilling over into everything.

He sighed. "What do you want to pay?"

"Nothing," I suggested, to tweak him.

"Oh, my God, Elizabeth." He became quite alarmed. "We couldn't possibly do that. Absolutely out of the question."

"What about two thousand dollars? That's twice what you said it would probably cost."

"Impossible. No. No." He meditated a moment. "At five thousand dollars, we are giving our services away. Absolutely free. Let's call it five thousand. How's the pension-plan specialist we referred you to?"

"Worthless."

"How's the accounting firm?"

"Worthless. They computerized my accounts in Chinese. I don't speak Chinese."

"I'm sorry you feel this way, Elizabeth. Is there anything more we could do to help?"

"Byron, you've done plenty."

The next day I received a bill for four thousand dollars. This time I didn't object to their incompetence.

Money was a constant worry for me. I made my living by doing surgery. I had seen patients in the office up to the last day before Lucy was born, but I had done no surgery for two weeks before that. You can't operate one day and go into labor the next. It's cutting it too fine. You might go into labor during the operation. I wasn't scheduled to operate my first week back at work either. I knew I would be tired. I didn't want to make a mistake at surgery. Altogether it had been seven weeks of no income. We had saved money in the office all year in preparation for this, but it was worrisome. Bills had to be paid. The rent, taxes, supplies, insurance — all had to be paid, in addition to Beverly's salary and mine. The legal bill was a severe blow.

My last patient that day was Pamela Dalton. Her cosmetic nose operation would be my first surgery since Lucy was born. Pamela was a shy southern lady with beautiful manners.

"I don't really care if you make my nose look pretty, Doctor, but you must make it look different." She tilted her head and smiled at me. "I had good parents, but they never loved me. I was the child they didn't want. My parents would tell me that my nose made me look ugly. My parents are both dead now." She sat for a moment. "So just give me a different nose."

There were so many things to remember now that I was a mother. After Pamela Dalton left, I made a mental note that I should never criticize Lucy's nose. It seemed silly, but who could tell what would really hurt a child? My own mother was always so gentle. I could be outspoken, almost abrasive. I didn't want to be like that to my child. I wanted always to be gentle and kind. I had to improve.

It was almost six when Beverly and I left the office. Six was early for me. Once the office was settled financially, I wanted to leave earlier, but that would take months.

It was a long day for Lucy to be away from home, I thought to myself, too long and too far for her to travel. I didn't see what I could do about it. Compulsively, I went over my other problems. I had to get a divorce. As much as I hated it, my mother was right. I had to start over again as soon as I could. That meant I needed time to talk with my lawyer. I desperately needed to look over my finances. We had to move, for Lucy's sake. Each day I saw a little more clearly what she would need:

friends, school, neighbors. I had to know what house I could afford. I had to get Lucy enrolled on my health plan. She needed new clothes. She was a big baby and she had outgrown her newborn clothes. And we were low on Carnation milk and diapers again. And Lucy needed to see Odette for her newborn-baby checkup. It was too much. I wiped my mind blank and drove to Nadine Hoskins's.

"Let me change her," said Nadine. "Don't take her home wet. She took four ounces a half-hour ago. She is a good eater. Does she sleep through the night?"

"Not yet." I picked Lucy up. She fell asleep on my shoulder. "Poor, tired baby." I kissed her and patted her on the way to the car. Brenda, her temporary night nurse, was still coming every night to look after Lucy. She was expensive, but she was worth it. With her, I could work. Lucy was awake three or four times a night, and sometimes all night. Sometimes she woke up to play, not to cry. One night I came downstairs and found her perched on Brenda's lap, grinning while Brenda chattered nonsense at her. I couldn't resist. I took her from Brenda and tickled her toes and cuddled her until my yawns forced me back to bed. I almost couldn't remember what life had been like without Lucy.

She slept on the way home. I continued my mental list of things to do. I stopped at a red light. Lucy squeaked in protest. She liked the motion of the car. "We'll move soon." I patted her tummy. She fell asleep with an approving smile when we started to move again. I reached out and touched her hand. I felt I had never been really happy until I became a mother.

⇒ *three*

A WEEK LATER, I settled myself cross-legged on my bed to study Pamela Dalton's nose. It was the night before her operation. Her new nose would be with her all her life. I had to plan it carefully. Lucy was downstairs with Brenda. I could hear Brenda babbling away to Lucy, who was in her bassinet in the little living room, and could picture Lucy watching her, amused, with huge, brown, roving eyes. My mother came in.

"Have you thought about tomorrow?" she asked me.

"How do you mean?" I spoke absently. I was thinking noses.

"Aren't you operating?"

"Yes."

"At the usual time?"

"Yes. Eight-fifteen." My mother said nothing. Baffled, I looked up. My mother looked pale and drawn. "Mother, is something the matter?" I felt callous to have ignored her.

"I'm a little tired. What about Lucy? Are you going to take Lucy to Nadine Hoskins's at seven in the morning before you operate? Isn't that too early for her? Wouldn't you like me to take Lucy over about nine?"

I sunk my head in my hands. "I don't believe myself sometimes. I forgot about having to take her. Would you take Lucy for me?"

"Certainly. She's so little now, it's easy to carry her." My mother's voice sounded flat. I looked at her closely.

"Have you been talking to Daddy? Was that who called you?" My mother looked sad.

"Is it that easy to tell?" she asked. She held up her hand to stop me from talking. "Don't tell me what to do, Elizabeth. I know what you think, but we've been married almost forty years. You weren't married that long. You don't understand."

I gritted my teeth. I hated to see my mother upset. I wanted her to be able to enjoy life. Maybe I couldn't understand. My marriage had not lasted long. Even so, I knew that my life and my husband's would be intertwined through Lucy, for years. Starting life over would be far more difficult for my parents.

"You have to let me work this out, Elizabeth. He's my husband. I didn't interfere with yours." She was right. There was little I could do to help her. Since her illness, stress quickly made her look wan and distraught. After forty years of marriage, she might find it easier to have her husband on any terms than to face life without him. She would always have a home with me, but it wasn't the same without her husband. I sighed. I wanted mine too.

"I'm sorry, Mother." I kissed her good night. Life was very strange. A year ago I knew my future. Six months ago I had my doubts. Now I had no idea. I tried to think about Pamela Dalton's nose, but I thought of my husband's face instead.

I yanked open my purse and opened my wallet. I sat staring for a long time at the snapshot I had of him. I had thought I was getting over him. I slapped the wallet shut. It reminded me of the night I left him. I sat cross-legged, my head in my hands, misty-eyed, going over and over my life with him. At last I returned to Pamela Dalton, and then I went to bed.

Lucy changed my life, and my mother's. We took turns feeding her because it was such fun. She was so delighted to be fed and had such a good time blowing bubbles afterward. I loved dressing her. All her clothes were pink, and she looked especially sweet in pink, ruffled rompers, but dressing and feeding her was time-consuming too. We started waking up an hour earlier than previously, and even earlier, once I was operating again. The morning of Pamela Dalton's surgery was the first of many times my mother took Lucy to Nadine's for me, because it gave Lucy more time to sleep. She needed it. When she was first born, she would sleep anywhere, but that changed. She was alert and watchful like a wren. Once she woke up, she wouldn't doze off again.

It felt strange to be back in the operating room. It was so far removed from Lucy. An operation made me inaccessible to the outside world and to Lucy if she needed me. I felt preoccupied with "ifs" as I walked into the operating suite. If she were too sick to go to Nadine's, what would I do? My mother would help me out. If my mother were away or sick herself, what then? I would have to cancel surgery. If I canceled out on surgery, I would soon not have a practice. When I was single, I had been impatient with divorced women who complained. It was very sad and difficult, but where was the stiff upper lip? How grossly ignorant I had been. It made no sense for me to try to manage alone as a single mother. My mother was the full-time live-in help that made my life possible. I changed in the nurses' lounge and went to see Mrs. Dalton.

"I'm terribly nervous," she told me when I met her at the operating room.

"It would be surprising if you weren't," I replied. I bent over her to mark her nose with a blue surgical marking pen. I outlined the bone I would remove from her profile. This was important. Her nose would swell during surgery. Without my marks to guide me, I could misjudge how much bone to remove. Rosemary, the circulating nurse, came in with a stretcher and we wheeled Mrs. Dalton into the operating room. A surgeon works with two nurses — a scrub nurse, who hands the instruments to the doctor and helps with the surgery, and a circulator, who looks after the patient and gets equipment as it is needed. I had always gotten on well with nurses. Without the advantages I grew up with, I might well have been a nurse, not a doctor.

"Hold on. These are cold," Rosemary warned Mrs. Dalton,

putting sticky foam pads for the heart monitor onto her chest. I turned up the speed of the intravenous fluid.

"Mrs. Dalton, I'll be giving you Valium now. It may make your arm ache, and it will make you giddy."

I injected the Valium slowly and watched the heart monitor. Her cardiac pattern bleeped steadily across the screen. I could tell Mrs. Dalton was sedated. Her shoulders relaxed from their tensed position. Shoulders are the first thing to show tension. You can see it even in professional ballet dancers. Only the best will dance with their shoulders relaxed, in a correct position.

"How are you feeling now?" I asked her.

"Yesh," she replied. "Interesh . . . intereshing."

She didn't move when I injected Xylocaine around her nose. Without sedation, this would have been intensely painful for her. Holding one of Mrs. Dalton's nostrils up with a hook, I put the long, fine needle inside her nose and injected into the skin on top, and into the tip. Then I put cocaine packing into the nose to numb it. Cocaine kills pain and stops bleeding in the nose, but it is rapidly absorbed. An overdose causes convulsions and may be fatal. I scraped away the hair in her nostril with a scalpel, cleaned the inside with an iodine solution, and looked once again at her preoperative photographs. Rosemary had spread them out on a table behind me. My headlight drifted out of line.

"Drat." I took a sterile sponge, adjusted the light, and tossed the sponge into the bucket by my foot.

"Sorry. The good one is out for repairs," whispered Camilla. She was the scrub nurse assisting me. Camilla and Rosemary were both working mothers, both happily married. Camilla had three grown children. Rosemary had a two-year-old.

I love to operate, but it makes me nervous. I felt my shoulders tense. Plastic surgery on the nose is difficult. Mrs. Dalton's nose was delicate. To remove too much would be a disaster; she might never breathe normally again. To remove too little would waste her time and money.

"Fifteen, please." Camilla handed me the scalpel. I poised the blade in the nose over the excess cartilage of Mrs. Dalton's broad tip. A horrible hiss broke out in the quiet room.

"Please clamp off the suction, Camilla. I hate that noise," I said, annoyed. The sound had broken my concentration.

"Sorry." She clamped the tubing and the noise stopped. She spoke patiently. Nurses are used to working with jumpy surgeons. An experienced scrub nurse ignores the surgeon's mood. I returned to the operation and sank the scalpel into the tip of the nose. Using fine scissors, I cut the cartilage free and checked her nose from the outside. It looked like the right amount. Camilla held the nostril up with a hook. I grasped the cartilage with forceps and carved off the excess from inside the nose. The cocaine was working; Mrs. Dalton had no pain and no bleeding. I removed the excess cartilage from her other nostril. She was so extraordinarily immobile that I wondered if she was oversedated. Camilla and I looked at each other and raised our eyebrows. Such silent conversations go on all through an operation.

"Take a deep breath," I asked Mrs. Dalton. Her chest rose and sank with a sigh. Camilla and I nodded to each other, reassured.

"It's all so fascinating," Mrs. Dalton drawled politely.

I turned back to work. My headlight lit up the cavernous recesses of her nose, making it possible for me to see inside. I sank the scalpel blade inside her nose along the roof. "Joseph elevator, Camilla." She handed me the fine, sharp instrument and I wiggled it down to the bone. Suddenly an earthquake erupted. Mrs. Dalton was coughing. I pulled out the Joseph so it wouldn't tear her nose apart. "Are you comfortable?" I asked her.

"Yes, Doctor, I'm real comfortable. Thank you. I had a little tickle." Blood from her nose had sprayed on both of us. Camilla wiped it off her instruments. I adjusted the cocaine packs. They probably had made her cough.

Pamela Dalton had a high, sharp hump on her nose. I pointed a finger at the 7-millimeter chisel. Camilla handed it to me and picked up a rubber mallet. Camilla and I worked together often. She knew what I wanted before I asked. It made surgery a pleasure.

I slid the chisel into the nose and I sank it into the hump of bone.

"Good. Tap, tap, please, Camilla. Very gently." Camilla tapped the chisel with the mallet. My chisel slid forward. I checked its position by feeling the nose on the outside. I didn't want the chisel to rip out through her skin. "One more time. Tap, tap." The chisel scooted to the root of the nose. I wiggled it and felt the bone come loose. I slid out the chisel and extracted the bone with bayonet forceps. With the hump of bone gone, there was still too much cartilage along the top of her nose. I sliced it off with a scalpel. This requires a wicked-looking blade that looks like a miniature machete. Now that the cartilage was gone, the bones felt too sharp. I rasped them down until they felt smooth. All this motion under the skin made the nose swell. It was puffy now, with no shape. My last step was to cut the nose bones free from the cheek to narrow the nose. This is done entirely by feel.

"The curved guarded Nievert, please." Camilla put the curved chisel in my hand. Doing this part is like being a sculptor. The bone is much thicker here, on the sides, than on top of the nose. I put the chisel into the left nostril and sank it into the bone. Camilla gave two taps. Nothing happened. "Harder — tap, tap," I said. She whacked the chisel and it surged forward. I felt it under the skin. "Just like that again." The chisel progressed. At the root of the nose, the sound of the striking mallet changed from sharp to dull. Blood streamed out of Mrs. Dalton's left nostril and down her cheek.

Camilla put a gauze sponge over the stream of blood and tapped my chisel along the right side of the nose. Now both bones were free. Blood was pouring out both nostrils. This part of a rhinoplasty looks like a horror movie. It makes my stomach turn to watch someone else do it, but when I do it, it's fun. Gently, I pressed the loosened bones together. The top of the nose became thin and narrow. The bleeding slowed to a trickle. The nose had no shape now, but I could feel the shape by pressing on the skin. I wiped the blood off Mrs. Dalton's face, sewed up the incisions, and molded wet plaster over her nose. Things had gone well. Her tissues were easy to work with. It hadn't been a struggle. Even so, although I didn't feel my blood pressure go up during the surgery, I could feel it come down now. I had done my best. The rest was up to Mrs. Dalton and how she healed.

We wheeled her out to the recovery room. "Not so bad, was it?" Rosemary asked her. "I have a bump on my nose, too," she continued. "If I didn't have a baby, I might ask Dr. Morgan to fix it, but I'm scared my son will hit me and break my new nose to bits. And my husband says he likes me the way I am."

Pamela Dalton was sitting up and sipping tea in the recovery room by the time I had written out her instructions.

"You did beautifully," I told her. She reached out for my hand.

"Everyone was so nice. I didn't feel a thing. I'd love to do the things you do, Doctor." I'd love to have a husband as nice as yours, I thought to myself. Happiness was more important than any career. I wanted to be happy again.

"Did you feel any pain?" I asked her. "Do you remember the injection?"

She paused. "Maybe I remember your saying something about an injection, but it didn't hurt, if that's what you mean."

I was relieved. She had needed so little sedation that I thought she might have been uncomfortable. "Where is your daughter today?" I asked.

"She starts high school this week," said Pamela Dalton

proudly. "Time goes so fast. I can't believe she's there. Diapers seemed like forever, and the rest went by in a flash." She shook her head. "I couldn't do diapers again to save my soul."

"The disposable ones are great, especially the ones with the elastic bands." I spoke with the authority of motherhood. Diapers didn't bother me. Perhaps my surgical training had inured me to smell and mess.

I left her to her solicitous husband, who had been hovering outside. I changed out of my bloody scrub clothes and studied my face in the mirror. I was pale, still. My hair was limp. My dresses looked dowdy on me. There was nothing I could do about my looks. I called Beverly instead.

"Don't forget the meeting at the hospital tonight, Elizabeth, to elect the medical officers. It's mandatory," she reminded me.

"Oh damn. What time?" I cursed myself. Nadine Hoskins wouldn't keep Lucy beyond seven. She had her own family. I had made no arrangements for Lucy. I couldn't ask my mother. An eternal optimist, she was going out to dinner with my father. Jim or Rob and Janice would take Lucy gladly in an emergency. My disorganized life as a new mother was a chronic condition, not an emergency.

"By the way," I asked Beverly, "did Mary Clinton ever call? She had her baby ages ago." Mrs. Clinton had a three-inch malignant tumor on her thigh. She had so far refused to have surgery.

"No," said Beverly. "Want me to call her?"

"I'd better do it." Beverly gave me her number. "And your brother Jim called. He says that if you had been investing in commodities and had gone long for four contracts of spring corn, you would have lost two million dollars. He says he knows you feel bad about some of your investments and he wants you to keep it in perspective."

I burst out laughing. Jim was very kindhearted and had a great sense of humor. Things would be definitely worse if I were two million dollars in debt. I had avoided getting myself into debt. Besides having Lucy, that was the smartest thing I had done.

"Also, Beverly, when can I see Donald Lamont?" He was my lawyer. "And I need time to sit down with you to go over finances."

"Will do," said Beverly. I heard her flip through the appointment book. "You don't have much free time, but I'll work it out for you."

Beverly was wonderful. She ran my professional life. Between my mother and Beverly, I didn't see why my life was so hard. I sat by the phone and thought for a moment. My pregnancy had left me sick and exhausted. That would pass. Someday my broken heart would mend. Lucy would sleep through the night, someday. When I had energy again, it would be easier doing the chores that seemed so hard — the clothes, the trash, the groceries, the cleaning. I would find a house. Somewhere. If I kept working hard, there would be money. But what about seeing my baby? Where was the time for her? I had to arrange my life so that being a mother came first, or I would grow old and Lucy would grow up, and we wouldn't know each other.

For now, there was work to do. I dialed Mary Clinton, my patient with the malignant leg tumor. She was young and had two children. The tumor had been growing for five years. Another doctor had removed it, but inadequately. It had come back, bigger than before. It stuck out on her leg like a black golf ball. It was probably a rare tumor called a malignant histiocytoma, which grows slowly and can be cured by a very wide excision. A neglected histiocytoma is fatal. My problem was getting Mrs. Clinton onto the operating table.

"Oh, Dr. Morgan." Mary Clinton answered the phone and sounded flustered. I heard her baby start to cry. "I can't talk now."

"Mrs. Clinton, you have to talk to me. Why don't you pick the baby up and come back to the phone?"

"I really can't. Oh, dear." She clicked her tongue. "I sort of hoped you'd forgotten about me. Okay." The phone clattered as she put it down. I heard the crying stop and she came back to the phone. "I'm here, Doctor."

"Mrs. Clinton, you know what I'm calling about."

"I know, Doctor. We're so busy. I don't have time to have surgery. Can't we just talk about it?"

"Mrs. Clinton, we've talked about it for six months. Talking won't solve the problem."

"I don't want you to operate."

"Someone has to."

"I can't stay in the hospital overnight."

"You may be able to go home the same day. I can't promise."

"Dr. Morgan, I'll be honest with you. I really do not want this operation. I don't want to die from cancer. No one in my family has cancer."

I raised my eyes to heaven and gesticulated at the telephone. Would she please listen to me? The operation should cure her. If she wanted to live, she had to have surgery. I felt frustrated. She was too young to waste her life. "Mrs. Clinton, listen to me." I spoke slowly and calmly. "I know you're afraid. This tumor will not kill you today. But if you don't have it removed, when your little baby is in high school you could be dying. You don't want that for your children."

There was a deep sigh. "I know, Doctor. It's just not the right time."

I thought of Rob and Janice. They couldn't find the right time for a baby. I thought of Lucy. She hadn't come at the right time. Things didn't happen in life at the right time.

"Mrs. Clinton, there is never a right time for an operation. I'm going to book your surgery. If you don't come for your operation, I can't help you. There's nothing more I can do."

She clicked her tongue again. "Oh, well, I can't have surgery now," she hesitated. "My husband can't manage a baby, but go ahead and schedule it, Doctor. Bye." She hung up quickly. I called Beverly and asked her to book Mary Clinton's operation. We would tell her when to come in for surgery. The rest was up to her. She was perverse to run around with an untreated cancer.

I arrived late at Nadine Hoskins's, just past seven. As I drove up, my husband was walking out of Nadine's house toward his car. He didn't see me. Briskly, he shot his cuffs, buttoned his coat, and pulled on his driving gloves. I knew those gloves. I chose them with him. I knew the clothes. I knew the suit. I knew he was going out, somewhere special. I waited, praying he wouldn't see me, feeling like an orphan in the cold with my nose pressed up against the candy-store window. I felt ashamed, watching him. I was intruding in a life in which I no longer had a place. When he had gone, I got out and went in.

"Nadine?" I called out. Lucy was in a playpen. She turned her head at my voice and smiled. Nadine came out of the kitchen and watched us.

"She's beginning to know you," she said.

"Do you think so?" I was thrilled. I wanted so much for Lucy to know it was me. Nadine helped me tuck Lucy in the car. As soon as I set off, she started to whimper. She was more active every day. "Don't cry, little bundle," I whispered to her at a stoplight as I adjusted her pink quilt. "Don't cry." The traveling to Nadine's bothered her now. It was a half-hour drive each way, every day — a lot for a baby. If only I had been more selfish for her. I should have made my husband travel to see her, not the other way round. Why hadn't I thought of Lucy first, and not of him? She calmed down on the weekends, but she was fretful during the week. Tonight it would be worse than usual. She would be out with me until the meeting was over. I had to go to the meeting. Doctors' hospital privileges are revoked if they do not attend required meetings. It felt like catch-22. Because I was a mother, I had to work harder. Because I worked harder, I wouldn't be a proper mother.

I fed Lucy in the car before we went into the hospital. She

blinked cheerfully, cradled in my arms, and drank down a half-bottle of Carnation milk and Karo syrup. She looked up at the bright lights when I stopped to sign in at the hospital desk. The staff secretary smiled. "Is that your baby?"

"Yes." Lucy's big eyes got rounder and she smiled into her quilt. I knew she liked the attention, little as she was. I signed in and went into the auditorium. Like a number of the doctors present, Lucy slept through the meeting. Franklin Grove, another doctor, sat next to me. He was a big, solid man, conservative and conventional.

"Are you back at work, Elizabeth?" he demanded.

"I've been back more than a week," I replied.

"It's too soon," said Franklin. He frowned. "Bad for your baby." I gritted my teeth and smiled. It was none of his damned business. I was Lucy's mother, and if I didn't have to be there, sitting next to him in a hospital meeting, I wouldn't have been. My baby and I would both be home. If Franklin Grove wanted me at home, he ought to pay Lucy's bills. After the meeting, Lucy woke up to inspect her surroundings.

"She's not allowed to vote, you know," said Odette, coming up the aisle. "She looks good. How are you?"

"Odette, I'm absolutely fine." My voice was as hard as glass.

"Tell me another one," said Odette mockingly. "And him?"

"It's over."

"For sure? No regrets?"

"Lots of regrets, Odette. It was a mistake, but I've got Lucy. I can't complain."

Odette patted my shoulder. "I knew it wouldn't work. I'm not surprised, but now you have the baby, and you have the struggle," exclaimed Odette. "Can you manage, Elizabeth?"

"So far. I wouldn't be here without my mother."

"What would we do without our mothers?" said Odette. "I can't wait for mine to come to visit." She laughed and we walked out together.

Lucy slept on the way home. It was past nine and she was

exhausted. As I drove, I thought about how important my family was — the ones who stuck by each other. There was my mother, Jim, Rob and Janice, me, and Lucy now. There was my aunt, my mother's sister. She was family, but far away in England. There was so much I wanted for Lucy. I wanted my family to get bigger, not smaller. I wanted her to have cousins. For her sake, I wanted Rob and Janice to have a baby. I wanted her to have a home. I had looked for houses. There were homes for families and homes for singles. It seemed that the single mother hadn't been noticed yet. There were lavish houses with grand master bedrooms and sunken tubs, and houses miles out in the country. There were ones with lawns we couldn't manage and ones that needed a "handyman" to keep them livable. I had looked at rental places again. I could afford a high-rise apartment, but I couldn't face an elevator every time that Lucy and the stroller went out and the groceries and the diaper boxes came in. At least now we had a front door. And after the teenage thugs on the patio, nothing had happened to disturb our peace. I had time to keep on looking. The house I bought might be the one we lived in for the next twenty years. It had to be right.

When we got home, I tucked Lucy in her bassinet in the living room, under Brenda's watchful eye. Lucy curled up, with her rump in the air and her head in her pink pillow, and fell asleep.

"You don't need me any longer," said Brenda. "She's slept through all week."

"Are you sure?"

She nodded. "I'm going to miss her. Your mom's already in bed, but Jim called." On the way upstairs, I came across a stack of garden catalogs. It was a good sign. My mother loves to garden and the collection of daffodils and tulip bulbs that she was ordering for next spring meant she was feeling happier.

I tiptoed into my bedroom and shut the door. I didn't want my call to Jim to wake my mother. Jim and I had grown up fighting. He got into trouble with my father. I got him into trouble. At times we almost hated each other and my mother had despaired. When we had grown up and sorted out our feelings, we found we were much alike. We got on well and we were very close.

"Hey, kid," said Jim when I called him. "I'm sitting here with my feet on the windowsill pigging out on peanut-butter ice cream. It's dinner. I'm in a great mood. I got a new client today. We're doing beans."

"Beans?"

"Soybeans. Futures trading in soybeans. How's my most favorite niece?"

"Sleeping through the night, Jimmy. She is so much fun. I never thought that a reasonable person like me could sit all day and go goofy over my baby."

"A reasonable person can't," said Jim. "What makes you think you're reasonable?" He laughed. "Has the 'ex' been bothering you?" Jim was protective. He didn't like the idea of my husband coming around.

"No, I don't talk to him much."

"Yeah. I'd like to talk to him. Listen, I know you're all broken up, but have you given up on marriage?"

"With him?"

"Hell, no. I mean someone else."

"No."

"That's smart. No point in being bitter. I found a guy who had possibilities, but he was married. That's the breaks." Jim talked about his new girlfriend for a while. She was immensely rich and couldn't see why Jim wouldn't take her to a dance in Rome over the weekend.

After we said good night, I started to make a new list of what I had to do: see my lawyer, get a divorce, find a new house, buy a bolt for the stroller and a high chair. The list grew longer. I felt like an ant struggling to carry a loaf of bread. I gave up and turned out the light. Downstairs, Lucy whimpered and Brenda babbled to her soothingly. I wanted to be downstairs with her. I thought about Mary Clinton and her cancer and whether she would live to raise her children. I wondered if I would live to raise Lucy. Car accidents, strokes, and cancer are part of life. If I died, what about Lucy? Every week I saw women who wanted breast reconstruction after cancer. Many were young mothers. Some had only a few years to live. Breast cancer is epidemic. I kicked off the sheets and sat up in bed, panicked. I did my first breast self-exam. It never seemed important before. I felt no lumps. Reassured, I fell asleep.

My appointment with Donald Lamont, my lawyer, was to take place on the same day as Mary Clinton's cancer surgery. Her operation was an "add-on" at the end of the day, the first time available. I had other operations scheduled that day. My first was a little two-year-old with a precancerous birthmark on his chest.

When I left in the morning, Lucy was seated on my mother's knee at our little dining-room table. She was being introduced to a cup and spoon.

"If you get her used to the idea early, she won't have trouble later on," said my mother. "Do you mind if I try?" She was already dressed, although it was not seven. Only on occasional weekends would she agree to breakfast in her bathrobe. "If you don't mind, Elizabeth, I'll dig up the rosebush in the front. It's quite dead. Roses won't do well on this street. There's not enough sun." She stopped to put applesauce in Lucy's mouth. "That white azalea and salmon impatiens would look nice against the brick."

"You're incorrigible, Mother." Her love of flowers was a standing joke.

I was watching Lucy, fascinated. She was trying to suck on the spoon in her mouth. She spat it out. She had applesauce on her tongue. She tried to eat it by smacking her lips energetically. It went up her nose. She sneezed applesauce across the table and beamed proudly at me. I applauded vigorously.

"Mother, try again. She loves it."

"You'd better go, dear. It's getting late." She was right. I kissed them both and rushed away, leaving them playing food games. I felt happy this morning, energetic and cheerful. We were beginning to do well.

"We need you on a stretcher now, young man," a pre-op nurse was saying to my first patient, Guy Brooks, when I arrived. His mother, a sturdy blond, stroked his head affectionately. Guy sat bolt upright, clutching a stuffed lion. Dr. Sheridan, the anesthesiologist, approached them. He was a tall man with grizzled hair. A mask dangled from his neck, and his crumpled surgical scrubs were covered by a white coat.

"Hello, I'm Dr. Sheridan. Guy looks like a brave boy. You aren't going to cry, are you?" He patted his knee. Guy frowned.

"He comes home today?" asked Mrs. Brooks.

"Yes," said Dr. Sheridan. "He's an outpatient." He checked the chart. "Everything's fine. See you soon." He disappeared through the automatic doors into the operating room.

"Dr. Morgan, you take good care of my baby." Mrs. Brooks beckoned me around the corner. "He's not going to die, is he, Dr. Morgan?" she whispered.

The horrible memory came to me of Lucy turning blue in the delivery room, on the verge of death. Anyone can die during surgery. What would Lucy's death do to me? An empty life after a painful marriage. "There is always a risk when anyone is put to sleep, but the anesthesiologists are excellent here," I replied.

"I've seen on TV about people being vegetables after anesthesia." Mrs. Brooks sighed. "I'm worried sick."

"As soon as Guy goes into the operating room, you have some breakfast and then go to the main lobby. I'll call you when he's in the recovery room."

Mrs. Brooks looked up at me. "Have you had breakfast? You can't operate on an empty stomach."

"I had breakfast."

"You don't have children," she said accusingly.

"I have a baby girl."

"You do? Oh, you were pregnant. I thought you were fat. So that's okay then." She sounded satisfied, as though with a child of my own I wouldn't kill hers. I left her with Guy and went into the operating suite and down to the locker rooms.

I stopped first at the men's locker room. I needed scrub clothes. At Smith Center, you get scrub clothes from the men's locker room. It was awkward. I pounded on the door. A sign said, "Absolutely No Women Allowed. Do Not Enter." A balding surgical resident opened the door and looked out at me. Beyond him, two surgeons in shorts sidled away.

"What size?" asked the resident before I spoke.

"Whatever comes first. They're all extralarge anyhow."

He closed the door and reappeared with a handful of scrub clothes. "You're in luck. I found two large and a medium." He tossed them at me. I thanked him and went to the nurses' lounge to change.

With blue paper shoe-covers over my sandals, a blue paper shower-cap on my head, and a blue paper mask over my face, I was ready to work. There's a thrill to passing through the second set of automatic doors. These lead out of the main operating hallway into the inner sanctum. Here the long, dark corridors are lined with towering steel autoclaves, steel sinks, racks of boxes filled with sutures, and carts with drugs. Doors lead off the corridors to the operating rooms themselves. I pushed open the door to Operating Room Three.

Guy was perched on the edge of the operating table, his short, fat legs sticking out from under his gown. I wanted to cuddle him. He held his lion with one hand and a black rubber anesthetic mask in the other. Children are allowed to bring stuffed animals with them to surgery. Strictly speaking, it shouldn't be allowed, but rules are bent for the sake of kindness. Dr. Sheridan stood by while Catherine Dove, the nurse anesthetist, told Guy what to do. Catherine was pretty, and also sexy. Her small waist and full breasts showed even in the baggy scrub clothes. She had magenta fingernails, perfectly manicured, and dark eyes outlined in black. With her face masked, she looked exotic, like a woman in a Turkish harem, but there was something wrong with her today. I couldn't decide what it was.

"Now put the mask over your mouth, just like an astronaut," Catherine coaxed Guy. "Does it smell bad?" She put her arm around him. Guy nodded as he held the mask over his face.

"What a good boy. Take a big breath and blow the smell away, honey."

Catherine twiddled the knob on the halothane control. I glanced at Guy's heart tracing on the monitor. It was normal. He took a huge breath and another.

"Blow it all away," said Catherine softly. "That's a good boy."

Guy's eyelids drooped and Catherine laid him back on the operating table. He was asleep. Catherine took the mask off his face and put a laryngoscope into his mouth. Two PVCs, heart misbeats, blipped across the screen. Children are susceptible to heart arrhythmias in the early stages of anesthesia. I looked at the monitor anxiously; so did Dr. Sheridan, standing beside me.

"Easy as pie." Catherine peered into the back of his throat. Dr. Sheridan put the endotracheal tube into her hand. The PVCs increased. Dr. Sheridan glanced at the screen and said, "He is in quadrigeminy." The room became eerily quiet. We braced for disaster in the form of a cardiac fibrillation. Dr. Sheridan pulled open the drug tray. Catherine pushed the tube gently into Guy's mouth and into the lungs, and she attached it to the anesthetic machine. Dr. Sheridan turned off the anesthesia and Catherine pumped oxygen into his lungs. Guy's heart rhythm returned to normal. Dr. Sheridan turned the anesthesia on again, and looked at me. "Kids are tricky. Were you worried?"

"Yes."

"Me, too."

Ten minutes later, gowned and gloved, I was ready to operate.

Camilla, the scrub nurse, handed me the ruler. I measured the nevus. Insurance payment depends on the size of a growth.

"Dr. Morgan, what is this?" Camilla asked.

"A giant hairy nevus," I said.

"A who?" asked Catherine from beyond the drapes. "It sounds like a video game. Don't let the giant hairy nevus catch you."

"Giant because it's big," I explained, "hairy because it's hairy, and *nevus* means 'spot present at birth.' Big, brown, hairy spot present at birth." I drew the outline of my surgical incision with the marking pen. I held out my hand and Camilla put the epinephrine syringe in my palm.

"Can I give him five cc's of one-to-four-hundred-thousand, Catherine?" I asked.

"We're using halothane." Her dark eyes appeared from behind the drapes as she stood up. "I'd rather you didn't."

Epinephrine can cause heart arrhythmias if it is used with certain anesthetics, including halothane. I put the syringe aside and held out my hand for the scalpel. "This is going to bleed a bit," I warned Camilla. I pulled Guy's skin taut with one hand and cut down hard, like a chef slicing a roast, straight through the skin to the muscle of the back. Camilla turned on the suction. I shook my head. She turned it off.

"I need some Kochers." She slipped a Kocher clamp into my hand. I clamped it into the nevus. "Can you hold these, Camilla, please." She took the handles and pulled up hard. I sliced the birthmark away, leaving smooth, pink muscle beneath. With the last cut, the birthmark jumped out of the wound and dangled from the clamp in Camilla's hand.

"Specimen," Camilla announced. She dropped the nevus into a cardboard tub that Rosemary, our circulator, held out.

Blood spurted from the wound. With epinephrine, there might have been no bleeding at all. I put a lap pad over the wound. The white sponge turned pink and then red. We worked our way around the cut skin. I sizzled each bleeding vessel with an electric cautery. In between, Camilla scraped the cautery clean. Then Camilla put a skin hook in my hand. We were a team. Things went smoothly. I hooked the skin, lifted, and, with a scalpel, sliced the skin off the muscle. This loosened the skin so that I could sew it closed. The dissection was done now. The wound had to be sutured.

"How's the baby?" Catherine asked me as I began to put in the sutures.

"She's a sweetheart." I had worked right through my pregnancy and everyone knew about Lucy. The nurses and I were friends and now we were all mothers, too.

"Has she started to eat her diapers yet?" asked Camilla. "Wait till she tries that one! Do you have a photograph?"

"In my briefcase." Rosemary opened it and started to hunt.

"And I bet your husband is proud as punch," said Catherine. "Seems you're the only one still married. Everyone else is getting divorced."

My heart started to pound. I tied another stitch. I might as well admit the truth.

"I'm joining the crowd," I said. "Things didn't work out." None of them spoke for a moment.

"I'm sorry," said Camilla at last. It's all anyone could say.

"I might as well announce my divorce too," said Catherine. With a start, I realized what had bothered me. She had looked different today. It was because behind the mask and the makeup, she looked sad. "Twenty-two years and four kids. You don't have to feel the way I do, Dr. Morgan. I've wasted my whole life." Her voice choked.

I tied the last stitch. Rosemary taped a gauze dressing over the stitches. Catherine turned off the anesthesia and let Guy wake up. He coughed, whimpered, wiggled his legs, and breathed normally. His mother would be relieved. Guy had survived.

"I'm sorry about your divorce," said Camilla, as we left the operating room. "I hope things work out for you and Lucy." She patted my hand. "Believe me, life's too short for a bad marriage." I was grateful. She had managed her life well. It gave me hope. In time I might learn to do the same.

In the afternoon, there was a delay before I could do my last operation. Mary Clinton had not arrived. I called my mother to check on the outcome of Lucy and the applesauce.

"She managed very well, considering," said my mother. "She's a very willing little baby. She doesn't refuse things." I felt a surge of pride. My child was unusually willing and cooperative. "It is a strain on her going to Nadine's," said my mother. "It is too long a day. We have to find a place to live where someone can come to the house, or at least where she doesn't have to travel so far."

"I know, Mother. I'm trying."

"Of course." My mother sounded tired. At her age, she was helping to look after a baby. It was a lot of work and there was no end in sight.

"You need a vacation, Mother."

"Perhaps I do, but how will you manage?"

"We'll manage. You look after your health first, Mother. That's your responsibility to me. I couldn't bear it if you got sick again." I remembered the days that became weeks and months as my mother lay in bed, with drenching sweats, heart arrhythmias, losing weight, her joints and tendons swelling painfully. All the tests were negative. She had probably had an unknown viral illness that someday would be "discovered." As it was, she had recovered after two years of rest. I had nursed her then. I couldn't nurse her now.

"Don't worry about me," said my mother.

"Sure," I said jokingly. We were worried about each other.

"How do other women surgeons cope?" demanded my mother.

I thought about it. I knew one who had no children. Another had never married. A third, a divorced lesbian, had no children. A fourth had a child, and she and her husband were separated; but she worked too hard and never saw her child. A fifth was rich and worked part-time. The list went on.

Was it impossible to do what I was trying to do? I was so pleased that I was coping — but I wasn't. I was surviving. I stumbled from one hurdle to the next. My mother filled in when I was too busy to take Lucy home before six. Weekends consisted of feeding, bathing, and cleaning Lucy and dashing out to buy diapers and groceries. What I wanted was a husband to be beside me. I fought down my resentment.

"What about women surgeons?" asked my mother.

"As a group, Mother, I don't think women surgeons are doing too well. My life isn't worse than the rest. It's just different. After I get my life settled, I have to change." I loved my practice, but a solo surgeon leads a loner's life. I wanted people in my life. I didn't want to be alone. It frightened me. The intercom came on. I was needed for my next case — Mary Clinton had shown up after all!

⇒ *four*

I HOPE YOU had enough sleep last night," Mary Clinton said, gripping my hand tightly. She was on the operating table, about to go to sleep. She had been talking from sheer nerves since I met her in the preoperative area. "I want everything to go right, Doctor. And I must be home by five. My husband would go insane if he had to feed the baby . . ." She yawned and was asleep. I pulled back the sheets to bare her thigh. My heart sank. The cancer had grown even bigger since I last saw her. Perhaps it was not a histiocytoma. It might be something much worse, a melanoma. I hoped this operation would not be an exercise in futility, a wide resection of a cancer that had already spread through her body. That was what had happened to my beloved secretary Clare. I felt the skin. The cancer had grown into the skin far beyond the visible tumor.

"If it's a histiocytoma, she'll raise her children," I said, and outlined the skin I had to remove. She would have a scar from her groin to her knee.

"What if it's a melanoma?" asked Camilla.

"She shouldn't live five years."

Camilla shuddered. "Grim."

"Life is grim," said Catherine from behind the drapes. Her voice was as haunted as her eyes.

"Count your blessings," said Camilla. "At least we're all healthy." I injected the epinephrine and Camilla put the scalpel in my hand. She was right. I was very lucky to be healthy.

Blood spurted as I sliced through the skin. Even with the epinephrine injection, there was blood over everything. Some cancers make a hormone that increases blood flow to the cancer so it can grow. Mary Clinton's looked like one of them.

I picked up the cutting cautery. Automatically, Camilla put a flat sponge on the leg and pulled, tightening the muscle to make it easier to cut. The cautery sizzled through the muscle. Smoke and the sickening smell of burning fat rose up beside the cautery. A vein spurted blood into my face. I switched the cautery to coagulate and sizzled the vein shut. Blood puddled on the sterile drapes.

"Are you going to have more blood loss?" asked Catherine, standing up to watch. She was responsible for blood transfusions.

"Not much." The faster we worked, the sooner we would stop the bleeding. I kept cutting. "It's out!" The cancerous skin and muscle leaped out of Mary Clinton's leg with the last cut. I dropped the mass of tissue into the specimen bucket.

"Frozen section?" Rosemary asked. As the circulator, she would call in the pathologist.

"Please." The wound was enormous. I stopped the bleeding and I cut the skin free, but it didn't loosen nearly enough. If the sutures were too tight, the wound would burst apart.

"Catherine, could you flex the table?" I asked.

She nodded and bent the operating table at Mrs. Clinton's hip and knee, letting her skin relax so the edges came closer together.

Camilla gave me a 2-O Dexon. This is a heavy suture. I like delicate sutures, but delicacy was not needed here. I dug the needle deep into the skin and tied the stitch. The skin came together.

"Dr. Morgan?" A pathologist with a bushy beard straggling out around his mask poked his head into the operating room. I didn't know who it was. "It looks like a malignant histiocytoma, but I can't be sure till I do the permanent section."

"And the margins?" I asked.

"The margins are clear. You're well around the cancer, whatever it is." He withdrew. The door swung closed.

Skin cancer can be hard to read on frozen sections. It would be days or weeks before I could tell Mary Clinton if she was probably cured or probably not. I finished the suturing and Catherine straightened the table slowly. Mary Clinton had lost weight after each pregnancy. She had stretched skin in her thighs and it helped. Her wound was snug, but not so tight that it wouldn't heal. I was tired but I was pleased. I had helped her as best I could. Her surgery had gone well.

"Is Catherine all right?" I asked Camilla in the nurses' lounge as she was changing to go home. I was on my way to see Donald Lamont, my lawyer. Camilla gave me a worried look.

"I think her husband is the problem." She shook her head. "But she's too soft on him. She wants to leave, but she can't leave the kids." I thought about it. I had left my husband when I was still pregnant, so Lucy had had to come with me then. And now? I loved him still, but I had left him. I felt I had to, for Lucy. I could never leave Lucy. My reaction was instinct, not reason. I was a mother. A primeval urge told me to protect and love and fight and die for my child. No one, but no one, could make me leave her. I was the most important creature in the world to her, and she was the most important to me.

I arrived at Donald Lamont's office early. He was not yet back from taking a deposition. His secretary let me use his phone. I had to call Jim. I needed his advice. Until now, I had managed my finances and hadn't done particularly well. Beverly had gone over them with me. I wanted to buy a house, but all my holdings had dropped in value. I had a knack: if Elizabeth bought it, it was a bad investment. It was after 3:30 PM and the markets were closed, so Jim wouldn't mind a call now. Before 3:30, I never called. He has total concentration when he's working. If it's not about a market price, he doesn't want to hear it. Jim had the most unusual diversity of talents. He was a natural athlete. (He had picked up jai alai as easily as tennis.) He had an extraordinary memory. (He could recognize a politician from a blurred photograph he had seen a year before; he knew who pitched for Boston in the '48 World Series, and the price of corn in 1973.) The one talent he lacked was a good singing voice, and it was the disappointment of his life that he couldn't sing the blues like Ray Charles. Whenever I had taken his advice about a stock, I had never regretted it.

He came on the phone at last. "Elizabeth, you wouldn't believe today." His squawk box chattered in the background. He sounded jubilant. "Gold went wild. Up the limit. London's crazy. Tokyo is insane. This is history. A gold trader in London lost one million dollars in a minute and made it back a minute later. My clients are fine. We're on the right side. How are you?"

"Jim, I need your help."

"Sure." He settled down. "I told you to keep away from diamonds and metals."

"You said gold was okay."

"At two-fifty, Elizabeth, not at six hundred dollars an ounce. Don't feel bad about it. Everyone else did the same thing. Listen. Didn't someone send you tickets for a charity benefit this weekend, a gambling-casino evening?"

"Yes. I'm not going."

"You ought to. It's healthy. Get mother to look after Lucy. I'll go over your finances and then we'll go gambling. It'll be good for you. Get you out and around and maybe you'll learn a thing or two." I agreed. Gambling seemed silly, but going out was fun.

Soon after that, Donald Lamont arrived. He was a former pilot, good-humored, good-hearted, and a good attorney. We sat down in his book-lined office. For a moment, I thought I would cry. I steeled myself.

"Donald, you know my husband and I split up? Permanently."

He nodded. "I'm sorry about it."

"'Cut your losses' is what Jim says." I tried to laugh. "I guess I did that. Anyhow, I need a quick divorce. I have to get this behind me."

Donald put his fingers together, tip to tip. "Do you own property jointly?"

"None."

"You were thinking of buying a house together."

"We didn't do it."

"Good. You can certainly get an immediate Haitian divorce."

"That's what I want."

"I don't think that's your real problem, Elizabeth."

"What is?"

"Lucy."

"In what way?"

"Child support, custody, and visitation, Elizabeth."

"Donald, let me tell you." I leaned forward urgently. "I would rather be on welfare than ask him for money."

He shook his head. "You will need the money, Elizabeth. You know you will have to limit your practice. You're a single mother. Besides, what you want really does not matter. You know he's important to Lucy. You want him to see her. Don't you think it's also important to have him share the financial burden?" I hadn't thought about the money. I was worried about what type of visitation agreement would be best for Lucy. She was so young.

"He sees her now. Nadine Hoskins's home is two minutes from his office. He's free to come. And he does come. He cannot take Lucy overnight until she's two. It wouldn't be good for her."

"How do you know that?" asked Donald gently.

"How do I know?" I felt indignant. Lucy was not a placid baby. She noticed everything and I knew she could easily become jumpy or nervous. "I'm her mother, Donald. I know my child, even if she is only a few months old. I can't let him do something bad for Lucy."

Donald looked at me sympathetically. "What I tell you, Elizabeth, is what every lawyer tells every man or woman getting a divorce. What you want and what the law will force you to do are very different things. Your husband will probably file for custody."

"Donald, he can't take my baby away from me." I was appalled.

"I don't think he will get custody. But you will have to fight to keep Lucy." He looked at me narrowly. "This is the era of no-fault divorce. A lot of scores get settled fighting over custody. All he needs to do is to claim you are an unfit mother."

"That's ridiculous."

"But you have to prove it's ridiculous. In court." He shrugged. "Even if it doesn't come to that, he will probably be allowed more visitation than you think is good for her. And it will be expensive. From a practical point of view, Elizabeth, I'm not the right person for you. I don't like divorce, and besides, you live in a different jurisdiction. I don't know anyone to recommend, but I know of a lawyer who is supposed to be good. Do you want to see her?"

"Please."

Donald made a phone call and took me down that afternoon to Ms. Jones. She was a bespectacled, older woman attorney with gray hair. She was very sweet and sympathetic. Donald explained my situation.

"My guess is," he finished, "that this is going to be a custody, not a visitation, battle."

"That's terrible," said Ms. Jones, reaching to pat my hand across her desk. "Terrible. Very, very hard for you. You seem to be managing awfully well." She made me feel like a Girl Scout of ten. "Now, I don't like nasty divorces. I don't imagine you do either, dear. I negotiate. Most of my cases are settled before trial. Going to trial makes for so much hard feeling. It's not good for your life. Or for Lucy's."

I agreed.

Donald Lamont intervened. "If it can be negotiated. Also, I think it will help Dr. Morgan to know how much it may cost her, in a general range. She has other bills to pay, too," he said with a smile.

"Your husband's not a lawyer, is he?" Ms. Jones asked me. "No."

"But he knows a lot about the law," insisted Donald Lamont. "And he's a very clever man."

"I see." Ms. Jones frowned. "For an all-out custody fight, maybe no more than fifty thousand dollars. Maybe as low as twenty-five thousand."

I stared at her. Was she crazy? Every penny I earned would go to taxes or lawyers. I would have to live on my savings, and I had no savings. I had to work harder. I had to earn more.

"It wouldn't be a problem if I robbed banks or sold cocaine for a living," I said jokingly.

Ms. Jones raised her brows. "Don't say things like that in a lawyer's office, dear," she replied coldly.

"I'm sorry. Anyhow, I suppose I can manage. I want the best for Lucy, and I want this done amicably. What if I didn't have the money?"

Ms. Jones sighed. "No one works for free. It is a problem. For the indigent, there is legal aid. Some women have rich husbands who are court-ordered to pay the bill. That's not too common anymore. Some don't have lawyers and do badly. Some sign agreements without a lawyer. Some simply leave with the kids to start over. Of course, it's illegal and a professional can't do that. You could be tracked down anywhere. It's tough, but it comes down to 'How much are your children worth?' "

"What about the average working woman who isn't eligible for legal aid and isn't going to run away?"

"They can have a problem, poor dears," said Ms. Jones. "I'm not saying this is a good system, but it's what we've got."

I thought things over when I got home. I decided my husband wouldn't file for custody. I was so boringly respectable, even too respectable. If I'd had more of a wild youth, I might have avoided such a belated and disastrous marriage. There had been conflict in our marriage. I was determined to have peace in the divorce, for Lucy's sake. I asked Ms. Jones to represent me and mailed off a check, her retainer fee.

That weekend, Jim came by to look over my finances. He was very fond of Lucy and bounced her on his knee while I lay out my books. She tried to chew his tie. "Look at this," said Jim. "She hasn't done this before." Lucy grinned, stared up at him, and started chewing on his tie again.

"Now the way I see it," I began.

"Now don't you tell me," interrupted Jim. I could almost see his mind go into gear. He was shutting me out, and Lucy. He was thinking numbers. "Just answer my questions. You own this house. Right?"

"Right."

"Okay. You own your car?"

"Right."

"You need it to earn your living, so we can't touch that. This house, I remember you paid too much for it. If you sell it now, you'll lose money. You have to move. So you can rent it out and let it pay its own way, and sell it at a loss to get the cash for your lawyer's bills if you need to. These are your stocks?" He looked them over. "Not a whole lot. You need to keep these for emergencies. If you get sick, you still have to feed yourself and bambina here." He started to bounce Lucy again. She waved her arms joyfully. "What else?"

"I can sell my jewelry to help buy a new house for us."

"Oh yeah?"

"It's worth a lot more than when I bought it."

"Oh yeah?" Jim gave me a sorry look. "Retail, sweetheart, retail. You buy it retail. When you sell it, you sell it wholesale. Insurance appraisals mean nothing. They are inflated beyond belief. Call the guy that sold it to you. He's honest. Tell him you want to sell everything. Ask him what you'd get. Before you call, I'm telling you, you'll get one-third of what you paid."

"Impossible." I reached for the phone and called Mr. Revere, the jeweler. It wasn't a good year to sell. Everyone was trying to sell jewelry. I could get a third of what I paid. A bit more, if I could wait for a year. I hung up. "Right again, Jim. You always told me jewelry was a loser."

"Don't feel bad, Elizabeth. You bought jewelry at least. That did better than investment diamonds. The people who bought them lost everything. That all you have?" He shook his head.

"I have money in my money-market, but I have to keep that for taxes. Last year I took a low salary, so I had a bonus at the end of the year, but half of that goes in taxes."

"When?"

"In six months."

Jim's eyes lit up. "Are you expecting another bonus?"

"Yes, but much smaller."

"Okay. You're all set. Sell jewelry for the first legal bills. Sell this house to pay the rest. Then take the money you have now. Put it in stocks. I'll tell you which ones. The market's at eight hundred now. It's going up. It's going way up. It'll double. In six months, if you do what I tell you, we can sell the stock. It'll pay your taxes and make a down payment on a house."

"Promise?"

Jim looked at me and shook his head. He spoke slowly, as though English was my second language. "Hell, no. I'm not crazy. I can't promise. You asked my advice. That's my advice. In six months, if the market isn't up, this country will be in such a mess everyone's going to be poor. Okay?"

I looked at Lucy. I had been in practice for five years. I had paid off my debts in under three years. I earned a lot of money for someone my age — more than an air-traffic controller, less than many pilots. I had saved money for ten years. I had lost more than half of it in poor investments. That didn't leave me poor, but I wanted a decent home for Lucy. If I took Jim's advice, I had a better chance. I knew his advice was good.

"Jim, I'll do it. I am very grateful. You know how much this means to Lucy and me." He looked embarrassed. "It's easy. Look, I couldn't do a skin graft."

"Skin grafts are easy," I protested.

"If they were that easy, you wouldn't get paid for doing them. Now get a pencil and I'll tell you the stocks to buy."

At nine o'clock, my finances were in order. Lucy was in her bassinet with her eyes closed and one hand dreamily fingering the ruffle on her pink pillow. My mother was doing a crossword puzzle in the living room. "Hanging from trees in the Book of Jeremiah?" she said absently when we looked in. "That's a difficult clue. Oh yes, 'Amenta.' I should have seen that." Jim and I looked at each other and shook our heads. We were utterly befogged by what seemed so clear to her. She focused on us. Like Jimmy, she has the power of total concentration. "What did you say?"

"Just good-bye. We're going gambling. We'll see you later."

"Have a good time. Stay as long as you wish. I'll be up a while with this puzzle." She looked very content but tired.

Jim and I left for the charity gambling benefit. It was held in a new hotel, all glass and glitter. The ballroom was a mob. Girls in skimpy, pink-sequined outfits strutted around in high-heeled shoes offering souvenirs of dice and playing cards.

"Where do you want to start?" said Jim, collecting a stack of chips.

"Roulette?"

Jim made a face. "We could. I don't mind, but it's throwing money away."

"That's what gambling is, Jim."

"No. It depends on the gamble. Roulette is strictly chance. The odds are against you. Chances are that you will lose. Now blackjack is different, if you count the cards. Let me show you." He surveyed the room and found, at the back, a blackjack table with two empty chairs.

"Sit down. Come on in," said the dealer with a lilt in her voice. She was heavily made up and her red fingernails and bracelets sparkled as she dealt the cards. She dealt so fast that the cards were a blur. Jim sat me down. He sat down next to me and pulled out our chips. He watched the dealer the whole time.

"Place your bets," urged the dealer.

"We're out this round," said Jim.

She looked at him sharply and then at me and gave us a dazzling smile. We joined the next time. Jim played my cards for me as well as his. His jolly face became blank. He looked indifferent.

"Three jacks are out," he murmured in my ear. "Pass." I passed. The house won the hand. The next time Jim passed but had me double my bet. "Eighteen," he murmured. "House will probably go over." The house did go over. I won. The dealer looked at Jim sharply. This was a charity game, but the dealers were professional. Jim won some. He lost some. Overall, his winnings began to pile up. So did mine.

"In this game, you have to know where every card is," Jim whispered. "See it in your mind. Where's the queen of diamonds?" He gathered in our winnings.

"I don't know."

"Not dealt yet."

Another dealer came up. "Time for a break, Meg." Our dealer stood up. The two women turned their backs briefly to the table and spoke to each other.

"Well!" The new dealer sat down. "What a great table we have. Now I don't feel like dealing. Let's have the gentleman here deal for me." She beckoned Jim behind the table and made him deal. I played cautiously and lost. After ten minutes, the house was winning steadily. Jim relinquished his seat to the dealer and we drifted away from blackjack.

"I don't want to upset them," said Jim. "This isn't for real money. But they're good. It's their job to get rid of a counter. I make a casino lose money. Not much, but to them it's the principle of the thing. I count the cards and the odds switch from the house to me, about 60-40. The essence of any investment is to find a gamble where the odds are in your favor — 51-49, 60-40. That way, you win, you lose, but overall, you win. The usual gambling sucker is playing at 80-20 or worse. Get it?"

I got it. I was the usual gambling sucker. If I took Jim's advice, the odds were in my favor. Skin grafts I could do, but not investments. We talked about mother on the way home. We both agreed she needed to get away.

It was cold at midnight when I got back home. The predictions were for an unusually cold winter. I looked at Lucy before I went to bed. The moonlight shone on her bassinet. She had burrowed facedown into her pink pillow. I covered her up with a quilt. She made a little squeak in her sleep. I went next door and woke up my mother. "Uh? Good time?" She said sleepily.

"Mother, it's me. Listen. You have to go south for a while or you'll get ill. You know that."

"I can't leave you and Lucy," she said, waking up.

"You have to. The best thing you can do for me is to stay healthy."

"Should I go with your father?"

"Oh, Mother, be serious."

She smiled. "I suppose you're right."

My mother left for Florida the next week. The night she left, Ms. Jones called me at home.

"Hope I didn't wake the baby, Elizabeth. I need to talk to you about this. Now your husband has filed for custody."

"What?"

"Oh yes," she said breezily. "He's saying you're an unfit mother. He wants a psychiatric evaluation of you. You don't have time for the child because of your career, et cetera. I've sent you copies. You know dear, his lawyer called me. I get the feeling from the case that there's hope for your marriage. Have you thought about that?"

Lose Lucy? He couldn't do this to me. Make our marriage work? What was she talking about? It couldn't work, but the idea was like tearing open a fresh wound. My heart started to pound. "It's ancient history, Ms. Jones." I said harshly. "I must keep custody." She wasn't my marriage counselor. I didn't need that. I needed a divorce — and custody of my child. Lucy needed me. I didn't want to fight, but never, never, never could I agree to let her go. I knew it would be wrong.

"I know. I know. It's so hard. I don't want your life ruined by this, dear. You could have such a lovely life. Anyhow . . ."

She asked me to come in to see her again. She needed all sorts of documents and copies of letters. She needed a financial statement.

Our phone call lasted an hour. When we were done, I realized that this would not be simple. There was a long, long way to go. I felt such a compelling maternal need to protect Lucy, to give her the loving, stable home she needed. I wanted to do something to protect her, immediately. There was nothing I could do but wait. I couldn't steal away in the night with Lucy and disappear. I felt sorry for the mothers who felt they had to, in order to protect a child. It wouldn't be fair to Lucy. I consoled myself. At least I had Ms. Jones. She would keep it amicable. She would not let it disrupt us.

I sat in bed that night reading the real-estate ads to take my mind off the question of custody. We might have to rent after all, but where? A studio apartment? A townhouse thirty miles from my office? I felt too upset to think. "Unfit mother" echoed in my mind. It was an outrage. How could

Ms. Jones be so cruel as to suggest in the same breath that our marriage might work? Love, indeed! Then doubts assailed me about our marriage. Was I wrong? Or hard? Should I go back to him? I turned out the light. Sitting in the dark, I made myself go back to the beginning. I remembered the moment we met. I remembered our first date. Step by step, I walked through our life together. Painful memories assailed me. I shut my eyes to ward them off. I wasn't wrong. Why must Ms. Jones torment me? Why couldn't she be my lawyer and nothing more?

I had to do surgery the next morning, and I got out of bed at five, shivering in the dark, to warm Lucy's bottle. I turned up the heat. I reviewed once again the chart for my first operation. My patient was Emily James. She was young, diabetic, and had had two mastectomies for cancer. One breast had been reconstructed, but it was unsatisfactory. She wanted both breasts reconstructed. Yes, I had problems, but they paled next to hers. I finished and went to Lucy's bassinet. She whimpered and burrowed deeper under her pink quilt. I leaned over and stroked her head.

"I know. No one likes to get up at six o'clock." I picked her up. "You are getting heavy, you fat little thing." Lucy grinned toothlessly and flung herself on her bottle, beating the sides happily with her hands. She was a jolly baby. If she wasn't tired, she was laughing. She squeaked or gurgled or giggled or laughed silently, which made me laugh out loud. Forty minutes later, she was fed, dressed, undressed, changed, dressed again, and put in her snowsuit; I packed her bag, washed the dishes, and we set off for Nadine Hoskins's.

"Good morning, Nadine," I called out, opening her front door at seven. "We're here."

She appeared at the end of the hallway. Lucy greeted her with a gurgle and a smile. Nadine didn't respond. She looked frail and ghostly white. Lucy suddenly clutched at me, frightened.

"What on earth's the matter? Are you all right?" I demanded.

Nadine stood frozen. "No. I'm not all right. Ken died last night."

"What? Ken? Your husband? Died yesterday?"

"He went out in the car. He didn't come home — I called the police. The next thing I knew they came by to see me. It was a freak accident. He was dead." Her voice rose. "They worked on him for an hour, but he was dead. He just died. He was so healthy. I don't believe it." She stopped and resumed quietly. "Now there's just me."

"Nadine, you can't possibly work today."

Her eyes widened. "I have to work," she said in a flat voice. "I have to. I can't bear it if I don't. Don't worry about Lucy. My aunt is here. She's going to stay with me. I wouldn't take Lucy today if someone couldn't look after her properly. Please, Elizabeth. I must work."

"Nadine, how will you manage?"

She looked past us, as though she was seeing someone I couldn't see. "We'll manage. Ken does not believe in insurance, I mean he didn't, but I can pay for the house. We've been married twenty years and the mortgage is low. We had some savings. We can manage. I have good parents and good in-laws. My mother wanted to come right away. She lives in Phoenix. I called her last night. I told her no. I told her to wait till spring. She hates the cold. I will be all right." She looked at me. "You and I, we are single mothers. Mothers always pull through." I put my arm around her. "Nadine, let me know what I can do to help you."

"I'm in shock now." She shook herself. "What am I doing? Give me Lucy." She took her out of my arms. Lucy looked at her, puzzled and frightened. I didn't want to leave her. I had no choice. I saw her gaze at Nadine, her brow crinkled.

"You have to work too, Elizabeth. Good-bye." I hated to leave, but I had to.

I got to Smith Center in time, but my operation was canceled. Emily James had woken up with a right-lower-lobe pneumonia. Her lungs were one of her weak spots, made worse by diabetes and cigarettes. I used to smoke two packs a day. I stopped ten years ago. Since my marriage had soured, I had often wanted a cigarette, to dull my emotions. I fought off the desire. I looked at the white patch on Emily Jones's X ray. Not smoking was something good that I had done. It was the least I could do for Lucy.

"Smoker?" said a passing radiologist, glancing at the X ray. "He has terrible lungs."

"It's a she."

"No it's not. No breasts."

"Bilateral mastectomy for cancer."

"And she still smokes?" He was amazed.

"There's no proven connection," I said in her defense.

"Does there have to be? Anyone who smokes these days is a moron or a psychopath."

"Or an addict. Tobacco is a real addiction. I should know. I used to smoke."

"All addicts are psychopaths," said the radiologist disdainfully. He walked away.

With the surgery canceled, my morning was free. I decided to go for Lucy. The thought of her puzzled face haunted me. But a Dr. Osbert Parks paged me. I had never heard of him.

"Yes, yes," Osbert Parks rumbled in funereal tones when I answered. "Yes, yes." He paused. "Yes. I'm so glad I reached you," he said sadly.

"Yes, Dr. Parks," I said, to indicate I was listening closely. Couldn't he hurry? I wanted to see Lucy.

"Yes, Dr. Morgan. You haven't received a call, have you, about this?"

"About what, Dr. Parks?"

"Yes, I see. Well." He got a grip on himself. "About this matter?"

"What matter?" I said.

"Yes. Well," and he plunged ahead. "We have a man in Concordia Hospital, Mr. Fairfield, I would like you to see. He had an infected splinter in his chest removed by his GP."

"I see," I said. I didn't see at all. Concordia was a private hospital miles away. I never went there, and certainly not for splinters.

"Two days later he had a necrotizing fasciitis of his entire chest and went into septic shock. He almost died."

"From a splinter?" Now I understood. With a freak complication like that, the hospital and everyone who treated him were likely to be sued. They were trying to bail out.

"Yes. We thought we'd lost him several times. The infection is better, but now he has another problem."

"Another abscess?"

"No. Gangrene."

"Good grief."

"Your colleague, Dr. Lorenzo, has been seeing him," continued Dr. Parks, "but now the gentleman wants another plastic surgeon."

"Oh, dear." Hank Lorenzo would not like my meddling with his patient.

"Do you know Mr. Fairfield?"

"No."

"He's Mr. Fairfield of Fairfield Industry."

"Oh, dear." This was worse and worse.

"I'd like you to see him for a second opinion," said Dr. Parks. "Dr. Lorenzo has agreed."

"I won't have anything better to suggest," I protested. Whatever Dr. Lorenzo had suggested would be reasonable. I didn't want to meddle, but at last I agreed. I called Nadine. Her aunt answered. Lucy was fine. Nadine was resting. I felt reassured.

Concordia was a small hospital, gray inside with some walls painted orange to try to cheer it up. I wandered around looking for the right ward. Mr. Fairfield had had radiation for Hodgkin's disease years ago, and had atherosclerosis and a high blood-cholesterol. Radiation makes the skin more susceptible to infection. He was in a private room at the end of the ward. I went in to see him. Mr. Fairfield was sitting on the edge of his bed like an implacable Aztec god wreathed in a cloud of smoke. His chest and arms were wrapped in white bandages.

"Who the hell are you?" he demanded in a throaty voice when I looked in. "I hate strange people barging in. If you think you're looking at my damned wound, young woman, think again."

"I'm Dr. Morgan." I went into the room.

"What of it?"

"I'm a plastic surgeon. Dr. Parks asked me to see you for a second opinion. I understand Dr. Lorenzo is your plastic surgeon."

"Lorenzo walks in here. Rips off my dressing. Doesn't tell me a damned thing. It's a damned wound. I don't want anyone looking at it."

A middle-aged nurse walked in with cheerful authority. "Hi, honey. Time for a dressing change. Let the doctor take a look." She handed me a pair of sterile gloves.

Mr. Fairfield glared at me but he lay back. The nurse cut off the bandage. From the left arm to the right, under the arms, up to the neck, there was no skin. Raw, red tissue, dripping with pus, lay directly over his windpipe, which was exposed just above the collarbone. I watched it move up and down when he spoke.

"Ever seen one like this?" demanded Mr. Fairfield. "Ever seen one heal?" Pus welled up from behind the windpipe and trickled out the wound. Gently, I pushed the windpipe to one side with my gloved hand. Underneath I saw the esophagus, the food pipe, bathed in pus, but I was relieved. The raw, red tissue was alive, if infected. The radiation he had had might have made him infection-prone, but the tissue was *not* dead from radiation.

"This will take a while to heal," I replied.

"I'll be in a box before it does, and I don't want Dr. Lorenzo looking after me."

"He's very good."

"I won't let him touch me."

"Well, if you won't, you won't."

"I won't let you touch me. I don't like you either. Hell, I don't like myself. I've looked at this in the mirror and it makes me sick. All from a damned splinter. Cutting down a goddamned tree. Can you believe it? A month ago I played golf. Now I'm dying. You might as well take me out and shoot me."

I looked at him. "This isn't going to kill you, Mr. Fairfield. It looks awful and you'll be badly scarred, but you'll heal. It wants to heal." I poked the raw tissue. It was like an old friend. I had seen hundreds of wounds like this. "You'll need some skin grafts."

"Oh yeah? You and Dr. Lorenzo been talking to each other? I ought to go home to die."

"You won't die. You'll heal. Even without surgery. Your body will pull your arms into your chest so you can't move them, but it will heal the wound. You'll look peculiar. You won't play golf, but you won't die."

"Oh yeah?" He turned stiffly to the side table and lit a cigarette. "Okay. Let Lorenzo operate. If you've finished with the sideshow." He blew a smoke ring.

I called Hank from the medical ward. He was going to transfer Mr. Fairfield to Smith Center and I would help him at Mr. Fairfield's surgery. Ten days later, Mr. Fairfield's wound was clean enough to book his skin grafts. My mother had returned from Florida, looking healthier than she had in years and more relaxed. Beverly had arranged my Haitian divorce. I had tried to do it. Then I asked her to make the phone calls for me. I accepted my divorce, but I couldn't look it in the face.

That Friday, I picked Lucy up early, at three in the afternoon. It wasn't often that I finished early, but it was a pleasure to get her before it got dark. Nadine was not expecting me. She was on the telephone, her eyes red from crying. A child stood by her, clutching her leg, but she ignored him. Lucy was in her playpen giggling excitedly at a little two-year-old boy who was poking a sharpened pencil at her through the slats. I snatched him away and picked Lucy out of the playpen. The little boy sat down and screamed. Lucy looked at me solemnly and grabbed on to my hair. Nadine hung up the phone. "You're taking her early?" She sounded annoyed.

"Yes. I finished early today. I don't think that little boy should be playing with pencils."

"No. That's dangerous." She took the pencil away. She seemed unconcerned.

"Is your aunt here?" I asked.

"No. I don't want her. I sent her home. I'm okay."

"Are you sure, Nadine?"

She looked at me, insulted. "Yes, I'm okay. Are you okay?" She was belligerent.

"I'm fine." I zipped Lucy into her green snowsuit and escaped. She fell asleep on the way home.

"Am I imagining things?" I said out loud. "Lucy, am I crazy?" She stirred and whimpered. If only she could tell me. Nadine was a widow. She needed my support. This was a hard time for her. I couldn't desert her. Lucy seemed content and well looked after. She smiled when she saw Nadine. She ate well. But was I going to get a call from the ER someday telling me that Lucy was blind because an unsupervised child had poked her eye out? I decided I was upset about the divorce and imagining things. Lucy woke up when I turned onto the parkway. She always did. She screamed all the way home.

It was a peaceful weekend. I rested. I played with Lucy. I read house ads. I read more house ads. I felt upset with Ms. Jones. Her reputation was good. She tried hard to help me, but when we spoke, I felt worse, not better. I didn't know why.

Jim stopped by to see us. Lucy was practicing rolling over. She had done it once by mistake and she now spent hours wiggling arms and legs to try to get onto her stomach.

"So how's your new lawyer?" began Jim.

"Fine."

"Expensive?"

"Very, but she's conscientious and thorough. She does the job."

"Any progress?"

"Not yet. I'm not expecting any yet."

Jim folded his arms. "I got a hunch she's not right, Elizabeth. Too nice. Too ladylike. Divorce stinks and a custody fight makes divorce smell sweet. No one likes it. Jones gets you upset. You need a rock-solid bull to handle this case."

"Jim, she's not a fighter, but I don't want a fighter. I want it friendly."

"You won't get it, Elizabeth. This is a war. You ought to hire a lawyer to stick up for your side, because you'd better believe it's what your husband's going to do."

"Jim, it's going to be okay." If I changed lawyers, I could end up with someone worse.

With a shriek of triumph, Lucy flopped onto her stomach. We cheered enthusiastically. She laughed, her head fell back, and she flopped onto her back again with a look of consternation. It was a happy weekend.

Room Six is an enormous operating room used almost exclusively for open-heart surgery. Mr. Fairfield's skin grafts were booked for Room Six on Monday.

"So why the heart room?" I asked Camilla as I came in to

prepare for the operation. She was sorting out instruments on the back table. I sat down next to the green analyzer that gave computer readouts for blood oxygen. The heart pump was in a corner, covered with a plastic dust-sheet. Four cardiac monitors hung from the ceiling.

"There are no hearts to do, Dr. Morgan. The emergency heart they had booked got worse and was done last night. Will you count with me?" She held up the large lap sponges and shook out the strings. "One, two, three, four, five," we counted together as she pulled each string, and then, "one, two, three, four, five," as we counted again.

"What have you heard about the infectious-disease residency at Harvard, Dr. Morgan? Do you know anything about it?"

"Yes, it's excellent."

She looked pleased. "My boy just got accepted there. He's thrilled." The door swung open.

"Good morning! Sorry to take so long. There's a traffic jam out there." Rosemary, the circulator, pulled in Mr. Fairfield while Catherine, the anesthetist, brought up the rear. She looked rather detached, as though life was pushing her along. She was present, but passive. Her heavy makeup made her seem remote and unreachable.

Mr. Fairfield gave me a lopsided grin of recognition. "Whatever the shtuff was she gave me, Dr. Morgan, it worksh better than beer," he said drowsily. "For the prices they charge here, you ought to give me a better mattressh." He moved onto the operating table.

"It won't bother you long, hon," said Catherine. She injected Anectine. "I'm putting a mask over your face. It's oxygen." She nodded to Rosemary. "Tell Dr. Sheridan we're going ahead. He needs to be here. This man will be a difficult intubation." Hank Lorenzo, bristling with X rays and a brace of special skin-graft knives, walked in with Dr. Sheridan.

"He's got a bull neck and it is too stiff to hyperextend,"

Catherine told Dr. Sheridan. "I hope I get the tube in." She injected the Pentothal. "Take a big breath." Mr. Fairfield's eyes closed.

"Go ahead," ordered Dr. Sheridan, scanning the heart monitor. "I'll hand you the tube." Catherine inserted the laryngoscope and looked into Mr. Fairfield's mouth. "I can barely see the vocal cords. The whole throat is pulled to one side. He's had radiation. I need a sharp curve on the tube. Here goes." She held out her hand for the tube. Shaking her head unhappily, she pushed it into Mr. Fairfield's mouth. "No, no good." She pulled it out. The tube was bloodstained. She wiped it off on a sterile towel. Catherine put the mask over Mr. Fairfield's face and pumped in oxygen.

I prepared for disaster. His neck had been infected as well as radiated. A few more failed attempts and the inflamed throat would swell and block off the lungs completely. I moved over to Camilla at the scrub table. "Do you have a tracheostomy set?" She pointed to it, open and ready. Camilla never let you down. "Good. We may need it." Mentally, I did a tracheostomy. Catherine took the mask off Mr. Fairfield's face.

"Give him some more oxygen," ordered Dr. Sheridan. "I've seen a few PVCs on the monitor." We waited. After more oxygen, Catherine set aside the mask once again. No one spoke. Once one person panics in an operating room, everyone is distracted and mistakes are made. She looked in through the laryngoscope.

"I can see something. Not much, and it's bloody." She held out her hand for the tube. "Everything it touches bleeds." She coaxed the tube down Mr. Fairfield's throat, attached it to the tubing, and pumped in oxygen. Mr. Fairfield's chest rose and fell. He was safely asleep. We all relaxed.

"In like Flynn," said Hank. He pulled bandage scissors from the back pocket of his scrub pants and cut the gauze on Mr. Fairfield's chest.

"This is one ghastly wound," he announced with gusto, "but a beauty compared to what it has been."

Mr. Fairfield's chest was better. The pus-oozing swamp was replaced by a cobbled surface of pale pink nodules.

"Holy smoke." Camilla slapped a sterile, wet green towel over the raw wound. "There is a fly in here. Rosemary, get the benzoin spray."

"That's all we need," exclaimed Hank. "How does a fly get into an operating room?"

"It's on the wall." Camilla pointed.

"Freeze," ordered Dr. Sheridan, holding a can of benzoin. He took aim carefully and fired. "Clogs up their side holes so they can't breathe," said Dr. Sheridan as Rosemary wiped the dead fly off the wall.

"I'm going next door to see how the meniscectomy is doing." Dr. Sheridan surveyed the room on his way out. "We could be in Soviet Russia. Women nurses, woman anesthetist, woman surgeon. Hank, what are we men going to do?"

"You could stop by my house," suggested Camilla. "There's lots to do." Dr. Sheridan made a face at her and left the room.

A few minutes later, Hank and I were gowned and gloved. He took the grafts. I put them on. Working clockwise from the right arm, I wiped crusts away with a wet gauze. There were little hills and valleys of healing tissue. Germs lurked in every valley, and each time I wiped the raw tissue, it bled. If it bled too much, a graft wouldn't grow.

"How does it look, Liz?" Hank asked. He was down at the thigh, cutting skin in sheets from Mr. Fairfield's leg. "Here's a piece. How much do we need?"

I spread the skin out over the raw wound. A human-skin graft looks like the underbelly of a frog — limp, white, and moist.

"More." I put the skin on the wound, slimy side down so it would grow. "What kind of suture do you want to use for the grafts?"

"Six-oh silk." Thin skin grafts are hard to handle. They crumple and stick like Saran Wrap. For two hours, Hank and I laid out the grafts and sewed them on. Each time my needle went through the skin, blood oozed from the needle hole.

"He's never going to look normal, is he?" said Camilla.

"Hell, no," said Hank. "He's lucky to be alive."

I visited Mr. Fairfield some days later.

"You tell Harry to call me," he was saying into the telephone when I came in. He was scribbling notes, a cigarette in one hand, the phone cradled to his ear. "You tell him to straighten this out or I'll kill him." He hung up, smiling. "Bank presidents," he snorted. "If I took out my account, their River branch would fold." He checked his watch. "Don't have time to show you my wound. It's fine. I'm closing a commercial deal here in twenty minutes, and then the boys from the country club. I can't play golf, so they're coming over for poker." He reached out to shake my hand. "Thanks. I was an awful patient."

"For what you had, I thought you were great."

He waved good-bye. He was indomitable. I wondered if the disapproving radiologist would classify him as a moron or a psychopath for his smoking. On the way out of the hospital, Josh McDonald, another surgeon, fell in step with me. "What are you two doing this weekend?" he began.

"Who? Lucy and me?" I asked.

"No," he laughed. "Not you and the baby. You and your husband. We've got some theater tickets for Saturday. Can you come?"

"Josh, I — wish I could say yes." I hesitated, "but we're getting a divorce," I blurted.

"Oh Jesus," he said wearily. "Not another one. Well, bring someone else."

"I don't think I'm ready yet, Josh, but thank you."

When I got into the car, I was surprised by how little it

bothered me. It always happened that way. In an hour, it would catch up with me and I would be thinking about my husband, running like a rat on an endless wheel of memory that led nowhere.

Mary Clinton's pathology report came in that afternoon. Her tumor slides had traveled up and down the East Coast. In the end, the pathologists agreed. She had a histiocytoma, low-grade malignancy, surgical margins free of tumor. She would live to raise her children.

"Do you want to mail this yourself?" Beverly asked me when I was about to leave the office. "Your divorce, for Haiti."

I shook my head. "Will you do it?" Haiti and my divorce were a good business decision, perhaps, but I didn't want anything to do with it. I didn't even want to hold the envelope.

"Absolutely." Beverly understood. She tossed the envelope in her "out" box. "And Ms. Jones called. Will you call her tomorrow? She wants to set a time for a court hearing for temporary support and visitation. That lady is a talker. You know, she's billing you for all that talk time, Elizabeth."

I put that out of my mind, too. I knew Ms. Jones was not the perfect lawyer, but she would have to suffice. I couldn't face another lawyer. Ms. Jones was friendly. She was nice. She was expensive. She would have to work out. I was trying to find a house, not a lawyer.

I needed somewhere safe, off the street. It had to be near transportation, so someone could come to look after Lucy. I needed schools nearby. Lucy had done enough commuting. It needed to be big enough for the three of us. It needed to be affordable. The problem wasn't money. The bigger houses suited us no better. I didn't need a formal garden and a library, but what I needed was hard to find.

I found it in a new townhouse cluster, near where I once had lived when we were married. I called the agent to make an appointment to see the unit. On my way home, I felt almost sick. I couldn't do it. I couldn't live close to my memories. I found that my hands were trembling. My mind wandered. Where was he now? What was he doing? Could we be just friends? "No! No! No! No! No!" I pounded the steering wheel, almost shouting. I didn't think I loved him anymore, but how could those brief memories revive that pattern of hopeless love? I was trying to break loose. I had to get free.

⇒ *five*

THAT WEEKEND, it snowed — the first snow of the year. Greta, a friend I hadn't seen in months, called up. Would I drop by for a late dinner? She had just moved to the Heights and wanted to show me her new house. It was a good omen. My social life was starting again, just before Haiti and my divorce. I left Lucy inspecting a slipper of mine in between yawns. She was on the bed, next to my mother, who was reading. It was a lovely sight. I had my child and my mother. I was lucky, indeed.

The drive to the Heights was beautiful. The falling snow, lit by the streetlights in the dark, made the trees along the avenue look enchanted. It was like being in a fairy tale. I didn't know this area. I drove up to the crest of the hill and turned left through the entrance gate in a high brick wall. This was Mayfair, a new development still being built. My car rattled on the cobblestone pavement. The colonial townhouses, nestled together in the snow, looked like Williamsburg at Christmastime. It was a peaceful place. I walked around Mayfair before I found Greta's door. Suddenly, I knew we had to move here. It was made for Lucy. Other children lived here. Folded strollers were parked in the snow in front of several houses. The children here were Lucy's age. Across the street was a church with a preschool. The slide and jungle gym in the preschool play-yard were covered with snow. I could imagine Lucy kicking in the sandbox with friends in the summer. Next to the church was the local elementary school. Lucy could walk to school when the time came. Major bus lines went by the development. It would be easy to get someone to come here to look after Lucy. On the other side was a park with snow-covered benches. A lone woman stood there while her dog frisked around her. This was right for children. The narrow cobblestone drive meandered through the development, with sidewalks on either side. Lucy could run outdoors without the risk of being hit by a careless driver. This had to be home for her. I could guess the price of living here. I probably couldn't afford it, but if I possibly could, we would move here. Not only would it be perfect for Lucy, but also it would demonstrate how I cared for her. Visible signs carry weight when a judge decides on custody.

"So where's the proud father?" demanded Greta when I went in. It was a shock. I had never told Greta we were separated. I had told no one.

"Oh yes. We split up," I said casually, almost lightheartedly. I felt triumphant. I had found the right home for Lucy. My husband paled in comparison to her. Greta shrugged. "Happens to all of us." She led me in. Her townhouse was perfect for us. Mentally, I started moving us in. This room for my mother, that one for Lucy.

My family had been quite poor while I was growing up. My parents had worked very hard, and in time things improved, but my father never moved. Our home had been a dark, battered house in the country, with no friends nearby, no school or parks. I would never spend money to live in Mayfair for myself. Lucy was different. I wanted to give her what I had missed as a child.

"Cheers," said Greta, handing me a drink. "To your new life." It was about to begin.

I left for Haiti a few days later. I couldn't leave Lucy with my mother. Lucy needed constant attention. She couldn't crawl, but she could squirm and she no longer stayed where you put her. It would be too much for my mother, even the one night I would be away. Lucy stayed with Beverly and her children. I took Lucy to them on my way to the airport. Sheryl, Beverly's older daughter, sat down, holding Lucy, and turned on the TV. A car ad came on. Lucy turned to look at Sheryl and broke out laughing.

"She's getting a tooth!" exclaimed Beverly. She pointed to Lucy's mouth. A tiny speck of white showed through the pink gum. Lucy kicked her legs happily and bounced in Sheryl's lap. I left detailed instructions with Beverly: when Lucy went to bed, what she had for breakfast, how often she needed changing.

"Mom, can we keep her?" demanded Jay, Beverly's son. He tickled Lucy's toes. She chortled and grabbed his hair. I left her reluctantly and dashed for the airport.

Haiti is a tropical island of breathtaking emerald green set in a sea of blue. The heat was a welcome change from the early winter I left behind. Lightning, my guide, met me in the noisy crowd of the airport. He was a busy, bustling, bureaucratic man with papers in both hands. As he greeted me, the crowd fell back like the Red Sea to let through two haughty, beautiful women escorted by burly men in black suits. Behind them came two little girls in pink dresses, holding on to their nurses' hands. Lightning grabbed my elbow hurriedly and pulled me back with the crowd. This was the land of Baby Doc and the Tonton Macoutes. One showed respect to the people in power.

"I pick you up at nine tomorrow," Lightning told me when we arrived at the hotel. "Do not leave the hotel grounds. You have no one with you, understand? Men may come and say to you that Lightning sent them. No. Lightning never sends no one. I see you tomorrow. Let me have the papers."

I handed them to him. He gave me a half-salute in acknowledgment and hurried away, pigeon-toed and self-important. He was one of Haiti's elite. He owned two cars and he could read and write.

The next morning I climbed out of Lightning's car into the

painfully bright sun and ascended the great marble steps to the
courthouse built under the rule of Napoleon. The strangeness
of Haiti was soothing. It seemed unreal. Soldiers stood guard
with rifles along the street and up the steps. You could disappear in Haiti and no one would ever know or care. I sat in a
vast waiting room outside the judge's chambers. My green
armchair had its stuffing coming out one side. Flies buzzed in
and out of the high-ceilinged rooms along with the lawyers
who passed by, negotiating in groups of two or three. An im-
passioned attorney leaned from the balcony of one of the french
windows, gesticulating furiously to heaven, and yelled indignant Creole abuse at a colleague on the steps below. A rotund,
disheveled man with a briefcase approached me. He looked
most disreputable. When he smiled, he revealed an assortment
of crooked and rotten teeth.

"Dr. Morgan, I am your attorney, Mr. Clay. Follow me." He
led me into chambers. The judge, a handsome man behind a
desk spread with papers, looked up and smiled briefly but
kindly.

"Sit down, please. You are Elizabeth Morgan Y?" Mr. Clay
said, standing with his back to me to face the judge.

"Yes," I replied.

"You are a doctor?" He shouted over his shoulder.

"Yes."

"Your spouse is Y?"

"Yes."

"By profession, he is an X?"

"Yes."

"You were married in Z?"

"Yes."

"There is a female child in issue of this marriage?"

"Yes."

"Congratulations." Mr. Clay and the judge in unison turned
to bow to me as though I had achieved something remarkable.
Considering Lucy, I had to agree.

I smiled. "Thank you." From then on, they addressed me, not each other.

"There is no settlement regarding support of the child?"

"No, there is not."

"But you are the legal guardian of the child?"

"Yes, I am." I hesitated. Or was I? Ms. Jones had assured me that custody would not change, but it was being challenged. I had not yet, legally, been given sole custody. Neither Mr. Clay nor the judge were interested.

"You will resume your maiden name?"

"Please."

"The grounds for divorce are incompatibility?"

"Yes."

Mr. Clay stopped to take a breath. "Mrs. Y, are you sure there are no grounds for reconciliation?"

"Positive."

He waited. The judge waited.

"Are you quite sure?" repeated Mr. Clay.

"I am." They seemed vaguely disappointed. I wondered if they often had people run out of the courtroom at the last minute.

Mr. Clay sat down and arranged papers in front of me. "This is the divorce plea. Sign here. Your married name." He turned a page. "Sign again. Your married name. This is permission to obtain a Haitian divorce. Your married name." He turned another page. "Sign here. Now you consider yourself divorced so put your maiden name here. This is your divorce decree. You and your former husband will each receive a copy." It was matter-of-fact.

"Thank you," I sighed.

Mr. Clay escorted me out of the courthouse. "You are a nice lady." He smiled broadly.

"Thank you." I couldn't take my eyes off his teeth, but I could identify his smell as whiskey, now that he was close to me.

"You would like to stay in Haiti a day or two?"

"Certainly, if I could. It's a beautiful island." I felt irritated.

"You could stay a few days with me." He winked one eye. I removed my gaze from the seborrheic keratosis on his left cheek.

"No, I don't think so," I said.

"Really, nice lady. I could show you a good time in Haiti. There are very good restaurants I could take you to." Mr. Clay flashed more rotted teeth. Lightning, my guide, stepped between us with a practiced air.

"You have to go back to the hotel now. You have a plane to catch."

My plane did not leave for five hours, but I hastily got in the car, a divorcée. I felt indifferent. I knew the reaction would come later. Along the crowded streets, chickens squawked, flies buzzed over piles of vegetable garbage, and women washed clothes in muddy streams of sewage. A little boy hobbled along with a cane. It looked as though he had a congenital hip dislocation. Lucy was healthy. I had much to be grateful for. I stretched out by the pool at the hotel and settled down with a murder mystery. I couldn't read. I let the hot sun beat down and tire me, so I couldn't think.

I flew home that afternoon. My marriage was over. It was strange to be legally single again, lonely but free.

That Friday, I picked Lucy up at Nadine's. Lucy and I had grocery shopping to do before we went home. Lucy loved shopping. She loved people and there are lots of new people in grocery stores.

At Nadine Hoskins's, Lucy didn't smile. She was solemn and subdued.

"Did you bring the diapers I told you to?" Nadine snapped, watching me get out of the car. There was a bitter wind but she stood in the doorway, her arms folded. A child played at her feet.

"Yes, they're right here. And I brought more food for next week."

"I don't need more food. She won't eat for me sometimes."

"She won't? Lucy eats for me like a horse."

"Of course she eats for you," barked Nadine. "You're her mother." She made motherhood sound like a sin. Nadine bundled Lucy into her snowsuit almost roughly. Life was hard for Nadine, but I was more worried for Lucy. There was a furious barking from a door deep in the house.

"Do you keep your Chow inside now, Nadine?" I asked.

"Yes. I do not like to be alone in the house."

"He sounds ferocious."

"He is. China is an attack dog, and my best friend. I will never give him up." She smiled. "That is why I keep the door locked between him and the children. Don't worry," she added grimly. "Yours is safe in a crib. It is the older ones who would get hurt."

I stared at her. "Are you all right, Nadine?"

"Why do you ask?" She glared back, outraged.

Lucy was very precious to me. I headed for the Safeway wondering whether I should keep her at Nadine's. Was Lucy safe with her? I wished that I didn't have to work, or that I could work part-time. Then I felt silly. Nadine was recently widowed. Of course she was touchy. Like Ms. Jones, my lawyer, she was not perfect, but was adequate for the time being.

At the Safeway, Lucy sat in the grocery cart beaming. She was a happy baby away from Nadine. A morose elderly man stopped next to us in the soup aisle. Lucy peered at him with interest. When he looked her way, she smiled delightedly, reaching her hands out to him.

"Is this yours?" he asked me, pointing to her.

"Yes, that's Lucy."

"Does Lucy smile at everyone or am I special?"

I laughed. "You must be special."

"She's the best thing that happened to me all day." I beamed.

Lucy was special. Other people had babies. Nobody had my Lucy.

Lucy cried all the way home. She was tired. She held up very well but her days were too long for her. She wanted to be good, but she was a little baby. I wanted to move soon, for her sake, and I hadn't even had time to sign a contract on the house. Abruptly, I felt tired and deflated. I fought the Friday traffic home. It seemed that everyone but me was going out to have fun. Parking on our downtown street was a problem. It was mobbed on Fridays. It was in the middle of the action. It took me half an hour to find a space. We ended up two blocks from the house. I balanced Lucy on my hip and lugged four boxes of diapers out of the trunk and four bags of groceries from the backseat of the car. I looked at them. Four trips. At least one grocery bag would fall apart on the way home. Soon I would be chasing soup cans on my hands and knees in the dark, while Lucy cried. Welcome, single mothers of America. A young couple passed me on the street. The girl was young, pretty, and obviously very happy. She glanced at me struggling with Lucy and the diapers as though I were an interesting zoological specimen. It made me feel faded, and sorry for myself. No one had ever had it so hard as I did.

"Now that's pure garbage," I snapped out loud. I shook myself angrily. I had so much more than most; there was no place for self-pity. It was destructive. Lucy stopped crying to look at me, surprised. I picked up a diaper box and we started the long trek home. My mother opened the door, still rested from her holiday in Florida. She took Lucy out of my arms and fed her immediately. By the time I had the groceries in and unpacked, Lucy was asleep in her bassinet, her bottom in the air. She snuffled when I tiptoed in to see her and burrowed deeper into her pink pillow.

"You ought to let me do the groceries," said my mother.

"Mother, these bags weigh twenty pounds a piece."

"I can do it," she said. "I did it for years."

"And you got sick," I argued. "First of all, they're too heavy. Second, you'll hurt your back. Third, you do too much for me already. Fourth, I won't let you."

My mother looked at me, with a glint in her eyes.

"And don't you dare go and do grocery shopping without telling me. Promise," I demanded.

"I shall promise no such thing!" she replied.

The doorbell rang. It was Jim. He wedged himself in past empty diaper boxes and grocery bags. I enlisted his help.

"Sure," he said. He steered my mother to the sofa. "Now stay there. I'll help Elizabeth get dinner."

"It's got," said my mother.

"Then we'll bring it to you. Why all the empty diaper boxes?"

"Where else?" I asked. "The trash pickup isn't till Monday."

"Who are you kidding?" Jim opened the door and heaved them out onto the edge of the sidewalk. "This isn't exactly a class neighborhood. A stray cat here, a diaper box there. It fits in."

He handed me a bag. "I bought dessert, and blueberry muffins for you two for tomorrow. I come over here so much, I eat most of your food. And some steaks." We had dinner in the living room. The dining room was too small for three people to be comfortable. Jim produced a *Wall Street Journal*. "Did you buy those stocks I told you about, Elizabeth?"

"The next day."

"Good girl. Have you been following the market?" I looked at him sheepishly. Jim laughed. "I'm following it for you. The market's at nine hundred now. It's a good trend." He turned to mother. "What are your plans when Elizabeth moves, Mother?"

"I was rather hoping your father and I will buy a house for our retirement and live together." Jim and I looked at each other.

"Oh come on, Mother. Get real," I said.

"Perhaps Elizabeth will rent me this house when she moves." My mother looked at us defiantly. "I refuse to live with my children. I refuse to be a burden. I won't do it."

"Oh, garbage," said Jim. "Of course you're going to live with Elizabeth. I tell you this, Elizabeth. You're pretty hopeless when it comes to business and investments, but you've always had a good real-estate sense. You won't make a mistake there." He paused. "What I really want is both of your advice on my future. I'm doing fine here. If I stay here the rest of my life, I'll have a good living. But it doesn't feel right. I need to expand. I think I have to go to New York." We talked about it, but we all knew Jim was right. He belonged in Manhattan. It was the center of trading. He needed the excitement and the challenge. I knew he would succeed. I knew he ought to. It was just that we would all miss him. Jim turned on me suddenly. "That lawyer of yours. She's got to go."

"Jimmy, you don't understand."

"I do understand," he interrupted, irritated. "You don't have a warm, sympathetic negotiation on your hands. They're saying you're an unfit mother. You've got a custody fight. You're making a business decision for emotional reasons. Change lawyers, Elizabeth."

"I can't."

He gave up. "If you say so. I know you're wrong. I'm telling you, Elizabeth. Why stick with Ms. Jones? I think you should have custody of Lucy and I don't think he should be allowed to raise questions about it."

"I won't lose custody," I said.

"Says who?"

"Ms. Jones."

Jim banged the table with his fist. "It's what the judge says that counts," said Jim grimly.

That next Monday, Beverly stopped me the moment I got to the office. "You won't forget about the lease, Elizabeth."

"What lease?"

"The office lease. It expires in four months."

"I forgot completely. We'll have to move," I said.

Beverly nodded. "I already called, in case you wanted to stay. They won't renew the lease. They want to sell you the building. For you, a special deal. A quarter of a million dollars at sixteen percent."

"Some deal. We have to move."

"Where do you want to go?"

"We'll stay in the area," I said.

"The office condos across the street are $330,000 at eighteen percent."

"Beverly, I'm not planning to buy. We're going to lease."

"There's a medical building a mile away."

"No. It's not a good place."

"There's the house on the corner," said Beverly.

"No. It won't meet the county codes for a medical office."

"There's three thousand square feet for twenty dollars a foot."

"No."

"That's it, for now," said Beverly.

I sat down. I didn't want another problem, but I couldn't avoid it.

"Pray, Beverly. We need fifteen hundred square feet right up the road at a price we can afford."

"Within four months," said Beverly. "I am praying, but I think there's another problem." She picked a letter off her desk. "Your old lease, when you first opened your practice. Didn't you negotiate out of that lease so you could take time off when your mother was ill?"

"I certainly did." I took the letter Beverly handed me. It was certified. It was a demand for a small fortune in unpaid past rent from years ago.

"Not a good way to start a Monday." This had to be some mistake. I called Donald Lamont.

"Read the letter," said Donald. "I have your file in front of me." I read the letter.

"Did I handle this?" asked Donald.

"This was from before," I said. He laughed briefly. "That's a relief, Elizabeth. I'd hate to be the one who did this to you. Your lawyer didn't negotiate you out of anything. Legally, you probably owe that money. I'd like to be wrong. Send me everything. Compared to what else you've got Elizabeth, this should be a piece of cake. It's only money."

It was cheering — in a way. "So what's money?" I said to Beverly. "Food, housing, clothes, electric bills —" she ticked them off. "Want me to go on?"

"Definitely not — wrong attitude entirely." It wasn't as though it affected Mother or Lucy. I classified it as a non-problem.

That evening my mother looked more thoughtful than usual.

"What is it?" I asked her.

"What's what?"

"What's on your mind?"

"Nothing at all." She looked preoccupied.

"Mother, something is on your mind. I can tell by your face."

"Yes, there is, she admitted. It's about your father."

"Like what?" I hadn't seen much of him.

"Well, would you rent your father and me this house once you move?"

"He hates this house, Mother." I felt resentful. When my tiny, little house had been all I could afford, my father had declared it a slum. Rent them the house he hated? It didn't make sense.

My mother took my hand. "We've been married almost forty years; we might try again." I sat for a long time, thinking. I was trying to be a good mother, a good example for Lucy, and to do the right thing for my own mother.

"Have you looked at the Mayfair townhouses, Mother?"

"Yes." She looked at me. She knew me well enough to guess what I would say.

"We ought to go and look at them again. I want to sign the contract as soon as I know I can afford it. Each townhouse has one floor with a master bedroom suite, like a private apartment. Why don't you and Daddy live with me first? If that works, you can find a new place to live. Living here won't work." I wasn't sure I wanted my father living with me, but I was willing to try it.

"Elizabeth." My mother took my hand. "I didn't expect you to offer, but I am grateful."

"Mother, I left my husband so Lucy would have a quiet, happy home. If Daddy fits in, I couldn't be happier. But Lucy's my baby and in my house, Lucy will come first."

My mother smiled. "I agree."

It was hard for me to fall asleep that night. The money problems didn't upset me as much as my father did. I didn't know how it would turn out if he came to live with me. Besides that, a court hearing on visitation was coming near, and after that the custody trial. Ms. Jones had to do her stuff. She had to protect Lucy. She had to convince the judge. Jimmy had to be wrong about Ms. Jones. Lucy snuffled in her sleep and turned over. She would be too big for her bassinet soon. A nightmare feeling came over me as I thought of my husband seeking custody. It might be only a negotiating tactic, but all sorts of doubts and fears assailed me. I was a normal, loving mother — it was obvious, surely. The impossible couldn't happen. It couldn't.

The morning of the court hearing was a chilly winter day. Lucy woke up laughing and I carried her down to breakfast in her pink quilt. The pink pillow and the quilt went everywhere with her. She greeted my mother with a shriek of delight, displaying her new tooth. She waved at a bird out the window. She had just learned to wave. Later, she waved me off to my car. I drove to court without enthusiasm. Today would settle Lucy's visitation schedule, until the trial. The courthouse was a vast, white building. The entrance was guarded by policemen, who searched my purse and directed me through the metal detector.

"Nervous?" asked Ms. Jones, meeting me inside.

"Very."

"Settle down. You'll have a lot of waiting to do."

We took escalators down to the ground floor and entered a broad room with a judge's podium like a stage at one end, flanked by flags. On the right were the pews for the jury. On the left, a small window looking into another room.

"That's for dangerous criminals," said Ms. Jones, pointing to the window. "If they get violent, the sheriff locks them up in there. They can hear, but they can't be heard unless the sheriff turns on the microphone for them. The judge's desk is bulletproof and there's a panic button for the judge on the floor under his foot." She opened her briefcase. "By the way, you'll have a surprisingly early trial. Usually there's a wait of a year. Sometimes more. I got the notice yesterday. Your trial is up in six weeks. Probably from a mistake." She looked nervously through her papers. "I'm hoping we can get this settled without trial. For your sake, dear. You're such a lovely lady. This shouldn't poison your life. Are you dating?"

"Dating? No, I'm not dating. At this point, when I'm not working to support Lucy, I'm with Lucy. I don't know anyone anyhow. I didn't lead exactly a sociable life when I was married."

"Not healthy, dear." Ms. Jones patted my hand. "I want to see you out and around more. You're young still. Have fun. You're a good mother. Lucy will be fine."

"All rise for the judge," boomed a bailiff in a brown suit.

Everyone got to their feet. I saw my ex and his attorney ahead of us. Judge Overbolt appeared from a side door, his black robes flowing around him. He was a squat man with a square, expressionless face.

"This will take hours," said Ms. Jones. "Relax. We may not be called until after lunch." We settled down to wait.

The first case was called. Two parents and their lawyers walked to the center of the courtroom. The wife's lawyer had a reddened, acne-scarred face. "Your honor, this is a question of visitation." The judge nodded and took notes.

"The two children are twins," said the attorney.

"How old?" asked the judge.

"Both four. They live with their mother. The mother objects to their being alone with their father. Until now, visitation has been restricted to being with the grandfather as well."

"Tell me why."

"Last December, the children, after a visit with their father, were taken to the hospital for anal tears, anal fissures, and genital swelling." There was a rustle of horror in the courtroom. "The father admits to being a homosexual, alcoholic, and to having sexual relationships with his brother and his parents."

The mother entered the witness box and took the oath. She described what she had seen her husband do to the twins. She faltered.

"Did he rub the baby's face over his penis?" prompted her attorney.

I felt sick. There were more details. A social worker was not allowed to testify. She had not done the original investigation. The hospital investigation was discarded as hearsay evidence.

At last, the judge leaned forward, bored. "The father will have the following unsupervised visitation: every other weekend, two weeks every summer. . . ." I stared at the judge, amazed.

"He's wrong," Ms. Jones said. "Absolutely wrong. You never know what will happen in court."

"Ms. Jones, that man is going to decide what happens to Lucy?"

Ms. Jones shrugged, sympathetically. "It's the system, dear. I can't help it." I didn't have time to reply.

We were called next. I moved forward. I knew we were sunk. Ms. Jones fidgeted with papers. She looked pale. She usually settled out of court. Did she hate being here as much as I did? Had Jim been right all along?

The two attorneys argued back and forth before the judge. "How old is the child?" demanded the judge, interrupting. "Nine months."

"Has the mother been confined to a mental hospital? History of mental illness?"

"No, your honor," replied Ms. Jones.

"She doesn't object to visitation. She just doesn't want overnight until the child is two?" asked the judge.

"Yes," replied Ms. Jones.

"What do the parents have to say? Put them on," said the judge. I looked at Ms. Jones, alarmed. I was totally unprepared. My former husband took the stand. He was calm, persuasive, convincing. Then Ms. Jones looked at me and pushed me forward.

"Say what you have to say!" It was my turn. I wanted to explain that I loved Lucy. I didn't mind her seeing her father. But she was high-strung. She needed stability. If she went away overnight, she'd be terrified. It would be bad for her, very bad. I knew it. I didn't know why I knew. I was her mother. I just knew. I wanted to scream at the judge. Please don't destroy my child, please! I tried to explain. The judge looked at me impassively. I saw Lucy's pink, fubsy face, wrapped in her quilt, asleep, so trusting and so vulnerable. I burst into tears. The judge's face froze in anger at my tears. I wasn't supposed to cry. He didn't like it.

I tried to calm down and explain. He didn't listen. I had just lost the case. He dismissed me from the witness box. Next came a child psychiatrist who testified that it would be bad for Lucy, or for any child under two, to have overnight visitation away from the mother.

The judge dismissed him. "Okay. Until the final trial, the father has her from four-thirty Friday until five o'clock Sunday, every other weekend." The gavel pounded. The next case was called.

"Not bad," said Ms. Jones as we came out.

"Not bad?" I was in despair. "What does he know? Where is his training in child psychology? How can he do that to Lucy?"

Ms. Jones gave me a stern look. "Don't play games with the courts, dear. A judge's word is the law."

"Ms. Jones, you don't know what it's going to do to her."

"It's not so bad, Elizabeth. From your description, Lucy is a strong child. She is a survivor. She'll do fine. Now some children couldn't handle visitation. My little grandchild, Tara, is much too sensitive, but Lucy will thrive."

I stared at her. Her grandchild was too sensitive, but my child could tough it out?

"Ms. Jones, you've never seen Lucy. How can you say that?"

Ms. Jones sighed. "Elizabeth, Lucy has to adapt. That's the system."

"It stinks," I said furiously. "It stinks."

"Maybe," said Ms. Jones, "I can try to get it out of the system. If your ex will agree, we can get a child psychiatrist to settle these things instead of the court. Until then —"

"Until then, Lucy loses," I interrupted. I tried to calm down. The more Lucy's life was disrupted, the more she needed me to be calm, cheerful, all the things I didn't feel.

I steeled myself to give her away that Friday, but by four-thirty, the court-appointed time, I could barely speak. I held Lucy and rocked her back and forth on my lap. The doorbell rang. I went to the door, Lucy in my arms. She laughed happily. I opened the door and looked at him. Once that face had meant something to me. The divorce had not changed my feelings for him. This had.

"Lucy, you're going to be with Daddy." She looked at him, bewildered, and clung to me. I didn't want to hate him. I knew that being taken away from me for two nights would be a nightmare for her. All her security would be destroyed. He took Lucy away. She craned her neck to look at me, her big, brown eyes round with confusion. I waved good-bye and watched them drive away. I had never felt more empty, forlorn, or desperately helpless.

"Mother, don't let me hate him."

"No, you can't do that," said my mother. She sat down beside me. "Don't be angry." I felt angry. What system of justice traded a child around like a commodity? I was powerless to stop it. "We'll go out for dinner," said my mother. "This weekend we'll buy the house. You can't think about Lucy if you're buying a house. Come along." My mother steered me out the front door.

That Saturday, my mother climbed up and down the staircases of the model homes in Mayfair.

"It is a nice place," she said. "Which is this one?"

"The Sheffield, and it won't do," I replied. "It would put Lucy's bedroom on the top floor. We cannot possibly climb all those stairs each time we need to change her diapers. Should I call him to see how she is, Mother?"

"Absolutely not. Don't interfere. You'll make things worse."

I looked at my watch. "She ought to be taking a nap now. Mother, I have to call and be sure he's looking after her."

My mother grabbed my arm. "As your mother, Elizabeth, I'm telling you not to. If she's not napping now, he won't put her down to sleep because you call. There's nothing you can do," she said sternly. "Don't interfere."

"I know." I forced myself back to the house plans. "I don't

think the Manchester house plan will work for us. The kitchen is in the basement and there's too little storage room." We studied the floor plans, the models, and the prices. I had worked it out that I could afford the mortgage — by a hair. It would leave money for groceries, baby-sitters, and not much else.

"Should I buy a cheaper house, Mother?"

"Certainly, but where?" We had looked. Schools and safety are important for children and the prices range accordingly. There were areas where drugs were sold and prostitutes roamed at night as a matter of routine. I could get a lovely house for almost nothing — and get robbed at gunpoint, too.

"You'll be surprised how small a house seems when Lucy is walking and talking," said my mother. "She's trying to stand now. One child plus toys will fill most houses. Besides, it's friendly, Elizabeth. When Jim goes to New York, we won't have anyone looking out for us. We need friends, the way Lucy does. We're both starting a new life." She knew things might not work out with Daddy. My mother had a happy temperament, but it didn't make her life easy. She had looked forward for years to a pleasant retirement with my father. I saw her face whenever she saw an elderly couple. It had a yearning look that touched my heart. The Mayfair development would suit her, too.

"If you can't afford it, let me help," said my mother.

"Never!" I was going to make it on my own. My mother had never charged me for living at home. I wouldn't dream of making her pay to live with me. If it weren't for my mother, I would no longer be in private practice. She picked up Lucy when I was late. She took her to Nadine's when I operated early. She looked after Lucy when I was out on emergency call. I owed her too much already. I signed a contract before we left. It was a big step, but I knew it was the right thing to do.

⇒ *six*

LUCY CAME BACK on Sunday. When I opened the door for them, she gave me a scared look, as though I had betrayed her. As soon as I closed the door, she began to scream, twisting in my arms, pushing me away. I put her down. She screamed, rolling on the floor, hitting her head. I picked her up and held her and rocked her while she struggled to get away. The screaming got worse, her little face screwed up in agony and her arms flailing around. My mother watched us. We looked at each other helplessly.

"Don't let me hate him, Mother. I don't want to hate him for doing this to her, but it's so unnecessary. It's so wrong."

My mother put her arm around me. "I don't like what it does to you, Elizabeth. You shouldn't hate. It's not good for you." I shook my head, unable to speak, tears in my eyes. I struggled to hold Lucy and calm her down. At last she fell asleep in my arms, drenched in sweat from screaming at me. With infinite care, I put her, limp and exhausted, to bed.

Jim came by that evening. "How is she?" he asked when he came in.

"Terrible. Jim, it makes me sick to think about it. I don't want to talk about it." He scowled at me. "I knew it. Elizabeth, listen to me. Junk Ms. Jones. Junk her."

"Jim, I'm going to think about it."

"Don't think. Do it."

"You don't realize, I have so much time and money invested in her. I don't know if I can afford to change."

"You have to." He scowled.

"Jim, Ms. Jones thinks we can settle this out of court with a psychiatrist advising us. I'm willing to try it, if it will work for Lucy."

"You've got a trial in six weeks."

"I know. The psychiatrist won't take long. If it works, it works. If not, I'll find someone new."

"Who?" challenged Jim.

"I'll ask Rob."

"I already have," said Jim. "He doesn't think you should change. He says it'll look bad in court. Poor image. That's what he thinks, so don't ask him."

I stared at Jim. "Rob doesn't think I should change lawyers? No matter what?"

"Right. He's wrong. I know he's wrong. Where's that list he gave you originally. Remember, he checked out Ms. Jones for you? He said she was okay, and gave you a list of other lawyers that he knew of to recommend. There was one, he called him the best tackle in town. What was his name?"

"Blackstone," interposed my mother. "William Blackstone."

"That's it!" said Jim. "You've got Ms. Jones, the warm, sympathetic therapist. This time get something made of steel, Elizabeth."

"If the psychiatrist doesn't work, I will, Jim."

"The shrink won't work, Elizabeth. I'm telling you." Jim pounded his fist into the chair. "He's challenging custody. It's absurd. And the trial is coming. A good lawyer won't take your case without time to prepare. Don't screw it up, you turkey. Lucy means a lot to me too. She's my niece."

I stared at Jim, paralyzed with indecision. I didn't know the right thing to do. I didn't want to fight. I didn't want Lucy's life settled in a trial. The judge had scared me. A judge wouldn't know Lucy. If only the psychiatrist would help us.

That night, Lucy woke up screaming at eleven. She screamed for an hour, while I rocked her in my arms. She screamed at two and again at five. She had never been like this before. She screamed at night all that week and by then it was only a week before she went away again.

On Saturday, Lucy looked more tired than usual. I put her down on the floor in the kitchen with her pink quilt, the rather grubby, battered one she had had since she was born. She put her head down on the pillow and I turned my back to get plates out for dinner. My mother came in from the dining room. "Watch out!" said my mother, alarmed. I turned around. Lucy had reared up and was falling like a log onto the floor. I dashed for her.

"She's all right." My mother got there one step before me. "Only a little bump." She scooped her up and sat down with Lucy on her knee. Lucy had bumped her head barely, if at all, on the floor, but she was sitting on my mother's lap awkwardly, her head down. "She's all right," said my mother. Lucy didn't look all right to me.

"Mother, give her to me. I want her." I took Lucy away from her and put her head on my shoulder. Lucy took a shuddering breath and I braced for the outraged squawl to follow. Instead her legs stiffened in my arms and went out straight. I looked at her. "Oh, my God. Oh no, no, no." This couldn't be happening. Not to my Lucy. She was dead white, rigid, her arms and legs moving out straight in tiny jerks. Her chest didn't move. She wasn't breathing. I put her flat on the floor and waited for a moment, hoping she would breathe again. My mind went blank. I couldn't remember how to resuscitate a dying child. Lucy shuddered again. Her eyes rolled up into her head under half-closed lids.

"Mother, call an ambulance." If Lucy didn't breathe soon, she would be dead before it came. A picture came to my mind of the resuscitation class I had taken almost a year ago, the week before I delivered her. Clear the airway. Her airway was clear. I put my left hand on her forehead, for mouth-to-mouth resuscitation. I couldn't feel a pulse. Either there wasn't one or I was too panicked to find it. I thumped her chest, briskly. I wanted to cry. I didn't want this to be happening. Not to my baby. I felt her arm. She had a good pulse at her wrist, so her heart was all right. If I breathed for her, she would live. I leaned down to begin mouth-to-mouth resuscitation, when a high, thin wail came from Lucy. Her chest moved. Another wail and her breath came in gasps. Her left arm moved, and then her left leg, but not her right side. Minutes later, her right arm and leg moved and she tried to struggle to her feet. For the next two hours, she sat in my lap crying, or resting her head on my shoulder, dazed and limp. "My darling, my little darling." I rocked her back and forth. "Poor, poor baby." She clutched me and tried to smile.

"What do you think it was?" asked my mother.

"Breath-holding," I said. "Children breath-hold." I was fooling myself. I knew she had had a seizure. I didn't want Lucy to have a seizure. It couldn't be true. I held her in my arms that night and rocked her to sleep. I tried to sing "Baby Elephant" to her. I couldn't. It made me choke and start to cry, so I rocked her instead.

I lay on my bed watching her that night. I dozed off, only to wake up frantically reaching out to touch her, to be sure she was warm and breathing. She didn't wake up that night. She slept as though she were drugged. At eight o'clock the next morning, I woke up to find Lucy looking solemnly at me from under her quilt with big, brown eyes, like a mouse peering out from a hole. I dialed Odette and took Lucy into bed with me.

"She's too young for breath-holding, Elizabeth. Your baby had a seizure," said Odette. "She has to see a neurologist. She may need to be treated, but, frankly, seizures and seizure medication both cause learning disability. I'll call Morris Zubek. I want him to see Lucy this week." I thanked her and hung up the phone. Lucy grabbed for it playfully. I felt too shocked for tears. My mother came in and I told her what Odette had said.

"Mother, no one will ever believe me, but she's having seizures because this visitation is frightening her," I said. "I know it. I know Lucy. She's terrified."

"I agree with you. And no one else ever will — except another mother," replied my mother.

There was nothing I could do.

Three days later, I sat in Morris Zubek's office, filling in a registration form for Lucy while she played on the floor with a red plastic cube. Beverly had rearranged all my midafternoon appointments. My mother had brought Lucy to my office so I could get to the appointment on time.

"He." It was Lucy, pulling herself up by my chair. She grabbed my skirt.

"Hello, Lucy." I leaned down to her.

"He," she said again. She had a plastic block in one hand. She tried to make me eat it, laughing.

"I aah oo aah," Lucy laughed. "I aah ooh."

"I love you, too." Lucy shrieked happily. She was trying to talk and I had understood her. I hugged her.

"Hu." She sat down with a bump and crawled over to another block, looking back at me to chortle.

"Hi." This time it was Morris Zubek. I picked up Lucy and followed him back to the examining room. I told him what had happened.

"You realize she had a major seizure?" he demanded.

"I know."

"Was she less coordinated for the first few days afterwards?"

"Yes. Today is the first day she could crawl without toppling over."

"Problems at her delivery?"

"Yes. She was briefly cyanotic. It was a long labor." He nodded, satisfied. "That's the most common reason for childhood seizures." I explained Lucy's court-ordered visitation, away from home.

"Psychological trauma has nothing to do with seizures," said Morris repressively. "Sleep disruption, yes — psychological stress, no." I explained how her sleep pattern had changed since her visitation began, how she screamed at night.

"It has nothing to do with her seizure," he told me. "It's not bad enough."

"Then why is she having a seizure now and not before the visitation?"

"I can't explain that." He smiled condescendingly. "Naturally you're worried. You're her mother. Believe me, it has nothing to do with it."

"Believe me," I felt like saying, "you're wrong!" I could see that her birth problems made her susceptible to seizures. Everyone has a weak spot. But ulcers, high blood pressure, headaches, every disease in the book can be precipitated by stress. I resigned myself. I was the mother. Mothers are foolish. I knew nothing. I knew how to stop the seizures: stop the overnight visitation until she was older. But I couldn't stop that. The courts had Lucy in their power. If they were going to destroy her, I could only stand by and suffer.

"We'll do blood tests and an EEG," said Morris. "If they're normal, she should not be treated. The drugs used to stop seizures impair brain development."

"Fine." I knew that already. I smiled and gathered Lucy up in my arms. "Thank you so much for your help." He had nothing to offer us. The seizures would injure her brain. The seizure treatment would injure her brain.

The blood-test results were all normal. The EEG was hell. Beverly once again rearranged my surgery and I spent all afternoon with Lucy in a neurology lab. I was forced to be strong, for Lucy, but I was desperate. I imagined her brain damaged by seizures, or doped by antiseizure drugs. I blocked it out. She needed someone calm to rely on and always turn to. It was me. I wasn't perfect, but I was trying. Dozens of electrodes were glued to her head while she sat in my lap and screamed at the lab technician. She had never been like this before visitation. She had trusted everyone.

"They never like it," said the technician. "Now you get her calmed down and get her to go to sleep."

"To sleep?" Lucy was purple with screaming, sweating, and sobbing. She would never sleep.

"Oh, yes. We want the waking EEG but the sleep EEG is so important." She turned down the lights and left the room. I rocked Lucy in my lap, electrode wires flopping around her head. At last she settled down, resting her head on my chest, with one hand clutching my hair — a curled up, sad little bundle. The door opened. The technician tiptoed in. The EEG machine clicked on, spewing out reams of paper tracings of Lucy's brain waves.

"Now we'll try the sleep one, Mommy. Put her down on the table," ordered the technician.

"She's not asleep, yet."

"Let's try, Mommy," ordered the technician. I put Lucy down on the table. She scrambled up, screaming in the dark room, reaching out for me in terror. I picked her up. This went on for two hours. I rocked her to sleep. The moment I put her down, she woke up screaming.

"I don't think she's going to sleep," said the technician at last. "We'll do the strobes. Then it's over." Strobe lights of increasing intensity flashed on in the darkened room. Lucy gazed at them from my lap, amused. I knew she hadn't had a light-induced seizure. She had had a psychological-stress-induced seizure. For all that I was a doctor, I hated the tests — a waste of time, another torment for Lucy.

After the strobe lights, Lucy was in a great mood. She liked strobe lights. My mother was waiting outside the lab. Lucy grinned and laughed excitedly when she saw her, reaching out her arms.

"Is your baby always so jolly?" asked a passerby in the hallway.

I shook my head. "Don't I wish!" If only they knew. Lucy had been a friendly, happy baby. No one who didn't sleep with her in the dark could know what a terrified child she was now.

That same week, I met Ms. Jones to arrange for the psychiatrist who would be advising me and my former husband about what was best for Lucy.

"How is Lucy?" chirped Ms. Jones.

I tried to be calm. "Now she has seizures." I clenched my fist to fight back tears. "She only screamed for two hours last night."

Ms. Jones winced. "Dr. Robinson, the child psychiatrist, is going to be a big help." She patted my arm. "I'm very hopeful. Now I should warn you, a child psychiatrist won't care a damn about what the parents want."

"I don't either," I snapped. "If it works for Lucy, it works for me."

Dr. Robinson was a child psychiatrist, an analyst. Usually analysts work with children old enough to talk, so they can be analyzed. He listened politely and took notes.

At the end, he said, "Your husband wants more overnight visitation, not less, Dr. Morgan. He says that way it will be less frightening for Lucy and it's what he wants."

"Dr. Robinson, what I want and what he wants is not the most important. What is it going to do to Lucy? She's mentally disturbed. You don't know what she's like at night."

He spread out his hands. "Maybe we need a test. I think I'll recommend a trial of midweek overnight visitation with her father." I was dubious, but I told Ms. Jones about his plan. She wrote it up as a court order. I signed it.

Lucy went away overnight the next Wednesday at nine-fifteen. She came back the next day, at nine-thirty. She didn't go to Nadine Hoskins's that day. My mother kept her at home because she wouldn't stop screaming. I got home at six. Lucy was still screaming. Seeing me made her worse. At ten she fell asleep in my bed, holding on to me.

At midnight she woke up. She was not like anything I had seen before. She screamed as though she were being tortured. She arched her back, her hands clenched, her eyes closed, screaming. I turned on the lights to wake her up. She wouldn't wake up. She screamed, twisting in my arms. My mother came in and held out her arms. Lucy looked at her for a moment, her eyes widened, and she went absolutely berserk. I couldn't hold her. She screamed all night. I canceled my patients for the next day.

Lucy screamed until ten that morning. I could not reach Dr. Robinson. I took Lucy to Odette. By then Lucy was limp with exhaustion.

"Overnight visitation at her age! She's not ill," said Odette, outraged after she examined her. "The poor thing's terribly upset. Give her some Benadryl. It will sedate her. It's all you can do."

I reached Dr. Robinson. He made an appointment to see Lucy in four days. When we went, Dr. Robinson sat Lucy on the floor and offered her two tiny dolls an inch high, one a man, one a woman. "Dada," said Lucy taking the male doll. "Dada," she said, taking the female doll. She banged them together.

"You see," Dr. Robinson looked up in triumph. "She's playing with the Daddy doll."

"Dr. Robinson!" I stared at him. "This is a baby. Remember how old she is! She does not know a Daddy doll. She does not know a Mommy doll. She said 'Dada' to a giraffe on television last night. And a koala bear."

"Let's see what more overnight visitation does to help," said Dr. Robinson.

"Dr. Robinson, it's not good for her. Believe me. Please believe me. She is worse. You don't understand."

Dr. Robinson shook his head gently. "Dr. Morgan. There are two sides to this. Your husband argues that you are a very manipulative woman."

"Do you think I'm lying to you?" I began to feel paranoid. Was the world out to destroy Lucy and me?

"Lying is a strong word," chided Dr. Robinson. "Let's say you exaggerate."

That night Lucy woke up screaming at two. At three-thirty, she was still screaming while I rocked her in my arms. I turned on the light. I turned to *R* in the phone book. I found Dr. Robinson. I dialed him at home.

"Hello." He was barely awake. Lucy screamed at me in desperation, shaking her head.

"Dr. Robinson. It's Dr. Morgan. I knew you'd want me to call you," I said firmly through the noise.

"Oh?" He woke up — now he was angry.

"What do I do? I have a disturbed child. You're her psychiatrist."

"I'm not her psychiatrist."

"Then what are you for Lucy? You ordered the visitation. You said I was exaggerating. She's been like this since two AM. What do you want me to do. Can you see her?"

"No! No!"

"Then tell me what to do."

"Rock her."

"Rock her? What do you think I've been doing for the past hour?"

"Talk to her."

"I've been doing that."

"A cracker?"

"A cracker!" I exploded. "She'll choke to death."

"A bath?" He sounded frantic.

"Oh, I haven't tried that yet. I'll do that and get back to you."

"Oh, no. There's no need to call me back."

"I'll get back to you." I was adamant.

"Oh, no." He protested. I hung up and gave Lucy a bath. It didn't work. She screamed at the sound of water. She sat screaming in her little plastic tub. At five she was still screaming. I called Dr. Robinson a second time.

"Dr. Morgan!" he shouted when he answered.

"Don't scream at me, Dr. Robinson," I snarled. "She's my child and you're doing this to her. I've been up since two. You haven't. I know the cause. Visitation. You increased it. You didn't believe me. Fine. I took your advice. Just tell me what I do now. You didn't believe that Lucy screamed all night. Tell me. Am I lying now? Am I exaggerating?"

"Dr. Morgan." His voice squawked through Lucy's tortured screams. "I believe you. This can't go on. We'll have to work something out."

I felt very bitter. What did a mother have to do to get help for her child? Beat peoples brains out? Have a live-in judge to testify that I wasn't a liar? At seven, Lucy fell asleep. I was worn out, but for the first time in months, there seemed to be hope. If Dr. Robinson believed me, maybe he could help us.

I called Ms. Jones that morning.

"I think Dr. Robinson is going to suggest decreasing visitation, Ms. Jones. At least no more Wednesdays."

Ms. Jones coughed. "I just spoke with your ex's lawyer. They won't agree to stopping midweek visitation. Basically, they think you're inventing Lucy's problem."

"I'm not. Dr. Robinson agrees with me. No more Wednesdays."

"But there's the court order, Elizabeth. You signed it. It's for every other Wednesday."

"For a trial period."

Ms. Jones coughed again. "I didn't write the order for a trial period," said Ms. Jones. "I thought you agreed to permanent Wednesdays. I'm sorry if I misunderstood. I wrote it. You signed it. You can't just change that, dear. That's a court order." There was a pause and I heard her light a cigarette.

"Ms. Jones, now what? At this point, I'm ready to bleach my hair and deny paternity. I want to save my child."

There was a pause. "You can take her away to England. You would have to plan on not ever coming back. And don't tell your ex. He can stop you at the borders. The border guards can arrest you, and your ex would ask a judge to give Lucy to him." I listened in amazement. She couldn't be serious. "But moving abroad," continued Ms. Jones, "will solve your problem. I have to be frank with you, Elizabeth. Your husband is a very intelligent man. He's determined to get custody." I turned cold inside. This was the twentieth century. This was America. I was mentally stable — at least I was before all this began. I was a respectable, divorced, self-supporting woman with a baby daughter. And my lawyer was telling me I had to run away? Over my dead body!

"Ms. Jones, have you heard of a lawyer called William Blackstone?" I interrupted.

Ms. Jones clicked her tongue. "Oh no, Elizabeth. Don't get bitter. I'd hate to see you ruin your life with a bitter divorce. Don't fight over your baby. You're a beautiful lady. Don't spoil your life. You've worked too hard for that." I could hear Jim snorting, "You've got a make-you-feel-good artist. She is going to make you feel good about giving Lucy away. Wait and see." And Jim was right. It was happening now. Lucy was at stake. I had blown it. I was a well-intentioned fool. A fool of a mother destroys her child. I had been totally wrong not to fight from the start. I had been totally wrong not to listen to Jim.

"Have you heard of William Blackstone?" I repeated coldly.

"Yes. He has always been most cordial to me but he is hated

by a lot of lawyers I know. I'm sad to see you do this, Elizabeth. You've got a lovely life to live."

"Ms. Jones, I want his opinion before we go to trial."

"Knowing how you feel, Elizabeth, I'm going to file to withdraw from your case. I can't represent you."

The trial was now three weeks away. It took me a week to get an appointment to see William Blackstone. He was a very busy man. He wasn't what I expected. He was an impressive man, when I met him — built like a football tackle, solid as a rock. He listened to me, watchful, attentive, studying my face. When I finished, he leaned back in his chair and said nothing for a long time.

"I would like to represent you, Dr. Morgan," he said at last. "I am in sympathy with your case. I cannot help you. I cannot possibly prepare for trial in two weeks." I had let it go too late. Ms. Jones had withdrawn. I would be without a lawyer at the trial. I would lose custody for sure.

"Is there anyone you know who could represent me?" I begged. I heard myself and knew it was a foolish question. No one could do a good job for Lucy in two weeks. "If the trial were postponed, could you represent me?"

For a long time, he didn't speak. He sat, his legs crossed, his arms folded, thinking. Then, he took out a pocket diary and turned the pages. Week after week flipped by. "If the trial is postponed four months, I could represent you." He looked up, impassive, clever, and uncompromising. He was tough. No one pushed him around.

"You are probably the only man in Washington who can save my daughter, Mr. Blackstone. How do I postpone a trial?"

"Ms. Jones will do it for you. She is legally and ethically obliged to represent you until a judge signs an order releasing her from her obligations."

I looked at him. "Assuming she won't, how do I do it?"

"First, notify the other side, your former husband and his lawyer, of the day you will be in court. Next, go to the courthouse. File a motion for postponement. The judge will hear you and decide that day. Explain that you have an attorney, myself, who is willing to represent you but who cannot represent you unless the trial is postponed."

"What do you think my chances are?"

He thought a long time. "You have left it very late. The judge will listen to you. All I can say is you have a chance."

"If it is postponed, you will represent me?" I wanted to be sure.

"No. Only if it is postponed four months or longer will I represent you," he replied emphatically.

I called Ms. Jones after that. She did not return my calls. I was on my own. I thought about my options that night. If I asked Ms. Jones to take me back, I'd lose Lucy for sure. If I went to someone else, I might lose, too. If William Blackstone took me on, I still might lose, but he was the only lawyer I'd met as clever and determined as my ex. If I wanted Lucy, I needed him. Four months of waiting was a long time, but the risk of losing custody would be worse. Lucy needed me to do the right thing for her now. I set my teeth on edge. My ex might be smarter, he might be richer, but I was stronger now. I would fight to the bitter end for her. And I knew that hell as it was for her now, she would come through if she had me. I was her anchor. Alone, I had to convince the court to give us a postponement of the trial so I could have the lawyer that she needed. If I failed, I would face my ex in two weeks in court, unprotected.

We had snow flurries that night. I stayed up late, watching the snow. I made lists — lists of what to say to my ex when I called him, lists of what to do in court. I couldn't go to bed. I could think of nothing else. What if the unthinkable happened and I had to argue my own custody trial? Jim had come by. He understood what I was up against. He said nothing. My mother said nothing. She went to bed early. Even Lucy understood. She lay in her bassinet, clutching her pillow and staring at the falling snow. I went over what I had to do in court. I went over what I wanted to say to my ex. I called Rob to see if there were other pitfalls I had to avoid. I relied on him a lot. "Want me to come?" he offered. "To see that you do it right. I'll walk you through. Don't thank me. You'd do the same. And by the way, Lucy's going to have a cousin. Janice is pregnant. We'll need your advice on working motherhood."

I couldn't believe him. "My advice? Rob, my advice is 'Don't ask my advice.' I'm doing it all wrong!"

Our tiny house in winter was warm and cozy — almost too cozy, like an animal burrow. When I pulled back the curtains at five-thirty the next morning, the city was quiet, muffled by the snow that had fallen during the night. These were no mere snow flurries. I had to look twice to see my car parked illegally near the alley, half-buried in the snow.

"My patients will probably cancel, but I have to go in," I said to my mother over breakfast. "Getting to Nadine's is out of the question." Lucy opened her mouth like a hungry bird and I spooned in the egg. She adored eggs. She grabbed the spoon and banged the table. She wanted more.

"Lucy and I will come with you, then. We won't like being shut in all day," said my mother. "It will be a little adventure for us." I hesitated. I had lived in the North for years. I should be able to drive well in this snow. It was barely snowing now. I dug the car out. We set off, dressed for an arctic expedition. Lucy threw her head back and chattered excitedly, like a chipmunk, when snowflakes floated onto her face. The car crunched along in the snow, sliding occasionally. The roads were empty. We made it easily to the office. "How great that I once lived in Boston," I remarked smugly. "Most people here don't know how to drive in the snow."

Beverly lived a block away. She was there when we arrived. She and my mother chatted over coffee. Lucy cruised. She had progressed from crawling on the floor an inch at a time like a tired snake, to being able to hoist herself up and toddle, holding on to the wall. I stood at the bay window looking out with dismay. It had begun to snow again. We ought to have stayed home. I had no business bringing my mother and my child out in a storm. I had decided to go back home when a patient, Mrs. Vernon, arrived, shaking snow off her ski jacket.

"I would have been furious if you hadn't been here," she announced. "This storm is perfect for me. My mother has the baby. I live a block away." She was a small, booted, birdlike woman, a corporate executive, used to giving orders, not used to listening.

In the examining room, she explained what she wanted. She was friendly but firm. "I've done my reading and I know all about this, Doctor. Nine months ago, I had a mastectomy for cancer, a modified radical. My right breast was removed. The pectoralis muscle is in, of course. The nodes were negative. Are you following me? Do you do this sort of work?"

"Yes, I do." My mind wandered to the snow outside. It had tapered off. I thought about court. I thought about Lucy.

"Good. You need to reconstruct my breast with one of those silicone implants under the muscle. Nothing fancy. Make it a 'B' cup."

"Cup size can be a little hard to predict."

"I know. As close as you can. And take off the other breast. I don't want it. Rebuild it too. All in the same operation. You can do that, can't you?"

"Yes, but why do you want the left breast removed?"

"Everyone in my family has breast cancer. Two sisters. My mother. My grandmother. An aunt. I don't want that breast." She was right: she ran a very high risk of getting a second breast cancer. For the next hour, Mrs. Vernon told me exactly how I was to do her surgery and the possible complications she might have. I listened closely but was preoccupied. Among other problems, if I remained absorbed with my own troubles I would ruin my practice; but fortunately, Mrs. Vernon didn't notice me. She was self-absorbed. I was a machine to do what she needed. She chose a time for her operation in consultation with Beverly, bundled herself up, and marched out undaunted into the reviving storm, snow eddying around her.

"Elizabeth, you can spend the night at my house if you'd like," offered Beverly. "Can you three get home?"

I yanked on my boots and looked out the window. I wanted to get Lucy home. Beverly had three children, plus house-guests. She didn't need us camping on her living-room floor as well. "In Boston, this would be nothing," I replied. "Once I hiked eight miles to make rounds in the hospital. That was when the Canadians had to send down their plows to dig out the Boston snowplows. That was a storm." Beverly and I trekked to my car. She helped me dig it out from the new-fallen snow.

I had brought emergency supplies — shovels and sand, in case we got stuck, and food and blankets. I went back to the office for my mother and for Lucy. Beverly sent us off with a wave. In the parking lot, a car in front of us floundered in a drift. I helped to dig it out. Then we got stuck when the car ahead stalled in a drift as we turned onto the main road. A passing gang of boys pushed us out. My mother waved thanks from her window. We were on our way home. We had the road to ourselves. We bumped slowly along the packed-down snow and turned onto the parkway.

"Halfway there, Mother. Good old Boston trained me well," and down the ramp we went. "Oh, Christ." I had been think-ing of what I had to say in court. Now, for miles ahead there were cars. Not one was moving. The federal government had ordered all its workers to come in to work as usual that morn-ing. While some were still struggling to get in, those who had arrived had all been ordered home early. "Let's get out of here."

"You can't," said my mother. "Look behind you." Four cars had come down after me. I climbed out of the car. A man in a business suit, carrying a briefcase, plodded up to me. He was red in the face with anger.

"It's a mess. It's a God damn mess. Left my car in a drift. God damned federal government. I'm supposed to catch a plane to Barbados at six. Only three hours. Can I make it by walking?" He consulted his watch.

"The airport is closed," I replied.

"God damn," and he trudged away.

A soldier in an army uniform came down to speak to us. His car was the one behind us. "What's it like down there?" He had a commanding air and seemed to assume he was in charge.

"Nothing's moving."

A burly, bearded man in jeans climbed out of the next car and approached us. "Nothing moving? Okay, what are we going to do?" We were a team. My mother amused Lucy in the car. I helped the two men to stop traffic at the top of the ramp and to direct cars backing out. The soldier gave the orders. The blue-jeaned man and I executed them, along with him. The third car behind us was empty when it was time for it to move. A pudgy man stood by it, flapping his hands. "I can't move it. It can't be moved. I've seen snow. Impossible. I can't back it up. I don't know what to do."

"We need your help," said the soldier. "You have to steer it. We'll push."

"No, no. I can't do it," he yelped.

"I can steer," I said.

"Good, get in," commanded the soldier.

I climbed in, numb with cold and with shock. Here we were in a mess again, thanks to me. The soldier and the man in jeans pushed the car up the hill, while the pudgy owner walked beside them. "Be careful. Be careful," he shouted. "You'll ruin my car." At the top of the hill, he examined it. "I don't see any scratches," he said grudgingly and drove away.

"What a shit-head," exploded the man in jeans. "Not even a thank-you. I'd like to punch his face in."

At the end of two hours, sweat was freezing on our clothes. It was my turn to be pushed up the hill. I had checked on my mother and Lucy at intervals. Lucy was asleep. My mother looked rather sick. Ever since her illness, she had been extra-sensitive to air pollution.

"It's not the cold." She coughed. "It's the car exhaust. I'll be all right." My mother is a stoic. She has to feel dreadful to complain at all. With her steering, we pushed my car up the ramp.

At the top, a truck had stalled, blocking our exit. "We have to dig him out," said the man in jeans, who had stayed around to help me out. "Otherwise you'll end up in a drift."

An irritated pair of drivers from behind the truck approached us. "What the hell are you guys blocking the ramp for? The parkway is clear up ahead. We heard it on the radio."

"Don't believe it," the man in jeans said. "We've seen it, and that traffic ain't going nowhere."

One of the men pointed. "Look down there. You can see the cars moving, you turkeys. Get going. We're trying to get home." I could see the traffic moving once again on the parkway.

"I'm going down the ramp," I said.

"Don't let him stampede you," said the man in jeans, holding me back.

"I'll make it," I insisted, but I knew I was stampeding all the same. The parkway was the shortest route home. Like a horse heading for the barn, I had to take it. I was tired, cold, and worried. I had to get Lucy out of the snow. I had to get my mother out. I had to talk to my ex about changing the trial. I didn't have much time. It was two weeks to the trial. Down the ramp we went. We crawled along. Then traffic stopped again. I got out and looked. Nothing was moving for miles ahead. My mother looked very pale. "Mother, we'd better bail out. There's a gas station at the top of the hill. Can you make it?" She nodded. I drove the car off the road into a drift and we climbed out.

Two more inches had fallen in the past half an hour. Blinding snow and the north wind bit into me. I wrapped Lucy in extra blankets. She still looked cold. My mother, coughing but determined, held on to my arm. We staggered back to the ramp we had recently driven down.

"Need help?" A chubby lady in an old camel coat waved to me halfway up the ramp. "Dickie! A lady with a baby. Help her," she shouted. Two boys in parkas rushed up. The local Boy Scouts. They grabbed mother's arm and like Saint Bernard dogs led us staggering into a gas station. It took us almost two hours to get there from our abandoned car. At least there was warmth. Lucy would not freeze. My mother could breathe. The Boy Scouts went off to help more travelers. I looked around.

"We're closed," said a man behind the desk. "I'm locking up."

"Not in a snowstorm like this, you're not," I replied belligerently. I pushed my mother into a chair. "Not to women and children." He looked mulish. The door swung open and three stranded bus passengers joined us. Nothing could travel in the chaos the snow had left. Only a big four-wheel-drive could possibly get through. I had to get help for mother and Lucy. My father was only a few miles away. I knew he would help in a crisis. Disasters brought out the best in him. He had a Blazer. I called him from the pay phone outside, as the wind whistled around me.

"Honey, where are you? I'll dig out the Blazer and come and get you," he said.

"Do you know the last station before the parkway, Daddy?" I tried to explain. He had never been good at directions. I could see him setting out and getting lost.

"Start digging, Dad. I'll walk there." It was eight miles to his house. I could make it there and back, with luck. My mother looked appalled when I told her I was walking.

"I got us into this mess. I'm getting us out of it," I said grimly. I walked up to the station manager. "I'm leaving my mother and my baby here. My father has a Blazer. We'll be back."

"You're coming back?" He sniffed and chewed gum. "Yeah. They can stay till then."

I trudged the first half-mile. Then two women picked me up in their car. We were stopped by a bus, on its side, blocking the road. I set out on foot again. I hadn't felt my feet for hours. Now my hands went numb. Wheels crunched behind me. A Blazer jammed with people bounced along, honking. A window came down.

"Hey, where you going? Climb in." The driver talked like a cowboy. He wore boots, an army-paratrooper jumpsuit, and a ranger's hat.

"That your mom and baby back there at the Exxon? I told her to come along, but I couldn't promise her how we'd go. She was afraid we'd miss you and decided to stay put. Too late to go back now. Hold on, folks." The Blazer accelerated and jumped the median strip.

"Learned to drive like this when I was deputy sheriff in Alaska." The Blazer roared and lurched back over the median strip to avoid another stranded bus. We veered off onto a side road. He gunned the engine and shot along the sidewalk past a clump of stranded cars. He waved to them, laughing, driving with one hand and chewing gum. "Ain't no one gonna stop me." He was true to his word. He dropped me at my father's, but by now dusk was falling. We would never get back to Mother and Lucy. I couldn't drive like that and neither could my father. Besides, my father's Blazer was still buried in snow. We called the police. They couldn't help. The squad cars were stranded. We called the hospital, but I knew the answer. There was only help for people dying. The Red Cross didn't answer. A towing service promised to come at two in the morning to free the stuck Blazer. Meanwhile, Lucy and my mother were stranded. I should never have left them.

"It's not your fault," said my father, stoking his wood stove in the living room. The ceiling was dark with smoke. "Have some coffee." He poured his home brew into a mug from an aluminum pot on top of the stove. The phone rang.

"So that's where the troops are hiding." It was Jim's deep, confident voice. I could see him leaning back with his feet up. "Am I glad to find you. I was getting worried."

"With reason," I said bitterly. "Mother and Lucy are in a gas station eight miles away. Thanks to me."

"Well." There was a munching sound from Jim. "Let me finish these Twinkies and think. Don't feel so bad. Remember the Boston storm when twelve died?"

"Jimmy. I don't need that right now."

"You were never a Cub Scout," said Jim scornfully. "This is just the kind of thing we were taught to do. Bye."

Ten minutes later, he called me back. "Spoke with the man at the station. He's just a bastard that shoots women and children when the going gets tough. He listened to me. He's with Mother and Lucy and about a zillion other people stranded there. Beverly's son, Jay, is going to get them with a Jeep, if he can. Meanwhile, a good samaritan at the gas station is taking Mother and Lucy to his house nearby, where his daughter is already getting dinner. Elizabeth, remember this next time — snow stopped Napoleon and Hitler, so chances are it'll stop you, too. On the bright side, this isn't Boston. When it melts, we'll dig your car out."

Fifty minutes later, he called again. "Your two lost platoons are safe and warm eating soup and chicken in company with a dachshund called Fido. Now, does that make you feel better? On the bright side, it's only snow. This is not the D.C. courthouse. Now you get some sleep. This time next week you'll know where you stand about the trial. Get ready for that. It's more important than the snow."

I fell asleep telling myself that what I once could do, when single and twenty-five, was not what I could do now. We should never have left home. Jim was a wonderful big brother. He looked out for me, but he was moving to New York. It had to be safety first for Mother and Lucy. I had to take care of them.

I wondered, for the first time, how other single mothers managed. In a crisis, there was always my mother or Jim to lend a hand. Besides, I had my practice. I could pay my bills. I could buy a home for Lucy. I could afford — even though it ate up all my savings — the most expensive lawyers for my child. There was no question that I could manage to pay William Blackstone if the court would postpone the trial. With all this, it was hard. And what about the single mothers who didn't have what I had? How were they protected? They weren't. It is almost unbelievable what the single mother goes through. I lay awake, thinking how neglected and how great a problem it is in our country. I fell asleep, acutely aware of my mother's advice to me when I was ten: to have a career and never be dependent on a man for money.

The next day, Daddy got his Blazer out and drove us home. I was grateful for his help. Lucy gave a shriek of delight and bounced in my arms when she saw we were home again. Between visitation and snowstorms, she didn't know what was going to happen next.

As soon as I could, I called my ex. He agreed to put off the trial for two months but not for four. I had a paper in front of me. Mr. Blackstone had told me what I had to tell him. I took a deep breath and steeled myself. I would do this right. "I am going to court tomorrow afternoon. I will ask for an extension of the trial. You should discuss this with your lawyer. If you do object to a four-month postponement, you should be there in court to object."

"I'll talk to my lawyer," he replied, "but you won't get it. You're wasting your time."

"If you object, you or your lawyer should be there," I repeated. He called me back later. He and his lawyer agreed — a two-month but not a four-month postponement.

"Will you be in court to object?" I asked.

"We're not planning to go. You waste your time, Elizabeth. We're not wasting ours." They were working from a position of strength. I was virtually defeated: no lawyer and a trial in twelve days. I was asking for an unreasonably long delay of the trial. I was unlikely to win the court appeal. If I lost, what then? I lay in bed that night, looking at the ceiling. If I lost, what then?

Early the next day, Jim helped me dig my car out of the melting snow. Then I had to go to the hospital to operate. I finished at twelve and drove to court, eating a take-out hamburger in the car. I had to meet Rob at the courthouse at one o'clock. He had set aside his afternoon to help me. Rob didn't even like me to thank him. He said it was a pleasure to help.

I stood in the courthouse lobby, a vast, modern expanse of marble, and waited for Rob. I knew what I had to do. I knew what I had to say. I felt tense, but I felt ready. I didn't know what I would do if the judge denied my request. I would face that when I had to, and not a moment before.

"Ready?" It was Rob, briefcase in hand. He patted my shoulder in triumph. "I'm sorry you have to go through this. We start in the clerk's room." The clerk looked up when Rob and I stopped at his desk. "Trial postponement? Sure. Agreed to by both parties? Sign here."

"Sort of," I said. "They agreed to postpone it, although not for four months." I picked up the pen to sign.

"Elizabeth, don't sign that," said Rob. "Let's not handle it that way. Let's assume they didn't agree. Make it watertight." I would have done it wrong without him.

"Contested," said the clerk without interest. "Get the folder and come back."

After the paperwork, Rob led me to courtroom II-J. We entered and sat down. The room was full, but the judge was not back from lunch.

"When you're called, go up there." Rob pointed to the microphone in front of the courtroom.

"What? I thought for a motion you spoke to the judge in his office. I go up there?"

Rob nodded. "It won't be fun. Don't talk. Answer his questions. For example, why are you changing lawyers?" I looked at Rob. I couldn't explain it simply.

"All rise for the judge," boomed out the bailiff. The simple motions came first. Mine was simple. I was called third. I walked the length of the courtroom like a lamb to slaughter.

"Stop!" said the bailiff when I reached the microphone. I stopped. The courtroom was silent. My hands were shaking. While I was being sworn in, I clenched them into fists. I had to do it right, for Lucy. The judge read my handwritten entry on the request form. He looked at me over bifocals.

"Where's the opposing side?"

"They're not here."

"Did you notify them?"

"Yes," I said. "Yes, your honor," I added hastily at the bailiff's prompting.

"They are opposed to a four-month postponement but not to a two-month one?" said the judge. "But they're not here? They can't feel too strongly about it. Why four months?"

I explained about Mr. Blackstone. "It's a long time. Four months," snapped the judge. "Does the father see the child now?"

"Yes." I explained Lucy's visitation schedule. The judge studied the legal file carefully, his pen poised.

"Okay," he said abruptly, "request granted. Be sure to give copies to the opposing side."

It was too good to be true. I clutched the precious order

and followed Rob outside. By pure fluke my ex's lawyer was in the hall. He saw me and scowled. I handed him his copy of the motion. He almost exploded. Suddenly we were back in the courtroom.

"Your honor! I respectfully submit this matter to be reconsidered. We are violently opposed. It would be harmful. Most harmful to the child. We had no idea this was being heard today."

The judge put on his glasses very slowly and glared at me. "Did you not testify that the opposing side was notified?"

"Yes, your honor."

"When?" he barked.

"Yesterday. I spoke to my former husband twice, once before and once after he spoke to his lawyer."

The judge turned to the attorney. "You were notified."

"We were," he retorted, "but we did not agree to a four-month postponement. We are violently —"

"If you didn't agree, then why weren't you here?" boomed the judge.

"We didn't think you'd —"

"You didn't think I'd grant the other side their request?"

"It's harmful for the child."

"I don't agree," barked the judge. "The motion stands."

"We —"

"The motion stands!" The judge's gavel pounded angrily. I turned away, triumphant. Rob gave me the clenched-fist sign of victory from the back of the courtroom. I had never cried for joy before. I had won the first skirmish for Lucy. When I finally stood up to fight.

"Are you allowed to go up and kiss the judge?" I asked Rob on the way out.

He grabbed me on the shoulder. "Good job. I thought you were a goner, but you were in the right and the lawyer put foot firmly in mouth. You don't argue with a judge. Poor form.

Tell me, should Janice have an amniocentesis?" I smiled. He looked so pleased to be an expectant father. It was nice to be able to be helpful, not helped, for a change. It was especially nice to know that Lucy would have a cousin near her age.

The courtroom had seemed like eternity. It was only three o'clock. I drove to William Blackstone's office and sat down in the firm's waiting area to compose a letter. It was brief: I had been to court; I had appeared "pro se"; I had gotten the trial delayed four months. I attached a copy of the judge's order. I sat thinking. Had I misread this lawyer? Would he, too, let me down? I didn't think so. I took out my checkbook and wrote out a check for $2,000 from my savings account. I wanted him to know I was serious. I tucked my note and the check into an envelope and approached the receptionist.

"Is Mr. Blackstone in, please?"

"And your name, please."

"Dr. Morgan."

She dialed and murmured into the phone. Then she looked up.

"Mr. Blackstone is in conference."

"Is his secretary in?"

She murmured into the phone again. "Yes, she is in."

"May I speak with her?"

There was more murmuring. "She'll be right out."

Mr. Blackstone's secretary, an efficient, attractive young woman listened politely as I handed her my envelope with strict instructions that it be given to Mr. Blackstone. She took it with surprise. "You know, Dr. Morgan, in the future, if you leave something at the front desk we will get it." She spoke to me as Beverly would speak to a difficult patient. I didn't care. There was no way I would leave Lucy's future at a front desk. I had hand-delivered it. Mr. Blackstone could not escape me now.

I walked over to Jim's office. The trading was over for the

day. He was doing paperwork, filling out orders. He jumped to his feet when he saw me. "Well, kid?" His voice was tight, ready for the worst.

"I got it. I would have done it wrong without Rob, but I got it." It swept over me what I had done. "I got it! I got it! I got it! I got it! I got it!" and I jumped up and down like a cheerleader.

"God damn!" He grabbed my hand. "First smart thing you've done in a year. Was I right?"

"Jim, you were right."

"Thank God." He smiled. "Now I can go to New York without worrying about my little sister."

"The nerve!" I protested. "Some people get no respect!"

≥ *seven*

I TOOK LUCY to see Odette that week. It was time for her next checkup. The appointment was squeezed in between morning surgery and afternoon office visits with my patients. I picked up Lucy at Nadine's and drove to Odette's office. Odette grabbed Lucy and tickled her tummy to Lucy's great delight. "Your mommy is going to take off all your clothes. Isn't that bad?" She handed her back to me. "How is she eating?"

"Like a little piglet. She is always hungry." Lucy began to tear the paper on the examining table into shreds. I stopped her. Defeated in this, she tried to eat her diaper. Thwarted again, she grabbed on to my hair with a shriek of delight and tried to swing off the table like Tarzan, hanging on to my hair. "Ba-ooh-da-da," she protested as I disentangled myself.

"Let's measure and weigh her." Odette looked thoughtful when she had finished. Then she turned to me, with her arms folded and her blond hair framing a stern expression. "Elizabeth, something is very wrong. Your baby is losing weight. Losing weight! That's very bad. Does she have diarrhea?"

"No."

"Does she eat?"

"Yes, like a horse." I was puzzled. "Visitation upsets her, but she shouldn't lose weight from that. And there was the snowstorm."

Odette shook her head. "Someone is not feeding her," she insisted.

"No, I don't —" and I stopped. How stupid could I be? I brought food to Nadine Hoskins's every day. This morning, when I picked up Lucy, the kitchen cupboard had been open. I remembered the long row of untouched cans of milk and food. That was weeks of Lucy's food, unused. It hadn't registered then. It did now. No wonder Lucy ate so much at night and screamed on the way home. She was starved.

"I think I know the answer, Odette. I have to change baby-sitters."

"Is that the problem! Yes, indeed. It's terrible." Odette's eyes flashed indignantly. "Believe me, I see it all the time. I want Lucy here in a month to check her."

Reluctantly, I took Lucy back to Nadine's. I had to go back to the office for a few hours. Lucy had to be somewhere. Nothing could go wrong in that time, in the two hours I would be away.

"What did the doctor say?" demanded Nadine suspiciously, cornering me before I left. I looked her in the eye.

"Lucy is not gaining weight." I said nothing more. I didn't want her to be angry with me and hurt Lucy. I added, "By the way, your driveway is a sheet of ice. It needs sand, or someone will fall." Nadine looked back at me coldly. It was clear to me now how she had changed. She seemed to hate the world. I called my mother from the office. She was at the hospital where she worked as a volunteer.

"Mother, Lucy can't go back to Nadine's," I explained.

"Of course she can't go back. I'll call Mrs. Petersen immediately," she said.

Hilda Petersen was a delightful woman, with grown children of her own, who looked after children occasionally. She loved them and was trustworthy and kind. Mother called me back. Hilda would be thrilled to baby-sit "little Lucy" until we moved into the new house. That was only a week away. In a lighter mood, I went to pick Lucy up from Nadine.

The roads were icy. Snow had melted and then frozen each day as the sun went down. After parking the car, I skidded to Nadine's front door and slid in over the ice. Nadine was standing, staring into space, with her arms folded and three toddlers tumbling around her. I hoisted Lucy up out of her crib. Still crying, she clung to me.

"You know, China gave me a big fright this afternoon," Nadine announced calmly. "I forgot to lock the door. Little Luigi opened it and China came into the room here. I had to move very quickly. Fortunately, little Luigi was not frightened or the dog would have torn him apart." She showed no emotion. "Lucy would not eat. She never eats."

"Did you try to feed her?" I demanded. I hugged Lucy closer, thinking of what might have happened. No more dogs near my Lucy. No more angry people near my Lucy. I turned to Nadine to tell her I was taking Lucy out of her care.

"I don't have time to play games over food," she continued. "I am busy. And don't come back tomorrow with your daughter. You told me this afternoon I should do something about the ice. You! Telling me! I don't need people like you!" she shouted at me. "I can fill your slot like that!" She snapped her fingers in my face, her voice rising. "You! You won't find anyone as good as me." The children stopped playing and stared at her, frightened. I was frightened, too. It occurred to me that two other mothers had recently stopped bringing their children to her. Those were children old enough to talk, to tell their parents what went on. I had seen the warning signs in Lucy. I should have acted sooner. At least Lucy was safe now, and I had learned another lesson: I had to trust my instincts. Months ago, instinct had told me to take Lucy away. After snatching up Lucy's things, I slithered, with her in my arms, over the ice, through the dark, to the safety of the car. Lucy screamed as usual, on the way home, but today it sounded like screams of pain, not hunger. She looked miserable.

"Thank God for Hilda Petersen," I told my mother when we got home. "Nadine fired me before I could resign." I put Lucy down to change her diapers and to see what was hurting her. I straightened up, appalled. Lucy had been scrubbed raw. Her groin and genital area were red and swollen, oozing serum and in a few places oozing blood. Lucy looked up at me, pathetic, frightened, as though she was begging me not to hurt her. First visitation, and now this. I picked her up and held her close. "That is since two o'clock this afternoon. My poor baby. A mother shouldn't make mistakes. I don't make mistakes like this with my patients. Why do I have to do it to my baby?" I wailed. My mother put her arm around me.

"You had seven years of surgical training. No one trained you to be a mother. You have to learn as you go." I put ointment on the raw red areas. It seemed to help. Lucy ate dinner and giggled as I played peekaboo with her pink pillow. Then the phone rang.

"Dr. Morgan, Mr. Blackstone here. Congratulations! Now we should arrange a time to meet. Fairly soon."

"Tell me when and I'll come."

"No, no," said Mr. Blackstone kindly. "This should work around your schedule as well as mine. What about next Wednesday at three o'clock?" I hesitated. "Wednesday at five," he suggested. "Will that give you time?"

"That's perfect." I hung up just as Lucy grabbed my ankle and tried to haul herself up on my leg.

"Cook! Cook! Cook!" She smiled hopefully.

"Is she asking for what I think she's asking for, Mother?" Solemnly, I opened the cookie tin and handed her a cookie while she tried to grab a handful. She took the one cookie at last and joyfully sat down, pudgy legs out straight, to eat it.

"She asked for a cookie. She really is talking!"

"I wouldn't exactly call that talking," said my mother. I strongly disagreed.

I spent the evening opening up packing boxes and taping the bottoms shut. We were moving in ten days. It seemed too good to be true. Lucy fell asleep on the floor. I took her upstairs and tucked her in her bassinet. She really was too big for the bassinet. She fitted in like a sardine, a darling sardine. I went back downstairs. Twenty minutes later, I heard her screaming. I dashed back up and rocked her awhile and tried to put her back to bed. She screamed in terror, clinging to me. I brought her downstairs. Amid the hubbub of packing boxes, conversation, and the light, she fell asleep with her pink pillow clutched tightly to her.

"She's become afraid of the dark," said my mother.

"And afraid of being alone. She was never like this," I said. "Look at the lawyer, the psychiatrist, the judge who made the decisions about her. They don't know about children. I don't think they care. It's not in their job description. It's not their business now that she's a terrified little child. She's just another case. I'm just another tiresome mother!" I yanked open a packing box angrily.

"It's the old King Solomon solution," said my mother. "If two people fight over a baby, you cut the baby in half. Children are always the ones to suffer, unfortunately, and their mothers suffer for them." She paused. "I hope that having your father live with us will work out. It may be the wrong thing to ask you to do. I feel I've too often put my husband before my children."

"Mother!" I sat down next to her, resting my feet on a packing box. "You are the best mother that ever was. If you start feeling guilty I will start to scream like Lucy. And that's a threat. When you look at me with Lucy, you can't possibly feel you ever did anything wrong."

"If I'd done things right, you wouldn't have gone through all this."

"Then I wouldn't have Lucy either, would I? I wouldn't trade her and I've learned from my mistakes."

"I think you've got life under control," admitted my mother, "and so do Jim and Rob, too. It makes me very happy." I felt happy too, and hopeful. Life could be fun again.

We were in bed at ten. I put Lucy back in the bassinet. She really had outgrown it. I took her out and tucked her in on a mattress on the floor. She woke up and looked at me disapprovingly.

"You're too big for the bassinet, silly." She yawned and went back to sleep, as I sat beside her, patting her back.

I was barely asleep when the phone at my bedside rang. I remembered I was on emergency call. "Dr. Morgan, Service calling. Emergency Room wants you." I took emergency call four days a month. It didn't sound like much, but it could mean some sleepless nights. Before Lucy, I was irritated to be called. Now I didn't mind so much. I needed the money. I had Lucy to work for.

I dialed the ER without turning on the light, so I wouldn't wake Lucy. I dialed the wrong number. I took the phone to the window and dialed in the moonlight. Three police cars and a fire engine raced by the house, sirens blasting. The street was so narrow, I could almost lean out of the window and touch them. It was really a crazy place for us to live. I couldn't wait to move. Lucy kept on sleeping.

"Emergency Room."

"Yes, it's Dr. Morgan."

"Yes?"

"You were paging me."

"We were? Who is this? Speak up. I can't hear you."

"Dr. Elizabeth Morgan," I said.

"Let me check." Click, and I was disconnected. It was a bad beginning. It was going to be a bad night. I dialed again, dialed for five minutes, and finally got through.

"Emergency Room."

"Yes. It's Dr. Morgan. You cut me off."

"I did?"

"Yes."

"I'm sorry. Can I help you?"

"Someone there is paging me for an emergency."

"Who?"

"I have no idea."

"Let me check."

"Don't you dare disconnect me," I told her. She sniffed, very offended. "Anyone paging a Dr. Norton?" I heard her call through the intercom. She returned to me, "No, Dr. Norton. No one paged you."

"Try Dr. Morgan."

"There's no Dr. Morgan here tonight."

"I am Dr. Morgan. I am not Dr. Norton. Ask if they paged Dr. Morgan — M-O-R-"

"Okay," she said wearily, and then, into the intercom, in a slow, bored voice, "Anyone paging Dr. Morgan?" Two seconds later, an Emergency Room doctor came on the line. He sounded annoyed.

"Elizabeth, what took you so long? We paged you half an hour ago."

"Believe me, I tried. What's the problem?"

"A boy leaned against a plate-glass window and shoved his hand through. He's cut his arm up pretty badly. He was bleeding like a pig when he came in. Not so much now."

"Drat." I had seen a lot of these injuries. If his arm was cut and he had bled a lot, it meant that the radial artery was severed and probably all the muscle and the tendons and the nerves as well. Most arm and hand injuries can wait. This kind can't. He could easily bleed to death.

"Jeff, it will take me twenty minutes to get there. Do this for me. Put in a huge I.V. Type him for blood. Give him lots of fluid. Call the OR for me and tell them we're coming. Put a tourniquet on his arm, but don't use it unless he goes into shock. It's bad for the arm."

"Will do," said Jeff. I hung up and almost stepped on Lucy. I avoided her, patted her, dressed, grabbed my purse, and walked into the bedroom door. I groaned. It woke up my mother in the next room. She turned on the light. A cavalcade of police cars screamed their way down the street. Lucy kept on sleeping.

"Mother, this is no way to live. I can't wait to move," I hissed. "Ten days isn't soon enough."

"Do you have to go out?" asked my mother.

"Yes, someone's bleeding to death. I have to go." My mother turned out her light. I went downstairs. I got my coat. As soon as I left the room, I heard Lucy turn over. Now I heard her wake up and whimper. Before I was out the door, she was screaming. Nothing bothered her — except being alone in the dark. I hated leaving. I heard my mother get out of bed. It was going to be a long night for all three of us.

I walked in to the ER and found four nurses, two orderlies, a college-student volunteer, and the ER doctor working on a young man who was spread-eagled on a stretcher with one arm wrapped in bloody bandages. There were pools of blood on the floor.

The doctor looked up. "He went into shock. He's getting his third unit of blood. Want to take over?"

"Yes."

An orderly grabbed the stretcher. We marched briskly down the dim corridor. The volunteer, an excited sandy-haired boy, kept a viselike grip on my patient's arm to control the hemorrhage.

"I'm Dr. Morgan," I said to my patient, a curly-haired teenager with a chubby face. "What happened?"

"We were celebrating."

"What were you celebrating?"

"I quit my job."

"What was your job?"

"It was trash."

"You didn't like your job?"

"No. It wasn't for me."

"What did you do?"

"Trash. You know. I was a sanitation engineer."

"Now I understand. I'm sorry."

We arrived in the OR. The stretcher went to Operating Room 12, leaving a trail of blood.

After he was asleep, I pulled great chunks of plate glass out of his arm. The boy had cut the radial artery and most of the tendons and muscles in his arm, but he was lucky: the nerves were not injured. I found the ends of the tendons and the muscles and the artery. I repaired the artery under the microscope. Then I sutured the tendons and the muscles, making myself work slowly so I did not do sloppy work.

At three-thirty, I was home. Lucy was asleep on her mattress, in my mother's room. She looked like a little dog curled up at the foot of my mother's bed. It was pathetic to have seen her be so frightened. I wondered what disruptive visitation would finally do to her. Would she have more seizures? There had been a minor second one, and then no more. Would she become seriously disturbed? The first psychiatrist had not helped. I gritted my teeth thinking of him. I stood looking down at Lucy. Her happiness meant everything to me. Circumstances might be threatening her emotional stability. It was up to me to protect her. I could pretend it wasn't true, but I knew. Lucy did need a psychiatrist, a good one, to help her and to help me. It was better that we get help now than to wait until she was older and things got worse. Mental illness wasn't going to be Lucy's future if I could help it. I went into my room and in the moonlight wrote down on my list of things to do, "Call psychiatrist."

I climbed wearily into bed. I was barely asleep when a crash outside my window woke me up. An engine roared and another crash shook the house. I peered out the window. A van was racing backwards down the street, trying to run down a man running away from it. A white man jumped out of a car and ran toward the van. A black man jumped from the van, charging him with a baseball bat. I called the police. The car and the van chased each other crazily around the block, again and again. A squad car pulled up. Two more squad cars charged down the alley, sirens wailing. Fifteen minutes later, a neighbor came by. He lived two doors down, and he watched over mother and Lucy and me. He had shoveled the snow off the sidewalk for us and kept a chivalrous eye out to be sure we were all right.

"Did it wake the baby, Elizabeth?" he asked solicitously.

"No. She sleeps through anything." Anything except fear and loneliness, I added to myself.

"A couple of rednecks with baseball bats jumped a delivery truck on its way to work. The delivery man got the bat away and decided to teach the farm boys a lesson. It's all over now. The van's back at work. The rednecks are in the cooler. Get some sleep."

"Never a dull moment," I said. He laughed. "You'll miss it when you move." Moving was only nine days away, I reminded myself. I went back to sleep.

I was feeding Lucy breakfast when the phone rang. Lucy yelped when I walked away to answer it, but I got back to her, cradling the phone with my shoulder. It was a ward nurse calling me.

"Dr. Morgan? I'm looking after the boy you operated on last night."

"Yes?"

"He wants to go home."

"What?"

"He's signed out, against medical advice, to drive home. It's four hundred miles. He said he didn't like the hospital."

"Can I talk to him?" Lucy dropped her spoon. As I tried to reach it, the phone began to slip from my shoulder. My mother came in, saw me, laughed, and saved me by getting the spoon and taking Lucy onto her lap. I grabbed the phone as it slid off my shoulder. "He's gone already," said the nurse.

"He's gone?" I said in dismay. For this I had worked all night. My work was wasted. Healthy young men hate casts as much as hospitals. He would drive home, cut his cast off with a table saw, use his hand, and rip out every single stitch. My work would be destroyed and so would his hand. Suddenly I shrugged. "That's life." There was nothing I could do. It served no more purpose to be angry with him than to be angry with a lawyer or with a judge. That was life.

"Gurk." With a hiccup and a pleased smile, Lucy spewed forth a volcano of cereal and poured milk all over my mother. She often did this after a disrupted night. I hung up and helped mop off my mother while Lucy tried to cross her eyes and get her feet into her mouth. I put her back to bed. "Cook? Cook?" she said hopefully.

"Not for breakfast, Lucy."

She gave me a deeply reproachful look and fell asleep.

She had screamed for two hours after I left to operate in the middle of the night. Now, in daylight, she wasn't afraid and she was tired. My mother and I, also tired, smiled as she fell asleep.

"What about a child psychiatrist, Mother?"

My mother nodded. "Better now than later," she whispered, and we tiptoed out of the room.

It made me feel tense even to think about psychiatrists. My Lucy was meant to be a jolly, carefree little baby, not this insecure child who screamed with fear in the dark and when I left her. If only she were old enough to understand why she went away every other weekend. It wasn't because I wanted to be rid of her. I knew she felt betrayed and abandoned every time.

A week later, I was finishing the last of the packing. I hate packing but I had a system. I had bought a hundred boxes. I had assembled them. I had thrown everything in. I had taped the tops down. "The new rugs come on Monday afternoon. The washer and dryer on Wednesday," said my mother. I felt my stomach go into a knot. I had never spent so much money.

With Jimmy's guidance I could afford to buy the new townhouse. I could also pay my legal bills, but I had borrowed money to furnish the house. Borrowed money, plus the mortgage, plus supporting Lucy, plus taking time to be with Lucy, which meant less time to work — I didn't see how I would have time to earn the money to pay it back.

"Are you all right?" my mother asked, looking at my face.

"Yes." I took a deep breath and shook myself. Jimmy had helped me work it out. I could afford it. It was dumb to make myself sick with worry. If it turned out I couldn't, we would sell and move, but only if I had to. I wanted Lucy to grow up in the Heights. It was right for her.

"Did you ever hear finally from the company about the mortgage?"

"Yes. The loan cleared."

"In writing?"

"Over the phone." My stomach went into a knot again. Lucy had to have a proper place to live. I couldn't have mismanaged the house loan. Impossible.

I turned to the sofa to pick up a stack of towels. Under the bright lamplight, a large, gray mouse sat on the sofa, washing its face. I jumped a foot off the floor.

"Good God!"

"Hush," said my mother. "Lucy is asleep."

"Look!" The mouse whisked away behind the sofa.

"It's only a mouse," said my mother.

"Only a mouse! Only a mouse! Lucy only sleeps on the floor! For all I know, mice walk over her all night, Mother. This place is a dump. This place is a God damn dump. We can't move soon enough!" I was not going to have mice walking on Lucy. The new house became an immediate necessity. We had to have it. Wednesday, moving day, was not a day too soon.

I tore up two packing boxes and crept into Lucy's room. Gently, I built a fence around her. At least this way mice would run around her, not over her. Shuddering, I went downstairs and I stopped again. "Mother, we're moving on Wednesday, aren't we?"

"Yes."

"Do you realize that I have booked surgery on Wednesday and also a visit to the child psychiatrist and the meeting with Mr. Blackstone?"

"Yes, dear."

"I can't leave you to move all by yourself."

"Why not?"

"You can't move my house. It's not fair. I'm going to ask Daddy to come and help."

My mother put out her hand. "I can manage, Elizabeth. I'd rather you didn't call him." I paused. I understood. Daddy ran things his way. This wasn't his house to run.

"I could ask Jim, but he's done so much for me already." My mother smiled. "He'll probably come to help us anyway." She was right.

I continued folding towels. "Mother, I'll do everything I can to get on with Dad, but no interfering with Lucy. It's my house. She's my child. It has to be that way. If he wants people to fight with, I'm not the one."

"I agree," said my mother. "All we can do is try."

My father is a knowledgeable man and I was very grateful when he offered to be with me on the afternoon that the foreman took me on the walk-through of my new house. It was a lovely brick townhouse, with green shutters. There had been building delays, but it was worth the wait. There were big closets, a bathroom for Lucy so the house would not smell of diapers, and even a dishwasher. As we were finishing, the front door opened and a sales agent looked in. "Dr. Morgan? I've been told to tell you that your loan is not processed. You cannot go to settlement. It may be weeks, even months. Sorry."

My mouth dropped open. She closed the door. I heard her footsteps on the walk as she hurried away. I turned to my father. "I have to move."

"Don't worry," said my father leading me away. "These things happen."

"But Daddy . . ." He didn't understand. It wasn't his house. He didn't have to move. We did. Lucy needed a mouse-free home, desperately. The visitation was too much for her. Everything else had to be perfect for her so she could cope with that. For her sake, I couldn't wait a month. I couldn't wait a week. I drove home in silence, thinking. This was the fault of the mortgage company. It was also my fault. I had complained, but I had never gone to the top — the men who owned the building company. I should have done that weeks ago. I called the sales office the moment I got home. The chief agent was most apologetic. The mortgage company was disorganized, but the matter was beyond her control. The builders owned the mortgage company.

"You can complain, Dr. Morgan, but I don't think it will do any good," she finished.

I called the sales manager at home. "Hey!" he interrupted me as soon as I called. "This is Friday. I'm not on the job now. It's seven-thirty at night."

"Listen," I begged. "Please, at least call the mortgage company for me on Monday and call me back. I need to move. If you don't have my number —"

"Listen, don't tell me what to do, okay? If it makes you happy to say your number out loud over the phone, go ahead, okay? But I'm not listening anymore. I've had enough." He slammed down the phone. What was going on? I began to feel besieged. Was this a conspiracy, a cabal of hostile builders?

"You really didn't deserve that," said my mother. She was

sitting on the sofa and Lucy was practicing steps. "You were most restrained." Lucy sat down with a bump.

"I know that kind of thickheaded gorilla," I fumed. "If I were a man, he wouldn't pull this stunt. If I were a man, the builder wouldn't let him. They told me six months ago I could get the loan." My voice rose. Lucy looked at me anxiously. "They're too lazy to do their paperwork for a woman. A divorced woman, a single mother, doesn't count!"

"Now, Elizabeth, it's not the end of the world."

"You're wrong." It was ridiculous and I started to laugh. With a relieved giggle, Lucy resumed her walking practice. I had frightened her. I went over and hugged her. There was no point in being upset. If there was a worldwide conspiracy, I couldn't change it. If not, they would possibly let me move in, despite the mortgage company's delay.

I composed a letter to the president of the construction company. I explained my problem, and my frustration. I asked for his help, or at least for a letter to explain to the movers, to the furniture and appliance stores, to everyone about the delay. I hoped my letter would work, but I didn't think it would. I hand-delivered it to the company's office that weekend and spent Sunday trying to resign myself to not moving. I was on the ward on Monday morning when Beverly called me.

"Elizabeth, you know that letter you wrote?"

"Yes."

"Don't ask me how, but it did the trick. The company president even called to apologize for his mortgage people. You don't know what this means. Builders never apologize. He says not to worry about settlement. He'll get it all arranged."

I sat down in a chair in the nurses' station almost not believing it. It shouldn't have been such a narrow escape. Still, I was learning, even if on an elementary level. I had spent so much time learning about surgery that I had had no time to learn anything else.

On reflection, I decided that what I had done right was to

deal with nice people. The builders wanted to do the right thing. They wanted to help. It was a simple lesson. I wanted to be able to teach Lucy how important it was to deal with nice people. I didn't want her to learn the hard way, as I had.

After finishing my surgery on moving day, I took Lucy to Dr. Oakes, the child psychiatrist I had chosen. I had already called our new home after surgery. The movers had come. They were nice. My mother sounded happy. As soon as trading finished, Jim had shown up to help, and so had Rob. "By the way, they're going to have a girl," said my mother when I called.

"Rob and Janice are going to have a girl? I'm so glad for them. And how nice for Lucy." It seemed just another aspect of Rob's and Janice's niceness that they were providing Lucy with a playmate.

Dr. Oakes was young and gentle. He was kind to Lucy. He had long legs that seemed to be in danger of knocking over the toys that he strewed around his consulting room to amuse her. Lucy crawled among the toys and discovered a telephone. She banged the top, grabbed the receiver, and began a conversation.

"Tell me everything," he began. I told him. He wrote it all down. I got to the other psychiatrist.

"Wait, wait," said Dr. Oakes. "Who suggested the midweek visitation?"

"The psychiatrist."

"The psychiatrist?" he sounded doubtful.

"Yes."

"Why?"

"He said she needed more, not fewer, overnights, to get used to her father."

Dr. Oakes tapped his note pad for a long time. "I don't know any other child psychiatrist who would recommend that for a child her age. Well. We have to leave changing that to your attorney."

Lucy dragged the phone over to me. "Tepoh?"

"Yes, Lucy, it's a telephone." She was still holding it out. I took the receiver. "I can't talk now." I handed it back to her. "It's for you." Pleased, she resumed her conversation.

At the end, we set up times for Lucy to come with me every week to see Dr. Oakes.

"This is a difficult time for her," he said urgently. "The older she gets, the more we can explain. Overnight visitation is definitely not good for the very young. It is disturbing to a child. But we can work on it. We can build her confidence. The next time she visits her father, send her pink pillow with her."

"I did once, but it didn't come back with her, so —"

"Didn't come back? Didn't come back?" Dr. Oakes's eyes flashed. "What sort of person doesn't return a child's favorite possession?" He looked murderous.

"I think he forgot," I hastened to add. "It wasn't intentional."

"Forgot," he almost shouted. "Forgot. What sort of person forgets a child's favorite possession? Does she have another pink pillow?"

"Yes. We got her another when the first one was lost. It was eventually returned."

"Well, we must try again. Lucy must go with something that means home and security. The pink pillow will mean that to her. The pink pillow must be returned." His nostrils flared slightly. "If it is not. If it is not." He shook his head. "I cannot conceive of such a thing, but she must be protected." Inside, I cheered. Children were important to him. He would help me help Lucy, even if it meant a fortune in pink pillows.

I disentangled Lucy from the telephone and we headed to our new home. I had to leave her with my mother before going on to Mr. Blackstone's office. Lucy knew the way to our old home and yelped from the car seat when I turned the car in a new direction. She knew the right way. A hundred times we had turned left. "Hup. Hup. Mummy," she announced urgently.

"It's all right," I called out over my shoulder. "We have a

new home." It didn't help. She yelped and protested all the way, sure that I had taken a wrong turn. She became quiet when I took her out of the car. She grabbed my hair and studied my face, puzzled but sympathetic, as though I had lost my mind. I walked up to the front steps. The last of the movers had gone. My mother was unpacking in Lucy's room. Lucy smiled at my mother, uncertainly. Jim was setting up a bed. She saw him and smiled a bit more.

We took her all around the house and then took her to her room. She grabbed her pink pillow with a happy shriek and burrowed into it. "This is home, Lucy. Our new house."

"Pillow," said Lucy firmly.

I looked out of the window. I could see a little girl going for a walk with her mother in the cobbled drive. Daffodils were coming up around the mailboxes. Lucy would have friends growing up here. It would be safe and peaceful and calm and we would all be happy, assuming . . . Assuming so much — that my father would settle in, that I could pay the bills, that I would have time to be a good mother, and, above all, that Mr. Blackstone could help me keep custody. I was counting on him.

⇒ *eight*

M R. *BLACKSTONE* shook my hand and led me into his office. His secretary brought us coffee. I felt nervous. If he wasn't the right lawyer, I didn't know where to turn for Lucy.

"I didn't think you would do it," he said when he closed the door. "Congratulations." He sat down. "Now we must talk. Ideally, Dr. Morgan, what do you want in the way of a settlement?"

"Ideally?" I thought for a moment. Various thoughts occurred to me. Should I suggest that I move to Moscow? Or that my ex become a Trappist monk? These weren't the things to say. This wasn't the time to joke. I calmed down. "Well, ideally, I would want no regular overnight visitation until she is five. An agreement from him that he will not repeatedly take me to court and that he will not seek custody ever in the future. An agreement that should I move from the area, he —"

"Stop!" commanded Mr. Blackstone as he held up a large, terrifying hand. "If that is what you expect, I would prefer not to represent you. It is unrealistic and you will not get it." He looked at me, awaiting my response. I looked at him. I was afraid he would throw me out of his office.

"You didn't ask me what I expected. You asked what I ideally would want," I protested. Mr. Blackstone continued to look at me, like an entomologist trying to classify a specimen. I knew he was trying to figure out if I was a troublemaking, quarrelsome, neurotic flake. I knew I wasn't, but somehow I had managed to make the wrong impression. I kicked myself.

"What could you live with?" he asked slowly, choosing his words with care, as though I had to lip-read to understand him. I restrained my usual impulsiveness. He was asking me a business question. I had to take a businesslike approach.

"The reason I am here is because Ms. Jones said my husband was determined to get custody. I cannot live with losing custody of Lucy. Lucy needs me. That is why I am here." He looked and waited to see if I had more to say. I waited. He already knew that Lucy screamed at night. He couldn't do anything about it. As a mother, I had lots to say. As a legal client, I had nothing to add.

"Child support?" he said at last. That was difficult. I didn't want money. I wanted my daughter. I wanted to see Lucy grow up happy and secure, not nervous and anxious. Yet, every dollar of child support was a dollar I didn't have to earn, a dollar's worth of more time with Lucy, a dollar more security for her.

"I could pay my bills with no support."

"Generous but irrelevant. Legally, a father is obliged to contribute to the support of his child. What you have is unsatisfactory. Would you be able to live with that, unsatisfactory as it is?"

I thought for a while. The more money he paid, the more time I had for Lucy. But if we agreed to visitation that was good for Lucy, would I balk because of money? Never.

"Certainly," I replied.

He jotted it down. "Visitation." This was the most difficult.

"Overnight is very bad for Lucy. It is horrible for her. I don't want to withhold her. She has to get to know her father, but she's still a baby. Mr. Blackstone, I have no idea why, but the overnights continue to upset her, for a whole week."

"And then she has to go away again every other weekend," added Mr. Blackstone. "Putting that aside, do you want Lucy to know her father?" he asked. "I have no idea what your ex is like, but, as a rule, should a child be exposed to a father, regardless?"

I thought of my own father. But I was better off having struggled with feelings about him than if I had never known him. "Yes. A child should get to know its father."

Mr. Blackstone nodded as though I had passed the test. "A judge will approve of that position. Now, what visitation could Lucy live with?" I was grateful that he understood that visitation was not a problem for me. It was a problem for Lucy. He seemed to read my mind. "You understand, Dr. Morgan, that I represent you. I am your lawyer. I am taking the position that you are a good mother." He smiled. "I don't know if you are or not, but that's my position." We both laughed.

"I try to be."

He shook his head. "You don't try. You are a good mother. And in as much as you are a good mother and your first concern is your child, I will try to arrange for you an agreement, with or without a trial, that — although not perfect, because nothing is perfect — will be, in your opinion, acceptable for your daughter."

"I would like overnight visitation to stop until Lucy is five, but I realize that is not realistic. Perhaps Lucy can adapt — painfully, but adapt as long as her present visitation isn't increased."

"So, the less, the better, but at worst she can live with what she's got. Right?"

"Right. But I must have custody." The pessimism that Ms. Jones had created hung over me like a cloud. Mr. Blackstone looked at me for a while. Then he read his notes and thought for a long time. "Dr. Morgan, I don't see custody as a problem," he answered.

"My ex is a very clever and determined man."

Mr. Blackstone looked at me. "I understand that." He read his notes again. "Now, when we first met, you told me about

Lucy and her screaming and her sleep disturbance and so forth. You are right to worry. You are her mother. If she needs a psychiatrist, take her to one. As your lawyer, I'm not inclined to emphasize her problems. Nor to use a psychiatrist's testimony. It doesn't sound believable. This should be kept simple. If you hear some mother in court going on and on about how the baby won't sleep, what will your reaction be? You probably won't believe it. It will seem exaggerated for dramatic effect. Agree?"

I had to agree. "That's been the problem. No one believes me."

He sat back thoughtfully. "My approach is very simple. No one ever finished taking your ex-husband's deposition. I want to talk to your ex at length. I want to get a feel for him. I don't like to fight. I'm a calm and peaceful man. I find fighting distasteful. I hope to find in him a similar distaste." He looked over at me. "Do you object to that plan. Do you agree to my resuming his deposition?"

"Of course."

"Fine. Now our position is that you're a nice person." He smiled. "I'll act on that assumption. I don't want you to worry about this. If you are worried about custody, I don't see that as a problem. Be friendly. Be polite and go on with your life. You and Lucy should not be disrupted by this. I am not bothered by it. You should not be. Do you date much? Do you have a social life?"

"Not really."

"You ought to. You're a working woman. There are lots of demands on your time. You have to make time for your child. You have to make time for yourself. And" — he leaned forward — "if you have a social life, your ex is really a free baby-sitting service for you. Besides, you don't object to visitation in principle. And you do need a social life. You do that. I'll arrange the deposition." He rose with a friendly smile and escorted me to the elevator. "I will be in touch about the deposition."

"Should I plan to come?"

"If you are my client, you will come," said Mr. Blackstone, and that was that. He was intimidating, but he inspired confidence. He made it all simple, and that was genius. Jim had been right. Now that Mr. Blackstone was in charge, I could relax. I rode down in the elevator, repeating his words to myself. "I don't see custody as a problem. I don't see custody as a problem." He was a very cautious lawyer. He might only have said it to reassure me, but the reassurance of those words made my eyes fill with tears. I didn't realize until now how oppressed I had been by the fear of losing Lucy. I wiped away my tears. I couldn't get my car out of the garage with a tear-stained face.

It was late by the time I got back to our new home. I was feeling happy for the first time since Lucy was born. It was more than that. I was happy for the first time since my marriage. Mr. Blackstone had shouldered the burden of Lucy's protection. I could go back to being me. I had been hard and tense, unsociable and preoccupied. I had had to fight my ex. I didn't like to fight. Mr. Blackstone took care of that. I could shed my protective shell, and see friends, and cuddle Lucy and tickle her toes, and be a nice person again. Jim and Rob had gone when I got home. My mother was cooking dinner.

"Mother, where's Lucy? You shouldn't be cooking. You just finished moving us in."

"Your father came over about an hour and a half ago to help. He's hungry and he wanted dinner. He took her out in the stroller."

"Mother. She's so tired. You shouldn't have let him." My mother looked helplessly across the counter at me. "I'm sorry, Mother."

"I can't stop your father from doing what he wants to do, Elizabeth. You know that. You tell him what he can and can't do with Lucy. I'm only her grandmother. I have neither the right nor the strength to control him."

I clenched my teeth. I wanted to get along with my father. I was happy to offer him a home, but Lucy was tired. She ought to be in bed. I wasn't going to fight, but I wasn't going to sacrifice Lucy, either.

"Elizabeth?" said my mother anxiously.

I held up my hand. "I'm fine." I knew what I had to do. I had learned from my struggles. I would insist on what was right as nicely as I could. The front door opened and my father and Lucy came in. She had chocolate on her face and she was waving a half-eaten cookie in each hand. She was covered with crumbs. She was flushed and half laughing, half screaming.

"You put the stroller away, Elizabeth," ordered my father. "She needs to be changed. She's wet."

"I'll change her," I said, but he was too fast for me. He whisked her out of her stroller and dashed upstairs with her. I put the stroller away.

"I'm not sure it's a good idea to let your father come between you and Lucy," said my mother. "She's a little girl and she needs you." I shut the front door.

"I know, Mother." I took my time going upstairs after them. I had to stay calm. I heard the water running. I walked into Lucy's bedroom. She wasn't there. I walked into the bathroom. He was giving Lucy a bath.

"Daddy, she had a bath this morning," I began.

"So?" He jutted his jaw out and rolled up his sleeves.

"She doesn't need a bath now," I said quietly.

"Her diaper was wet." He lathered up the soap in his hands generously.

"She doesn't need a bath everytime she has her diapers changed."

"She's my granddaughter. As long as she is in my care, she gets a bath every time she gets her diapers changed. Now get

· 176 ·

out or you'll get wet." Lucy shrieked excitedly as he splashed his hands into the tub.

"She's in my care, not yours, Daddy."

Lucy looked from my father to me. "Mummy?" she said pathetically, looking worried. "Mummy? Okay?"

"Yes, Lucy. It's okay." I stroked her head.

My father turned toward me. "Do you want your daughter dirty?"

"No. I don't think she's dirty. I want her in bed." I picked Lucy up and wrapped her in a towel. She started to cry. I rocked her in my arms, and waited until he left the room.

I put Lucy in her nightgown and sat on the bed and rocked her. "Wock a bye, mummy?" I sang "Rockabye, Baby," over and over. "Mummy nice." She put her head on my shoulder and relaxed. She whimpered with fatigue. Her eyes closed. I put her to bed and tiptoed out the door.

"And Daddy," I said as we sat down to dinner. "Please don't take Lucy out and feed her cookies at her bedtime. It's not good for her."

"She loves it," he answered.

"Please don't do it."

"Rules," said my father. "Why don't you write them all down for me!"

"Certainly. If it helps." We ate dinner in an awkward silence. Afterward, he pulled himself heavily to his feet and limped to the stairway. Slowly, one step at a time, he climbed the stairs. There had been no limp when he ran upstairs with Lucy two hours ago.

"Is he well, do you think?" asked my mother anxiously.

"No. I make him feel sick."

"Don't be hard on him, Elizabeth."

"Mother, I don't mean to be. I want to get along with him, but this is my house. Lucy is my child. She has plenty to contend with. I don't want her confused by what happens at home." I stopped talking. Talking about it made me feel more upset, not less. I wanted us all to get along.

My mother put her arm around me. "I know, my dear, I only want the best for you." After a while, she said, "I think I'll go and see if I can't smoothe things over. It's the least I can do."

My mother came into my bedroom later that night. I had been thinking of my father and myself since she left. "He's asleep, Elizabeth." She sat down wearily on my bed.

"Mother, I hope I'm not the problem. Sometimes, after Daddy and my ex, I wonder if I'm the problem. Maybe I'm just a bitchy, bossy surgeon — but Lucy has to have stability, doesn't she?"

My mother nodded her head. "You're right."

"I learned a lot from Mr. Blackstone today. I'll try to stay calm and let Daddy decide what he wants to do. Is that fair?"

My mother looked at me as though she saw a new person. "Very fair. I really think you've grown up."

"Well, it's taken me a damned long time," I said, and we both laughed so loud that Lucy woke up and yelped in protest. We tiptoed in and patted her bottom and she went back to sleep.

"She loves this house," whispered my mother as we went out. "Isn't it nice to see her in her own room, sleeping so serenely?"

My room was next to hers, and I slept with my door open and the intercom on in case she woke up frightened. She slept right through the night and well into the morning, with her face in her pink pillow, her rump in the air — a picture of peace.

The house was all we had hoped. Best of all, Beverly's daughter Sheryl had asked if she could baby-sit for Lucy at our home while I worked. She was the answer to my prayers — someone to come to the house, someone whom Lucy knew and liked. Sheryl had baby-sat for Lucy occasionally and Lucy crowed with pleasure when Sheryl arrived the next morning. "Hi! Hi!" Lucy waved her spoon, splattering yogurt on the floor. Sheryl was taking a break from college. She wasn't a permanent sitter for Lucy, but she gave us a chance to settle in and catch our breath. Above all, with Sheryl, Lucy had peace and calm. Sheryl was gentle and kind and calm. Lucy didn't have to commute anymore. She didn't have to get tired. She would have a chance to enjoy life, the way a baby should.

Sheryl came over to Lucy. "Hi, Lucy. Do you like your breakfast?"

"Hi!" squeaked Lucy. She suddenly began to scream. She had attacks like this, arching her back, screaming for no reason at all. I picked her up. "When she's like this, Sheryl, I show her the cat." I walked Lucy around to the living room to inspect a framed print Jim had given me. It was of a Siamese cat coolly surveying a blue china ginger-jar. Lucy found it soothing.

"Cat," she said through her tears. "Mummy, cat." For some reason, it comforted her. I left for work while Lucy contentedly let Sheryl spoon in the rest of the banana yogurt. It was peaceful. Lucy improved every day, losing her nervous excitability and becoming a jolly, carefree little baby. In fact, I realized with surprise, she wouldn't be a baby for long. She was becoming a little girl. Along with words, and walking, she had grown some hair.

She went away the next weekend. Sunday evening she came back. This was not her first time away, but the present visitation still upset her. Her distress upset me, no matter how I schooled myself. My parents waited with me — my mother feigning calm by reading a book, my father pacing with his arms folded. He checked his watch. "One minute late. I'd better straighten this man out. Let me handle this, honey." He folded his arms. "I'm a man. You shouldn't have to speak to him." It was nice to feel protected. I was grateful for my father's being there. The doorbell rang. Lucy was back. I opened the door. My father stepped up beside me.

"Come right in," he ordered. I took Lucy. As usual, she

didn't seem to recognize me. She looked dazed and bewildered. "Come in," repeated my father. My ex came in. My father closed the door.

"I'm taking her right upstairs," my mother said in a whisper to me. "You'll have to stay." She gently took Lucy in her arms and whisked her upstairs.

"Sit down," ordered my father, taking out a note pad and sitting down at the dining-room table. "I have a few questions I want answered. Sit down, Elizabeth," he said. I sat.

"Sit!" ordered my father. He had been an army colonel. My ex sat.

"Where did you take her?" my father demanded, his pen poised above the note pad.

"I don't think I'll answer that." The two men glared at each other, like angry bulls. My father turned up the volume in his voice. He infrequently shouted, but when he spoke loudly, plaster fell.

"When did you feed her?" The volume of my father's voice rose again. My ex got to his feet.

"I don't think —" but he was drowned out by a tidal wave of noise.

"When did you change her diapers? When did you bathe her? This is my granddaughter. What sort of father won't answer a few simple questions?"

"Don't shout at me!" shouted my ex. He didn't understand. My father had not yet begun to shout. My father filled his lungs with a gigantic breath.

"Shout? Who's shouting?" My ex stepped back into the wall as though the sound had slammed into him. He turned and fled from the house.

"Shouting," said my father when he had gone. "He doesn't know what I'm like when I shout. I wasn't shouting."

My hands were trembling.

"Please don't be like that here, Daddy," I said in a shaky voice.

"What if I can't control myself?"

"Then you can't be around."

"I can help you," insisted my father, his voice rising again. "I want to talk to your lawyer. I know how to handle this man. I want to get involved."

"I'll leave that up to Mr. Blackstone." I wanted peace for my daughter. It was useless trying to explain. I went upstairs to Lucy. "Did you hear what went on?" I asked anxiously. Lucy clung to my mother.

"We couldn't help hearing."

I folded my arms and stared out the window. "This is our safe house, Mother. For you and me and Lucy. I won't have our sanctuary invaded." I stroked Lucy's head. She took my hand and made me stroke her face. She was so sweet and gentle and vulnerable. Lucy would be most hurt by this conflict, not me or my mother, not my ex or my father.

"Can I take Lucy out to the carousel?" asked my father one Saturday at ten. "We'll be back in twenty minutes. I want to take her for a ride."

I was washing up after breakfast. "Of course, Dad. Have a good time. Don't be long though. I want to take her out to get new shoes. She's grown out of the old ones already."

"My shoes!" said Lucy pointing to her own. "Mummy shoes." She pointed to mine. They were a jolly sight as they set off, Lucy clutching my father's hat, laughing happily.

After an hour, I became impatient. After two, I felt annoyed. After three hours, I began to worry. Four hours later, my father called.

"Elizabeth, she's quite tired. I'll keep her here for the afternoon. Okay, honey?"

"Daddy, where are you?" I asked anxiously.

"I took her out to my place."

"You were going to be back in twenty minutes."

"The traffic was bad."

"What about the carousel?" I relaxed. "You didn't take her to the carousel," I said matter-of-factly.

"Well. The traffic was so bad it was easier to come over here."

"Easier to take her for an hour's ride in the country than a five-minute drive?"

"Don't talk to me like that," he replied. "Treat your father with respect."

"I do what I can, Daddy."

"Well, we'll be back this evening."

"Okay." I hung up and thought about it. It wasn't okay. I couldn't let this go on. I had Lucy alternate weekends. I missed her when she was away. Outside, a little boy hopped beside his father while his sister rode around on her bicycle. A dog chased a ball. I knew Lucy needed time with me. She needed peace and quiet and friends, and she needed to be home. I called him back.

"Daddy, please bring her back to me. Now." An hour later, they returned. Lucy was tired and excited, jumping up and down, grabbing and hitting and shouting. She finally fell asleep.

"Now, I don't think you're fair," complained my father when I came back downstairs after putting her to bed. "I think you're very inconsiderate." I turned to face him.

"Daddy, from now on, I would rather you didn't take Lucy out alone."

"What?" His voice rose. I stood my ground, waiting. He looked me over. "I know when I'm not wanted." He turned and left the house. He came back later to get his belongings. He had decided to live alone.

Lucy was still sleeping when there was a knock on the door. It was Jimmy. I let him in. "Hello, stranger! Have some lunch. Where have you been?" Ever since Jim decided to move to

New York, he had been out of town on interviews at every spare moment.

"Have you had lunch?" he asked.

"Not yet."

"I'll join you." He looked around. "Where's Dad?" My mother looked at me.

"He left," I said.

"Did you have a fight and throw him out?" asked Jim. He sounded anxious.

"No. I laid down the law about Lucy. He didn't like it and he left."

"What did you tell him about Lucy?" Jim interrogated me. He had a right to ask. Daddy was his Daddy, too.

I explained. Jim shrugged. Jim and I were close, and if he thought I was in the wrong with Dad, he'd let me know.

"Listen, Elizabeth. I need to change the subject," he said as we sat down over bread and cheese. "You know I'm moving to New York in about three months. My apartment lease is up in a few days. I could get an extension but . . ."

"Come and stay with us," said my mother and I in chorus.

He looked at us suspiciously. "Have I talked to you about this before?"

"It's been perfectly obvious for months," said my mother.

"And we have a spare bedroom," I added, "but you'll have to put up with Lucy. She can be very difficult after visitation, and I'm not the easiest person to live with, if you ask Daddy or my ex."

"What do you think I am?" said Jim. "I've been living alone. At least you've had Mother to civilize you."

"We'd love it," I assured him.

"Mummy?" wailed Lucy's voice over the intercom. She was awake from her nap. "Mummy?" I dashed upstairs and brought her down. She was rubbing her eyes and was rumpled from her nap.

"Look who's here. Uncle Jimmy."

She smiled sleepily. "Dinny." She scrambled down and got her book about Jemima Puddle Duck from her toy drawer. She solemnly brought it to him.

"Duck frying?" she asked, hopefully. "Up, peese." He picked her up on his knee and turned the page.

"Ah yes," said Jimmy solemnly. "See the duck running? Run! Run! Run! And now she's flying! See — fly, fly!" and he flapped his hands in the air.

"Duck frying!" said Lucy, happily flapping her hands. Jim produced from his pocket a battered crow-call. "See, Lucy. Duck sounds like this. Quack, quack," and he blew into the crow-call. It made a frightful squawk. He gave it to her. After a while of making quacky sounds, she climbed off his lap and made her way to me.

"Mummy? Duck frying? Up, peese? Quack? Quack?" She handed me the crow-call and climbed up on my knee. "Mummy," she said, pointing at me. "Ga-mama." She pointed to my mother. "Dinny." She pointed to Jimmy.

"Uncle Jimmy is coming to stay for a while, Lucy."

"Hi, Dinny. Duck frying?" she asked hopefully.

Jim obliged, flapping his hands and quacking the crow-call to her great delight. Jim chuckled.

"Janice is due soon, isn't she?" he said. "Wait until Rob and Janice have a baby. They'll never know what hit them. It's the best thing you ever did, Elizabeth. Whatever else your ex is good for, he's got good genes."

Lucy scrambled off his lap and approached my mother with her duck book in her hand.

"Ga-mama? Duck frying?"

"Later, Lucy, not now. I'll read later. We're talking."

"Eei-eei-oh?" asked Lucy hopefully. "Sing?"

"Later, Lucy."

"Cookie, peese. Ga-mama? Cookie, jus one?"

"No cookie, Lucy."

"Peese, Ga-mama. Duck frying? Quack? Quack? Read, peese, peese?" she looked up meltingly, disappointed.

"Well, all right."

Lucy clapped her hands vigorously at her triumph.

"She needs her baby cousin," said Jim.

≥ nine

I KISSED LUCY. "Bye, Mummy. Good time." Lucy waved me good-bye while Sheryl stood by her at the patio door. "Bye. Bye. Bye," she called out. I blew her a kiss for each "bye," got into the car, and drove off. Once again I had wrestled with the problem of who was to look after her. Sheryl was going back to school soon. After much thought, I had decided that Lucy needed a nanny — a proper English nanny, someone to live with us, who would give Lucy the training and stability she needed. It would be expensive but worth it. The London agency had called the night before to confirm that Miss Hawkins would arrive that Wednesday. Finding a nanny was this morning's ray of sunshine through the clouds. The clouds were my deposition. I was on my way to Mr. Blackstone's office to spend the day having my deposition taken. It was horrid. If only they would get the trial over with, slaughter me at one fell swoop, let me know what I had to live with and what Lucy had to live with.

"You don't look nervous," said Mr. Blackstone when I arrived. He studied me critically. He had prepared me for this for hours. He was like a professor sending a pupil into a national exam.

"I am."

"Don't be. It's easy. You should enjoy this. You're a loving mother, a respectable professional woman. All you have to do is answer the question. Answer only the question. Remember, if yes or no will do, say yes or no. Tell the truth. The questions are simple ones. Keep your answers simple. I expect this lawyer to treat you well. On the other hand . . ." Mr. Blackstone rubbed his hands together, dusting them off for battle. "He is not legally entitled to get nasty or to argue with you. I don't think he will try. I think he's a good lawyer. But if he does . . . If he does" — a gleam came into his eye — "I'll stop the deposition right then. I'm there to protect your interests within the law. You have nothing to worry about." Having instilled in me what confidence he could, he led me into the conference room.

"Elizabeth, you sit there." Mr. Blackstone steered me to the chair opposite my ex's attorney. Mr. Blackstone sat opposite my ex. The court reporter sat at the end of the table. I was getting used to the routine. I had sat rigid and nervous through my ex's first deposition and through his second one. That had been disagreeable for him. I was sure that this time it would be equally disagreeable for me.

The opposing attorney gave me a most unconvincing, sharklike grin and the session began. I raised my right hand and swore to tell the truth, the whole truth, and nothing but the truth. The sharklike attorney leaned forward, grinned again, and fixed me with a fishy eye.

"What is your name?"

I was relieved. That was easy. "Jean Elizabeth Morgan."

"Where do you live?"

I knew that too. I recited the address.

"What is your date of birth?"

How easy. I realized that if you lie habitually, with practice you could create a fictitious persona. Perhaps I would be Silver Star, a disco dancer. I could claim to be rampantly promiscuous. I could swear that my ex was not the father. It was too late now. I had been raised to tell the truth. The questions came relentlessly, like machine-gun fire.

"Do you have a specialty?"

"I am a plastic surgeon." The court reporter didn't hesitate. He didn't care what my words meant. He simply had to get them down accurately.

"Have you ever lied?" I hesitated. Of course I had. I had lied to my parents when I swore I wrote to them every day from Camp Kanuga. I was seven.

"Yes, I have," I said evenly. The attorney grinned.

"Have you ever cheated on an exam, Dr. Morgan?"

I considered this. "No." I never had. It was a simple question. It was a simple answer, but it rattled me. My mind wandered afield. The attorney asked me another question. I didn't listen. My answer was confused. The attorney asked again. I argued with him. I wasn't thinking of the deposition. I was remembering. I remembered eighth grade and a history test. The girl sitting next to me seemed to know all the answers. I was new to the school. I knew nothing. I remembered looking over at her test. I couldn't read the answers. I was too nearsighted. Was the intent to cheat in fact cheating? If I had had normal vision, I might have cheated then. This deposition had the force of law. Was I telling the truth, the whole truth, and nothing but the truth? I couldn't concentrate now. I couldn't answer a simple question. I was floundering. I fought to concentrate. I couldn't listen anymore. The thought of Ms. Jones came back to me — the time when she had set me adrift in front of the judge. I couldn't cope with the law. I couldn't do it right.

"Don't argue," said Mr. Blackstone irritably, intruding on my panic. "It's a simple question. Answer his question."

I focused in a snap. That was exactly what I needed. Mr. Blackstone was my professor. He had taught me. I knew what to do now. My mind cleared.

"How many days have you traveled out of town this past year?"

I thought. "Do you mean for the day, or overnight?" I asked.

"Why not tell me both?" grinned the opposing attorney. It seemed to me that he hated me. He was like a torturer. I have read that torturers are nice to you, to get you on their side so that they can hurt you more. I wouldn't be conned. I concentrated and counted. The answer surprised me. "Out of town overnight. Not more than five." He didn't like that. I saw his eyes crinkle. He was trying to figure out if I was lying.

"Has your father been present when Lucy's father gets her or brings her back from visitation?" I readied myself. My ex knew all about my father's past problems.

"Yes."

"Have you ever heard your father shout at him?" I almost laughed.

"No." He had not shouted. They didn't know my father.

"How would you describe it?"

"He talked in a loud voice."

"Have you been named in a lawsuit brought by your father against your mother?"

"No." He was near the mark, but the shot had gone wide. That was not my life they were intruding on. That was my mother's. Unhappy memories surged up, all my mother had lived through and all she had nearly died for in those two years of her illness. Having my ex across from me didn't help. Why had our lives turned out this way?

"What was the answer again, please?" The attorney came in for the kill.

"The answer was no. I'm sorry. I'm upset," and I burst into tears.

"Have another Kleenex," suggested Mr. Blackstone during a short recess called so that I could blow my nose. "You're doing very nicely. I don't mind the tears at all. This sort of thing always happens at depositions. You were a bad girl in the beginning. I had to speak to you; then you settled down. Ready?" I was ready and I faced the sharklike grin once more.

"For the record," said the sharklike counsel facing me. "We

took a short recess because the last question seemed to be distressing to the witness."

"There is no need for you to correct the record," interposed Mr. Blackstone sternly. "Dr. Morgan already stated that she was upset." The other man nodded and leaned across the table toward me again.

"Do you have a will?"

"Yes."

"Who inherits if you die?"

"Lucy."

"Is your father excluded from your will?"

Mr. Blackstone's outstretched arm came down like a portcullis in front of my face.

"I advise Dr. Morgan not to answer that question. The question is irrelevant to the current matter. It is harassment." I began to feel like a pony, not a pupil. I trotted merrily along until Mr. Blackstone tugged on the reins and told me to "Whoa!"

"What is your answer?"

"I decline to answer on the advice of my attorney."

"You refuse to answer?"

I hesitated. "Yes." That was exactly what I was doing.

"How would you describe yourself? What are your worst qualities?" resumed the attorney. Mr. Blackstone cleared his throat.

"While Dr. Morgan is thinking . . . While she is thinking," he repeated emphatically in a clear voice. "While she thinks about her answer, I'd like to say that's a very good question. Very good." And a very good play for time, I realized while I thought about my answer. He really did protect me.

"I tend to be very anxious. I tend to worry. I tend to be disorganized."

"You will have to ask your client to stop making faces at Dr. Morgan," interposed Mr. Blackstone abruptly.

"I can't see him making faces," retorted the other lawyer.

"Of course you can't," said Mr. Blackstone cheerfully. "You're not looking at him. I am. He is making faces at my client. Ask him to stop."

I wasn't looking at my ex. I wasn't sure if he was or if he wasn't. The other attorney turned to look at my ex. "Okay?"

The deposition resumed. He must have started again. Mr. Blackstone objected again.

At one o'clock, we broke for lunch.

"Are his faces bothering you?" Mr. Blackstone asked solicitously on our way to get something to eat.

"I'm really not aware of him at all. I'm concentrating too hard."

"Well, whenever he doesn't like your answers, he makes a face. If he is bothering you, I'll stop the deposition. Legally, he isn't allowed to make faces. Making faces certainly constitutes interfering. He's allowed to glare. He is not allowed to react. Still, you're doing so well, unless it bothers you, I'm inclined to let him go on."

After a quick lunch, we reconvened.

"Have you obtained a divorce?" asked the opposing attorney.

"Yes."

"Did you obtain it in Haiti?"

"Yes."

"Do you have a copy of the divorce decree?"

"Yes."

"Please supply us with a copy," snapped the attorney.

"But I did already," I protested. "Last October, along with everything else."

The attorney looked embarrassed. "We received so much material — boxes of it! Would you be kind enough to send us another copy of the divorce decree?"

"Certainly." Again I thought of my father. He had taught me much that was useful. When his taxes were investigated, he sent fifteen shirt boxes of jumbled papers to the IRS. Rather than read them all, the tax men settled. I had nothing to hide, but I was pleased to think that the shark had seen all my laboriously copied checks and bank statements and credit-card bills and grocery receipts — and had given up. He began to sound weary after that. At five o'clock, he threw in the towel for the day. My deposition was over and Mr. Blackstone led me back to his office. I was worn out. Mr. Blackstone looked ready to start again.

"I think it went well," he said. "Now, for the trial. It's coming up on a Wednesday." He took out his book. "I'll be preparing on Monday and Tuesday. Can you be here Tuesday at eleven o'clock?" I nodded. He wrote the appointment down and escorted me to the elevator. "You described yourself in the deposition as worried and anxious. This is a difficult time. If it helps, let me reassure you. I think things are going well. Let me know if there is anything more I can do to help relieve the anxiety and worry that are a necessary part of all this. How's Lucy?"

He was kind to ask. He loved his own children very much and spoke of them often. He knew what Lucy meant to me. "She's sleeping better. In fact, since you took us on, I feel more relaxed and I think she knows it. You've been awfully good for both of us." He did shield us. I didn't worry so desperately anymore. The past seemed too bad to have really happened. It had. Remembering those days chilled me.

I drove home thinking of Lucy. The visits with the psychiatrist had increased her confidence. We were about to stop seeing Dr. Oakes. Lucy was no longer deteriorating. Her screaming fits had lessened. She was unable to sleep in her bedroom at night, so she had to sleep in my bedroom. Her bed was next to mine. That way, she crawled up into my bed if she got frightened. Often, at two or three in the morning, she woke up crying and climbed into my bed to be held for a while. Sometimes she would get in my bed to play, saying, "Mummy! Mummy!" at two AM and giggling. The first or second night after visitation, I sometimes had to hold her all night, but at least she wasn't screaming anymore. And the seizures had not recurred. She was terrified of the dark and of being alone, but now she could say, "Mummy, I scared. Don't like it," instead of screaming in wordless terror. She was afraid of strangers. Running water and thunderstorms sent her running to me for safety. They terrified her too, but she was better than she had been. She was sweet and affectionate. When the trial was over, things would settle down. The nanny and I could work on making her happier and more secure.

My mother and I met the nanny, Miss Hawkins, at the airport that week. It was Sheryl's last day with Lucy. College began the next day. We didn't know what Miss Hawkins looked like. Her work record looked good and we knew she had a visa. She was legal and she was an experienced nanny. Her self-description was "average height and blond." A black-and-white photograph showed a female face of indeterminate age, with black hair and dark eyes. We arrived at the airport and waited in the international lobby, leaning against a wobbly guardrail. People around us shifted from one foot to the other, chewed gum, and checked their watches. The doors from Customs opened. A pair of Arabian diplomats came through, flanked by airport officials and bodyguards. Then the flight crew passed through. Finally, the regular passengers appeared, a steady stream of weary businessmen, vacationers clutching large plastic shopping bags, and a group of students. At last, a lanky, young bleached-blond came through the door pushing an enormous yellow suitcase. She straightened up to look around. Her eyes were heavily made up in peacock blue. "This has to be her," I said despondently.

My mother gasped. "Oh no" was all she said. This was not our idea of an English nanny.

"Miss Hawkins?" I inquired.

She smiled. "I'm Marsha. You must be Dr. Morgan."

"Is this all your luggage?" I asked. "Let's go to the car." My life and Lucy's seemed destined to be muddled again. Maybe

Marsha would be better than she looked, but I didn't think so.

"I was terribly anxious in Immigration," said Marsha in a high-pitched English voice as we drove home.

"Why?"

"Well, I'm only here on a visitor's visa, you know. I'm not supposed to work. I had to invent my story pretty carefully. I said I was staying with friends and my family would send money as I needed it. It was a nervy time."

There was a long pause. "You're illegal?" I asked as cheerfully as I could.

"Oh, yes. The agency knew that."

Now I had an illegal alien to cope with. I looked at her reflection in the rearview mirror. She looked like a disco dancer, not a nanny.

Once we got home, we arranged for her to see a lawyer, to make herself legal. In the next few days, she seemed more interested in traveling than in Lucy. We were interrogated as to bus routes, social clubs, and plane schedules to resorts. Lucy simply ignored her.

That Saturday afternoon, I left Lucy with Marsha to make hospital rounds. Marsha was in the kitchen reading when I returned. She was barefoot, in a housecoat, with her eyelids painted a brilliant blue. "You're going to be rather cross with me," she began, "but I've decided to go and get a different kind of job." I blinked. "This job is too boring, really," continued Marsha. "It doesn't suit me." She gazed at me.

"You can't just leave," I said crossly. "Where's Lucy?"

"Hi, Mummy!" Lucy was exploring the fireplace in the living room. I pulled her out of the chimney and looked at Marsha. For weeks, I had waited for a nanny. I had paid an outrageous fee. She had to stay until I could replace her. There was no one else to look after Lucy. My mother helped, but she couldn't do full-time child care. At the same time, I didn't want Marsha in my house. I couldn't trust her with Lucy. She was irresponsible.

"I'm leaving tomorrow," said Marsha. "This just won't suit."

"I'd better call my brother, the lawyer," I told her. Rob groaned when I explained. "Oh, Elizabeth, when I think Janice and I will be in the same boat in a few weeks. Anyhow, you can employ an illegal alien. That is legal. But you cannot harbor one. To let her leave your house to work elsewhere is illegal — harboring an alien, a federal crime."

"Wonderful." I didn't need to go into the trial for custody guilty of a federal crime.

I turned to Marsha. "If you want to go home, that's fine. But I can't let you walk out to get another job."

She stared at me. "Why not? I want to live with a friend. I can get a job as a secretary."

"I can't let you. It's illegal. We'd both get in trouble."

"Lies, bloody lies," yelled Marsha. "No one cares that I'm illegal. You can't do anything to me. I'm walking right out."

"Marsha, you don't understand. It's legal for you to work for me if we're trying to make you legal. But it's illegal for me to let you leave to work elsewhere illegally."

Marsha rushed to her room and reappeared, in skintight pants and more makeup, lugging her gigantic suitcase. She was at the door when it opened from the outside. It was Jim. He had been playing tennis. He swung his racket cheerfully.

"Let's not fight about it," he suggested, when I explained. "Let's go ask Immigration. The airport is always open. Okay?"

Marsha looked at me triumphantly. "I know they'll let me do what I want."

"Fine." Jim hoisted her suitcase into his trunk. When Lucy realized we were going out for a ride, she chortled with joy, then fell asleep in the car. At the airport, Jim casually walked through a door marked "No Admittance" and reappeared with two immigration officers, a crisp Hispanic woman in a business suit and a willowy black woman with her hair in beaded braids.

"What seems to be the problem?" asked the black officer. She smiled at Lucy and looked at Marsha consideringly.

"I'm here on a visitor's visa and I want to visit some friends in Atlanta," said Marsha. "She won't let me." She tossed her head in my direction.

"Sure. And you've been looking after this baby until now? Have you been paid for it?" Marsha didn't answer.

"How much?" the Hispanic officer asked me. I told her. "Not bad money," she said, and turned to Marsha.

"Did this lady pay you that amount of money for looking after her baby?"

"Yes," she said sulkily.

"Then you're not a visitor, are you?" She studied Marsha's passport. "You're working, on a visitor's visa. This lady can't let you walk out of her house. She's legally responsible for you."

My divorce had taught me to respect the law. Until then, I usually had taken it lightly. Unless you were a criminal, the law gave out traffic fines, at worst. Now I knew what the law wasn't. It wasn't a game. I felt sorry for Marsha, but I wasn't fooling with the law.

"Now look," said Marsha angrily. "I'm here to see friends." The two officers looked at each other and then at her.

"I think you need to come and have a talk with us, miss. I don't think you understand," said the black officer. Her voice was silky but she was used to being obeyed. Marsha followed.

Marsha went back to England that night. Her choice was to leave or to be arrested. I felt sorry for her. The agency had lied to me and robbed me, and Marsha. She had paid them a fee, too. I decided it was no more nannies and called an employment agency. I doubted that they would do better, but there was nothing else to try. Somewhere I would find the right person, the kind, loving, responsible woman who would treasure Lucy. She had to be American, I decided. And, after a week of

Marsha, I had decided that whoever looked after Lucy had to live elsewhere. I wanted Lucy to myself when I got home.

My mother spent that Monday calling more employment agencies and looking after Lucy. Beverly spent the day rearranging my schedule. I took Tuesday off to interview people for Lucy. Beverly rearranged my schedule so that I saw my Tuesday patients on Monday, after surgery. It made for a hectic day.

My mother arranged fourteen interviews with women who might look after Lucy. We wanted someone who spoke English and who could come five days a week, from eight to six. If I had to leave earlier or come home later, my mother would be around to cover the "swing" times. Our phones rang madly with all sorts of people eager to come for an interview. Half of them did not speak English. We had interviews with those who did. For six hours that Tuesday, my mother and I talked with various women. There was a charming Peruvian who spoke no English — a friend had called and set up the interview for her — and a delightful Jamaican nurse who was recovering from a major operation — quite unfit for running after Lucy — and an elegant young woman from Liverpool whose father owned a car dealership in London. She wasn't a serious worker. An Italian woman arrived, waving her arms excitedly. She wasn't interested in work, but she wanted to meet the baby. She cooed over Lucy and dashed away. Our last interviewee did not show up. We sat on the sofa. Lucy sat next to me, reading *Peter Rabbit* upside down, saying, "Puddeput rabbit. Quack quack," while I turned the pages.

"The only possible," my mother began.

"Is the nurse," I finished.

"And she won't really do," we agreed.

The doorbell rang. A handsome, dignified black woman in her thirties was on the doorstep. "I'm Mrs. Taylor." She held out her hand rather shyly. "I'm sorry I'm late. My bus broke down." She came in. She had a slight southern accent. She had raised six brothers and sisters. She liked work. She always had worked. She was trained as a secretary, but she preferred looking after children. Lucy walked over to her. She lifted Lucy up on the sofa beside her and put her arm around her. "Now I like housework, too. I keep a clean house. I could clean the house if you want to pay me for it. If you don't have anyone, that is." Her eye fell on the undusted coffee table. I did have a cleaning lady, but her idea of clean wasn't mine or Mrs. Taylor's. Mrs. Taylor was gentle and reassuring. She exerted a calming effect on Lucy. Mrs. Taylor was an American working mother and she knew what I needed.

"Would you" — I leaned forward — "like to come to work for us?"

Mrs. Taylor considered us for a moment.

"I'm a Witness. A Jehovah's Witness. Are you prejudiced against them?" she asked bluntly.

"No, I don't know much about them."

"We believe that the word of Jesus is Truth and that God will bring Heaven to earth for Heaven on earth. We believe in the brotherhood of all men."

"That's fine," I replied fatuously.

"Are you prejudiced against blacks? Some people don't like us."

"Of course not. You're American," I said fervently. Marsha Hawkins had made me a chauvinist.

I hired Mrs. Taylor without misgivings. She was the right person. She was in the same boat I was — working, on her own, trying to do the best for her child. She knew my struggles and I knew hers. Lucy would be all right with her. She wouldn't let us down. She agreed to start work in two days. We escorted her to the door and saw her off.

"Good-bye, Lucy," said Mrs. Taylor.

Lucy waved and followed her out the door. "Bye, Taer." She leaned forward on the railing, waving until Mrs. Taylor vanished around the corner. "Bye," she shrieked. To Lucy's immense delight, Mrs. Taylor turned back to wave her a last good-bye.

"Now come on in, Lucy," I said as Mrs. Taylor disappeared.

"I wun away," she announced and started down the steps.

"Lucy!"

"Wun away!"

"Lucy!" She looked back at me laughing.

"Good-bye." I closed the door, almost.

Disappointed, Lucy came back up the steps looking for me. "Mummy, wun away? Mummy?" Then she announced importantly, "Luwee inside," and came back in the house.

"Mrs. Taylor is wonderful," I said to my mother after Mrs. Taylor had gone. "She's wonderful. Why didn't I find someone like her before?"

"Until we lived here, you couldn't very well. You had to take Lucy out. Sheryl was delightful but temporary. We knew that. As for the nanny — live and learn. Everyone goes through this. Rob and Janice will have their turn."

"We've dealt with a lot, haven't we?" I reflected. I had thought that leaving my husband would destroy me. I had survived. My practice had survived with me. I loved my work. Many of my patients came to me at a time of crisis. My own suffering helped me understand theirs. I had thought visitation would destroy Lucy. Lucy had survived, at least so far. Mr. Blackstone had brought us peace of mind almost overnight. He was forceful and in command of our destiny. My relations with my father were clear, which was a relief. My mother was healthy and happy. And now, Mrs. Taylor, like Mary Poppins, had come into our life, an answer to my prayers.

We sat talking after Mrs. Taylor had gone. "I would like," said my mother, "I would like to see you have more social life. You couldn't until now, but it's time you did things."

"I know." I wanted friends. I wanted to do things, but I had been in a cocoon for so long that I had forgotten how to be sociable. "I can't do anything until after the trial," I said, but really I was afraid. My looks were average. I was out of shape. Lucy was my only hobby. Starting a new social life sounded to me like swimming in winter: I knew it would be harsh and cold when I first got in. I didn't want to get in. The phone rang. It was the Emergency Room. I had to see a little girl who had burned herself at home. I set out to the hospital with a feeling of reprieve. Decisions on my social life were temporarily postponed. I was slipping into the trap that snares so many doctors. Willingly, I was letting my profession edge out all hope of a normal life.

Cecily Carter was the burned girl. I pulled back the curtains around her bed. She was a little brunette, about Lucy's age; her chest and abdomen were wrapped in wet dressings. Her mother sat by her, a look of shock on her face, while Cecily slept. "We gave her Demerol," whispered the nurse, coming in beside me. "She was exhausted from screaming."

"I have to take a look," I explained to her mother. She simply nodded, clutching Cecily's hand and gazing at her face. There were red, splotchy, burned areas on the child's face and neck. It wasn't even blistered. Gently, with gloved hands, I pulled up the dressings. Cecily whimpered and stirred but the Demerol and her own fatigue had overpowered her. Her eyes opened and she looked at her mother with glazed, unseeing eyes. I put the dressings back down. I had seen enough. Cecily would not ever want to wear a bikini. There would be too many scars on her chest from the burns and from the skin grafts that she would need.

"What happened?" I asked in a whisper.

"Doctor, I . . . ." Mrs. Carter bit her lip.

"Hot water?" I asked.

She nodded.

"Boiling?"

She nodded again. "She's seen me make coffee. That's what she wanted to do. She got hold of the kettle." I sat down on the bed. Cecily's eyes closed wearily and she went back to sleep.

"She is going to be in the hospital three weeks, at the least," I explained. "She's very lucky. Her face and her neck and her arms are fine. She will probably need skin grafts on her abdomen. She will have scars on her lower chest and abdomen."

"Bad ones?"

"I don't know. It depends on how she heals. She'll go to physical therapy every day, before she's grafted."

"Oh, my baby." Mrs. Carter shook her head, rocking back and forth, grief-stricken. "My beautiful baby girl. Doctor, can I stay with her?"

"If you can afford to. If you work, you may lose your job if you take so much time off."

"Thank God, I don't work. My husband doesn't like it. At least it wasn't her face. I'll keep telling myself that. It wasn't my baby's face."

I held her hand for a while, small comfort for her, and reassured her as truthfully as I could. At last I went to the record room. I had hospital charts to sign out. How would I feel if it were Lucy that was burned? Would I exchange her struggles with visitation for painful burns, scars on her breasts and abdomen, and three frightening weeks in a hospital? I didn't think so. I could help her cope with visitation. Her continuing problems with visitation puzzled me, but I put them down to the upcoming trial. Lucy was perceptive. She had to be affected by the tension that the custody trial created in me and, presumably, in her father. But, nevertheless, a physical injury was final. No matter how you coped, it was always with you. It occurred to me that Lucy's psychological injuries also would leave traces of their own kind, inside rather than out. Perhaps little burned Cecily and my Lucy were not so unalike. I sat down with a cup of coffee and a stack of charts.

"Dr. Morgan!" said a cheerful voice from the chair next to me. "What are you doing here?"

I looked up. "Dr. Knowles! What are you doing here?"

"Trying to stay off the suspense list," he said.

"Me too," I replied. It was four years since I'd seen Elliott Knowles. He had tried to get me into riding and fox hunting. In Virginia, foxes got chased. It was poor form to kill them. I hadn't had time then, with my new practice, to take up riding. In the meantime, Elliott had married and fathered a son.

"Didn't you just have a baby?" I asked.

"No, Elizabeth." He shook his head sadly. "What do they teach in medical school these days? I didn't have a baby; Penelope, my wife, had the baby — a bouncing boy. You did too, didn't you?"

"A little girl. I think yours and mine are the same age."

"Why don't you bring your husband out and come riding sometime?"

"Well, for one thing, Elliott, I'm not married anymore." It didn't bother me now. My ex's charge that I was an unfit mother was so outrageous that it obliterated all my tender feelings for him and for our marriage.

"Then don't bring him. Seriously, you ought to ride. We need to get new blood in the hunt. Now I'm not much of a teacher, but Penelope is a fantastic rider. Olympic material. She'll have you jumping like that." He snapped his fingers. Then he slapped his thighs. "I'm fit. You look kind of flabby to me." He leaned back and laughed at my expression of dismay. "Seriously, I'll tell Penelope that you'll call."

"I don't think I can until after my custody trial."

"Got a good lawyer?"

I nodded.

"Then the heck with it. Why can't you ride a horse before a custody trial? Make you feel better. Perk up your looks. Circulate. Don't let me down. I'll make a rider of you yet." The horsey people were the nicest, most gregarious, friendly people I had ever known. Jim called them "shirt-off-their-backs people," and they were. Assuming that Elliott's wife didn't mind a horseless rider turning up on her doorstep for lessons, it was a chance I couldn't turn down.

I called Penelope Knowles that evening. She seemed quite content with having an uncertain hunt-hopeful thrust upon her.

"Sure. Come down this weekend, Elizabeth. I'll take you out and see what you can do."

That Friday, Lucy left for visitation. The next morning, I was out at the Knowles estate. I saddled King George, one of the Knowleses' horses. I got the bridle hopelessly tangled and Penelope untangled me.

"Your left stirrup is too long," she said with a glance at me from her prancing thoroughbred. I tried to adjust it. King George moved sideways. I stopped him and fixed my stirrup. "You'll get the hang of it," said Penelope. We went down to the ring. "First," said Penelope, "can you post?"

"I can try." King George struck out in a trot and I bounced around like a sack of potatoes. King George did not approve of me and he shook his head angrily, like a fierce beast.

"He's a great horse," called out Penelope. "Keep your heels down. Sit up. Hands down. Knees in. Relax. He's perfectly safe. We call him the baby-sitter. You don't need to know how to ride to stay on King George." It was a good thing.

Two hours later, we were back in the stables. I fell off King George as gracefully as I could. My legs were much too stiff to move. I followed Penelope back to the house. Elliott was on his way out to play polo. "She's all right," said Penelope. "Much better than I thought."

"She'll be hunting next season," said Elliott, grabbing a polo mallet off the hall table. "Keep it up." He took a swing and clicked happily as he hit an imaginary ball.

"Come on, Philip. Go riding with Daddy?" he called out.

"Polo!" shouted Philip, running in from the kitchen. He ran after his father. "Daddy! Horsey! Polo!" He was not yet two, but Philip was already a horseman. Penelope and I watched Elliott lift Philip into the saddle with him. He sat balanced perfectly in front of his father, and they went cantering off after imaginary polo balls.

"What a little ruffian," said Penelope proudly. "My next is going to be a quiet little girl. Why don't you bring Lucy out next time?" They were real friends, and friends were what I needed. I had an image of Lucy riding her own pony with the same skill and verve that Philip had displayed. I took her and my mother out with me the next weekend. I rode and Lucy and Philip played with my mother. When I came back to the house, Elliott was hooking up the horse trailer in preparation for a polo game.

"Okay, now her first lesson." He got on King George and led Snowflake up the drive. "Put her on, Elizabeth."

"Mummy, see horsey!" chattered Lucy. "Mummy wide."

"Lucy ride." I put her up in the saddle and held her on, staying beside her while Elliott led Snowflake at a slow walk. It was a very long way up for a little girl who wasn't yet two. Lucy looked around, beaming, and then made the mistake of looking down at the ground. "Mummy, Mummy, Mummy!" she shrieked in a panic. I lifted her off. Philip rode without being held, looking very proud. Then he got off and pushed Lucy and then Lucy pushed him and they both sat down on the grass with a bump.

"Love at first sight," said Penelope. "You know, you're going to do well. We'll have to take you out with the hunt."

We drove home and found Jim reading the *Wall Street Journal*. "Dinny. Mummy boots. Mummy wide. Horsey, wide!" explained Lucy with enthusiasm.

"And did Lucy ride?" asked Jim courteously.

"Horsey wide!"

"Very good, Lucy." He looked at me. "She's really full of beans, isn't she? She has really improved."

"Since Mr. Blackstone took over," I said, "thanks to you."

Jim nodded thoughtfully. "I called that one right. Listen. Look at this." He handed my mother and me a stapled stack of multi-colored papers.

"What impression does that make? If you were a prospective client, would you open an account?"

I took the papers and leafed through the dozens of forms. It seemed like a federal report. "Speaking for myself, I'd never fill these in."

"Strike you as sloppy?"

"Yes."

"Unfriendly?"

"Yes."

"I thought so, too." Jim leaned forward, his elbows on the table, and sunk his head in his hands. "This is what the firm I signed on with sent me. The one I'm going to in New York. The people I work for in ten days. It's a lot of money up front — but a firm that gives you this!" He tossed the papers aside disdainfully. "For a new account. Completely unprofessional. I can't go with them. I can't do it." He was having to discard a year's work. He had interviewed, negotiated, and bargained. This had seemed the best firm, the one he wanted most, next to Cartwright and Cartwright, who had been polite but gave no offer.

"Stay here, Jim," I urged him.

He shook his head briefly. "I want to manage money. I can't do it from here." For a moment, he had the look of longing that haunted his face when he was the teenager whose one ambition was to be the greatest miler the world had ever seen. A knee injury had knocked out his hopes as a miler. Now he wanted to be a force in the world of investment. All I had to offer was to tell him that he was a wonderful brother. It wouldn't help. Then his expression changed from one of dashed hopes to one of calculation. He looked the way he had when we had played blackjack. He was figuring the odds.

"I'm due to move to New York in two weeks." He was almost talking to himself. "I've got to go back to Cartwright on Monday. They've just got to give me a slot. I want to be in New York, and I can't trade for high-class clients with this garbage." He flung the papers on the floor. "I'm going to have to figure this one out."

"They'll take you," interposed my mother. "You're too good. There aren't enough good people to go around. Cartwright will take you."

"We'll see," said Jim tersely. He was already thinking of the best approach to use on Monday.

"Garbage," murmured Lucy happily, under the table with the papers Jim had flung down. "I want garbage." It was not funny for Jim. My struggles had never threatened my livelihood. I had the security of being a doctor. For Jim, there was the excitement, the profit, and all the risks of investment. His whole career rested now on the cards fate dealt him. Cartwright's New York office was the dealer. I was certain Jim could play against the house and win. I knew he could. He had all the talents that I lacked. If he made money for me, he could do it for anyone.

"You'll do it, Jim."

"Australia needs brokers," he said thoughtfully. "You may be visiting me in Australia."

I shook my head. "It's a real gift to be able to make money, Jim, and you have that gift. New York will not let you go. You're too good. I know I'm right."

Going to Cartwright on Monday was a gamble, but whenever Jim gambled, he won. All the same, I had been wrong about so many things. If it didn't work out, what would happen to Jim? Worry lurked in his eyes and in my mother's while he sat contemplating his strategy for Monday.

⋑ ten

ONE THURSDAY after Mrs. Taylor had gone, the doorbell rang. A motherly black woman stood on the doorstep holding a little girl by the hand.

"Hi, I'm Mrs. Robbins," she began. "Can Lucy come out and play?"

"My Susie!" squeaked Lucy running to the door. "My friend." She and Susie embraced with such affectionate energy that they both fell down. "George's mother's taking him to the sandbox across the street and the twins may come. Can Lucy come too?" asked Mrs. Robbins.

"Sandbox, Mummy!" Lucy took me by the hand and tugged me to the busy playground across the street, while Mrs. Robbins and I talked. Not only were the twins and George and Susie and Lucy all there, but also an Elizabeth, two Marias, an Adam, and a Carol. They all lived in Mayfair. They were all about two years old. I had had no idea how many children were in my development. I knew Lucy had a lot of friends, I had met most of them — but this was a gang. It was good for her.

"And is Lucy going to enroll in Playtime this summer?" asked Mrs. Wood, George's mother. She wore an electric-blue silk dress, but she was so pretty that it looked charming instead of loud.

"Yes, I enrolled her for Tuesday mornings." Playtime was a preschool play group in the church across the street.

"Is anyone else going?" I asked.

"Oh, surely, they're all going, aren't they?" replied Mrs. Wood, gazing at me in kind reproach. "It's only a question of what days."

Mrs. Wood didn't work. I felt bashful. I was not the only working mother in the group, nor the only single mother, but clearly the nonworking married mothers considered themselves a notch above the rest of us in the nicest possible way. It was partly financial. They were better off, so they didn't have to work. It was partly snobbery. They, along with the baby-sitters, were an integral part of their children's social group. The working mothers like me were peripheral. My social standing was simply "Lucy's mother"; Mrs. Wood, like Mrs. Taylor and Lucy, was known by her name. I had a sudden yearning to be married to a man of means and to lead an idle life, able to spend all my time with Lucy. And, as always, now that my own life seemed to be under control, I wondered how other single mothers managed. I had had an easy time, compared to most.

"Susie's having a birthday party on Tuesday," said Mrs. Robbins, coming over. "Is it all right if Lucy and Mrs. Taylor come?"

"Of course." I felt included again. Even if I wasn't a necessary part of the group, I had power of veto. Mrs. Lane, who looked after Carol, approached me.

"I'm taking Carol to the zoo tomorrow," she began.

"Gaffe," Lucy told me loudly, stopping for a moment from her assault on Carol's sand dune. "Hellerfan."

"Can Mrs. Taylor and Lucy come with us to the zoo? We're going in a cab, if you approve," said Mrs. Lane.

"Gaffe," Lucy told me urgently. "Owl frying. Hellerfan in zoo."

"Of course it's all right." I turned to Lucy. "Do you mean a giraffe, Lucy, and an elephant?"

"Gaffe and hellerfan in zoo," said Lucy, correcting my pronunciation. She upturned her sand bucket. "My cake," she said proudly. "My Carol eat my cake," she announced, and approached Carol with a handful of sand. Carol fended her off with a plastic shovel. I had pieced together Lucy's days from what my mother and Mrs. Taylor told me. It wasn't until this visit to the playground that I was struck by the social whirl of which she was part. She went out walking in the morning with her friends. She lunched out with friends in their houses or in local coffee shops. She visited friends in the afternoon after her nap, or they came to see her for tea. And now, parties, summer school, and the zoo. I sat in the sand and made sand cakes, under Lucy's direction. Then she took away the bucket and directed me to make imaginary sand cakes for her. Then she rushed after George, a sturdy blond boy who was in the swing. She was having a lovely time. I had chosen the right place for us to live. Lucy was awash with friends. Lucy's friends all came with mothers and sitters, and gradually I was becoming friends with them. It was an easy, sociable atmosphere that I had missed all my life.

George and Lucy, Marilyn Wood and I meandered back together from the sandbox. On the Woods' doorstep was a theatrical, impatient woman, younger than us, in riding breeches. She was ringing the doorbell and stamping a booted foot impatiently. Marilyn Wood introduced us. This was Cynthia Danvers. She also lived in Mayfair, but we had not met before. She and Marilyn were both blonds, but they were completely unalike. Marilyn had gigantic blue eyes and glossy, almost white, blond hair; she never made an unnecessary move. Cynthia had cascades of energy and curly blond hair. She had the type of willowy figure that I had always envied. Her long, graceful arms talked with her.

"Marilyn, where have you been? I thought you were a housewife. Housewives stay at home!"

"We were out," said Marilyn.

"You have to come to lunch next Tuesday."

"It's my tennis day," said Marilyn.

"Tennis! What's tennis? We are starting a new club. A network. For women. By women. To help women." She gestured the invitation while she talked. She bent down to say hello to Lucy.

"Boots off," said Lucy sternly. "Mummy's boots."

"Not my boots, Lucy. Mine are home," I told her.

"Do you ride?" asked Cynthia.

"Sort of." I wasn't in her league, clearly. Only very good riders wear custom-made boots. She and Lucy and I left George and his mother and we headed home. Our townhouses were near each other. She and Penelope Knowles knew each other.

"Do you work, Elizabeth?" asked Cynthia.

"Yes, I'm a doctor."

"You must be the plastic surgeon Marilyn told me about!" she exclaimed. She threw her arms wide. "You must join our club. You must. I have women lawyers and economists and consultants by the yard, but a woman doctor would be great. Would you be interested?"

I hesitated. Was I up for women's clubs? Was I a club type? Would they be my sort? Wouldn't they all be more social, more successful, more attractive, just more of everything than I was? What would my mother do in my place? Accept at once. "Of course, I'd love to join," I said. If the club members didn't want a busy, anxious, overworked single mother, that was their lookout.

That evening Penelope called to ask if I could join them "hill-topping" on Saturday. "Keep your mind off the trial," she urged. Hill-topping is riding in the hunt for beginning riders. You run with the hunt, but you don't jump the fences. I had no excuse to turn her down. Lucy was away that weekend. Riding would make it impossible to think of her and the trial. I had blocked the trial from my mind, but Wednesday was the day.

The next morning, I dressed for my first hunt — a yellow vest, a white stock, yellow breeches, and boots. I felt snappy until I arrived at the Knowleses. My boots were clean; Penelope's glistened. She retied my stock under Elliott's critical eye. I brushed Sweetpea, the horse I was to ride. Penelope came into her stall and brushed her again. I knew the hunt would be fun. I hadn't grasped what an important event it was to be. I began to feel fat. I always feel fat when I feel self-conscious and awkward. Who was I trying to fool? What I did on a horse could barely be dignified by the word "riding"! My assortment of riding clothes — some from twenty years ago, some secondhand — would not do in horsey circles. I felt as gauche and fat as I had the first day at the new school in tenth grade wearing my gray flannel skirt and the brown tie shoes. It wasn't for me. I was in the wrong place at the wrong time. I almost fled. I would take up fishing. That way I could sit alone on a rock all day and hide.

"Load her up!" boomed Elliott Knowles, resplendent in a scarlet jacket. It was too late to go fishing. I led Sweetpea from her stall. She looked at Elliott and the horse van and obediently clattered into it.

"Want to ride with us in the truck?" asked Elliott.

"I'll follow."

"Not on call, are you?"

"No, but you never know." Some utterly unpredictable emergency might save me from sociability. I felt like an ostrich or a mole or an owl or any creature that wanted to shun the world. I got fatter every moment that went by.

"Fine." Elliott led the way out of the drive and I followed, my ear cocked for my beeper. No one needed me. It remained silent all the way. I had no escape. It was a lovely day for hunting. I followed the Knowleses to the hunt on a vast farm in the country. The rest of the hunt was gathering already. Cars and trucks pulling horse trailers lined up in the field. Elliott and Penelope waved to friends. "Help us with the horses, Elizabeth." He let down the back of the trailer and Sweetpea crashed out of the truck, tossing her head. I grabbed the halter.

"She's nervous," said Elliott. "Get on her and walk her around. It's only the second time out for her." I saddled her, and he boosted me up. She was a big, chestnut horse, a brood mare until six months ago. A horn sounded. Other horses and riders swarmed around us. Sweetpea tossed her head and pranced. I kept my knees in, my heels down, my hands down, and prayed. I prayed that I wouldn't get killed by my horse. I had no time to feel gauche and fat.

"At the back, Elizabeth," called out Elliott, when Sweetpea pranced to the front of the assembled horses. "Hill-toppers keep to the back."

At the back of the field of forty horses, Sweetpea pawed the ground. I walked her around in circles to calm her. Each time I stopped, she bounced sideways.

"Okay," ordered Elliott, "hill-toppers follow me. Keep back from the pack." The hunting horn sounded for the last time. The field of hunters galloped off after the barking hounds and the red-coated whip. We cantered behind. Sweetpea surged forward. She wanted to do some jumping. I tried to hold her back. I pulled on the reins. I yanked them desperately. Sweetpea was stronger than I was.

"Keep her back," shouted Elliott. "Behind me." I would have kept her back if I could. She weighed twelve hundred pounds. She careened across the stream after the hunt. She was trying to catch up with the field. Sweetpea wanted to be out in front. Elliott galloped after me frantically and pulled along side. "Ride her in a circle. Circle her, Elizabeth," he shouted. Sweetpea reared. I pulled her to the right to bring her around in a circle. She galloped madly to the right heading straight for the trees. At the edge of the woods, she stopped dead and I lurched ungracefully across her neck. Penelope cantered up beside me on her thoroughbred.

"We're changing horses, Elizabeth," she said calmly. "You ride Elliott's." Gratefully, I slid off Sweetpea and scrambled onto Elliott's horse, Sir Nigel, a seasoned polo player and hunter. Elliott got onto Sweetpea. Her neck was covered with foam. As soon as he was on, she calmed down. Horses can tell when you're inexperienced.

"Shorten your stirrups," said Elliott. I leaned over to do so.

"Look out," called out Penelope. "Heads up. Out of the way."

I looked up. The hounds had scented a fox in our direction. Forty horses were coming down on me at a gallop. First Sweetpea, now this. I was paralyzed. The end had come. Sir Nigel wasn't bothered. He trotted off to the side to let the hunt pass. Anyone can hunt if the horse is smart enough. I don't like hunting or killing, but by the end of the day, Sir Nigel had convinced me that "hunting" was a lovely sport. I spent four hours chasing across fields, stopping to talk when the hounds got lost.

"See that," called out Elliott once when we had gathered in the middle of a cornfield to try to find our hounds. "See that! A fox, a lovely red one." The hunt turned to watch the fox. The fox stopped to watch the hunt for a while before he loped across the field. "A beauty." The hounds were busy and by the time they were rounded up, the fox was long gone. In this hunt, foxes are chased but not killed. Their purpose is to give the hunt a direction to run. The Knowleses' hunt went out twice a week on the same land. The foxes seemed to know it was a lighthearted business. It was the cows that didn't like it. I was warned to always walk my horse through a field if it had a cow, so as not to upset the cow.

At two o'clock, we loaded the horses back in the vans and drove off to breakfast at the clubhouse, a log cabin on a lake. It was now surrounded by suburban houses, but once it had been in the middle of a farm. Breakfast was beef stew and buttermilk biscuits, and we sat around talking for the rest of the afternoon. I forgot about fishing. I felt saddlesore but I didn't feel fat. I had old, clumpy boots because I didn't have the money to spend on swank new ones. I wore a cheap, secondhand riding coat for the same reason. My money went for Lucy and the new house and I didn't have much left over. If I looked frumpy, then I looked frumpy, but no one cared. "Elizabeth, meet Chuck Forester," said Elliott, introducing a big man, built like a bull, who had joined our end of the table. "Chuck's a guest, too."

"That Sweetpea is one crazy horse. What were you trying to do, putting her up on that mare, Elliott?" He turned to me. "Does he have a life insurance policy out on you?" We laughed. "So what do you do?" he asked me later.

"I'm a doctor."

"What kind?" he asked, staccato.

"A plastic surgeon. And you?" I asked hastily. He was interrogating me like an attorney, and I was sensitive to that.

"A contractor. Married?"

"I'm divorced," I said slowly.

"Children?"

"Yes."

"How many?"

"Fifteen," I said quietly. He shouldn't have been prying into my life. His jaw dropped.

"You have fifteen children? How did you ever get through medical school?" he asked, awed. "Oh no, I can't buy that. You're lying to me." He chuckled.

"Yes, I only have one," I admitted.

"Boy or girl?"

"A girl. And you?"

"Three, grown-up. Do you date?" he demanded.

"Yes."

"Anyone special?"

"No."

"I might call you for a date if I feel like it."

"All right." I said slowly. I didn't like this. Was I a cement mixer to be contracted?

"What's the matter?" he said impatiently.

"I don't even know if you're single, for one thing," I said tentatively.

"No, I'm not." He seemed insulted and moved away. A chill settled over me. Were all men like this?

As I was leaving the club that afternoon, I chatted on the club steps with another man, a pleasant attorney. He didn't interrogate me, but somehow I learned he was widowed and he learned I was divorced. He walked me to my car. I drove home feeling triumphantly horsey and a social fledgling. I had made a beginning. My life as "a woman" had started up again — shakily, but it had started.

I was home at four. At five o'clock, the doorbell rang. It would be Lucy. I opened the door and took her into my arms. I had kept on my riding gear because it usually made her laugh. She was crying. My ex handed over the pink pillow without a word. As usual, he and I had nothing to say to each other. What was part of our marriage had all been said. What needed to be said now was best said by our lawyers. He left and got into his car.

"Close the door, Mummy, close the door," ordered Lucy. I closed it. Then I held her and rocked her and talked to her. Her visits had such a bad effect on her. The Wednesdays were the worst. I blamed myself for ever agreeing to them. I could blame my ex. I had no idea what happened once Lucy left me. But I felt the biggest damage was simply that she was being taken away. She needed, like any child, a safe, secure home. She had been forced away before she was a year old. It was unnatural. It was wrong.

She clung to me and I walked her around the house. "Cat," I said, pointing to her favorite picture. "Cat." She looked at me and tried to smile. She whimpered instead. I took her to her room. She looked around, sadly. I gave her the teddy bear and the pink pillow. She screamed with delight, bouncing excitedly in my arms. She was home. I undressed her and put her to bed, exhausted. I stayed awhile. She was fast asleep. I tiptoed out of the room.

Twenty minutes later, I heard her over the intercom. "Mummy? Mummy. Peese, Mummy. I scared," and she started to cry.

I ran to her room and held her and rocked her. For an hour, she stayed in my lap, clutching her pink pillow and sleeping or whimpering or looking at nothing with big, sad eyes. She no longer screamed all night — at least, not often. When, oh when, would this improve, and how much damage would it do to her in the meantime? And was there something more, something I didn't know? She fell asleep in my arms. Suddenly, in her sleep, she arched her back, twisted her head, and screamed. "Lucy, wake up. You're home now. You're with Mummy. Wake up." She woke up, looked at me in unseeing terror, and screamed and screamed, hitting me, kicking herself free in a frenzy. I couldn't hold her. She twisted and fought to get loose and scrambled to the floor, still screaming. She was too tired to stand. She sat down facing me, doubled her head over on her knees, and screamed.

"Lucy." I got up to get her.

"No! No! No!" She beat me away, her little arms flailing, and raising her face to me in anguish, she screamed.

"Lucy. Lucy," I said urgently. I sat down. "I'm not going to touch you, but listen to Mummy. Listen to me. Please listen. I love you." Her screaming increased violently as though to deny it. "I love you, Lucy. It's true. You're a good girl. Mummy loves you. Grandmother loves you. Mrs. Taylor loves you. Uncle Jimmy loves you." My voice choked as I talked. She had stopped screaming. She was looking at me, tears in her eyes, but she was listening. I wanted so much to protect my baby. I couldn't. I could only explain. "You're a good girl. Mummy loves you. Your daddy loves you too. You have to be with him." You're too young to go away so much, I thought, but I kept that to myself. "I love you, but you have to see your daddy. I don't want you to be unhappy, Lucy. I love you." I put my arm around her. "Understand?"

She looked at me for a long time. At last, she let me pick her up and rock her. She wasn't angry anymore but limp and fearful. And how could I explain this to a judge? If I were a judge, I would not believe what Lucy had lived through, but I knew Lucy was not alone. I was not the only divorced mother in Mayfair with an infant and court-ordered visitation. What Lucy was made to live with was unnatural. We needed guidelines, from people who knew enough about children to make the rules. I do not think judges, whose experience is largely in trial law, are the ones who should decide a child's fate. But until the system is changed, a mother can only guard her child from harm as best she can.

That Tuesday morning, I sat in Mr. Blackstone's office to be instructed on the trial. "Preparation will take a while," he began. "I asked them to send up Cokes and sandwiches. Is that all right?"

"Certainly."

He took out a pen and a pad of paper. "Now, the first question will be your name."

"Okay."

"Tell me your name," insisted Mr. Blackstone. "Answer just as you will tomorrow."

"I'm sorry. Jean Elizabeth Morgan."

"Where do you live?"

I gave the address.

"The judge doesn't know you. By my questions, I am telling him who you are and what you are. We want him to believe you, so that what you have to say about Lucy as her mother will help him decide what is in Lucy's best interest. Do you work?"

"Yes."

"What do you do?"

"I'm a doctor."

"Good. Do you have a specialty?"

"I'm a plastic surgeon."

"Do you have a child?"

"Yes."

"What is her name. And" — he looked up — "I want her full name, including her father's last name. A lot of mothers won't say their husband's name on the witness stand, and judges don't like it."

We worked on through lunch and into the afternoon, going step by step through my life over the past two years.

"Why did you move from your old home?"

I hesitated. Why had we really moved? "It was too small and not very safe. I couldn't get a baby-sitter to come. It was on a main street and dangerous for a child. There were no parks, no playgrounds, no churches, no other children."

"Where did you move to?"

I said the address.

Mr. Blackstone looked up and waited and waited.

"Oh, I'm sorry." I added the state. He smiled. "That's why we go through this. It's important. Describe your new home, please."

I was at a loss. "It's a brick townhouse, do you mean?"

"No. I mean that you moved for certain reasons — size, safety, et cetera. Is your new house large enough, safe . . . do you see?"

"Yes, my new home is large enough and safe. We have Mrs. Taylor, who comes to look after Lucy. It is off the street in a development. There are five parks and two playgrounds within a half a mile."

"Does Lucy have friends?"

"Yes."

"Name them, please."

"Well, there's Maria and George and the little Andrios boy, Michael and Carol and the twins and Susie and —"

Mr. Blackstone held up a hand. "Does she actually see all these children?" he asked in wonder.

"Every day. They have lunch together in each other's homes, and go out to lunch at the local cafés, and go to the zoo, and they visit each other's patios."

"And they are her own age? And they all live in Mayfair?"

"Oh, yes. They're all between two and three."

"Quite a busy life being a child at Mayfair Place. I like that. The judge will like that." He grinned. "If I knew nothing about where your ex lives, I would still bet he couldn't produce ten playmates the same age in the space of a city block." He nodded his approval and went on.

At six we took a break. I had been planning to meet a date for a drink at six-thirty. This was not the contractor — who never called — nor the attorney, who did, but a man I had met at a show with some friends. My social life, once I started, seemed prepared to flourish. I was pleased and surprised to be somewhat in demand. I had to call my date to tell him I was held up.

"I may be as late as seven-thirty," I warned him.

"I've got *Barron's* to read and lots of time."

Mr. Blackstone looked at me sternly when I hung up. "You are making a date the night before your trial?" He changed to a smile. "Good girl. One of the first things I told you was not to let this disrupt your life."

Just before seven-thirty we finished. At eight-thirty the next morning, my mother and I arrived in the basement cafeteria of the courthouse. Mr. Blackstone stepped forward to greet us. "We're number two," he said. "That means we may not be heard. It means a lot of waiting. I want to be sure you have breakfast. Don't go to a trial hungry." After breakfast, the three of us sat on one side of the hearing room all morning, waiting. My ex and his family filed in and sat on the other side. My mother read a murder mystery. I read my own deposition. Mr. Blackstone read my ex's deposition. At one o'clock, we had lunch. Mr. Blackstone stretched wearily in the cafeteria. "We may not get heard today if they don't have a judge. It looked promising this morning, but I have my doubts now." My mother looked at me anxiously.

"It's fine with me," I said. "I am sure I am going to say the wrong thing and ruin Lucy's life. I wouldn't mind if this were put off until 1990."

"Six months maybe. But not six years," said Mr. Blackstone, smiling.

"I don't suppose that as a lawyer you like to read for relaxation?" asked my mother over coffee in the cafeteria.

"I do!" protested Mr. Blackstone. A gleam I had never seen came into his eye. "Shakespeare, of course. But Dickens is my favorite. Do you read Dickens?"

"Oh yes!" said my mother.

"*Nicholas Nickleby* is good," he said.

"*Little Dorrit*," countered my mother.

"*A Tale of Two Cities*, of course."

"*Great Expectations?*"

For the next hour they argued the merits of Dickens's novels. I listened. I had read several of Dickens's novels. I remembered little about them. My mother had the mind of a scholar. So did Mr. Blackstone. They had a wonderful time.

At three-thirty the court clerk told us we had no judge. Mr. Blackstone and the other attorney agreed to a new trial date a month away.

"You have done nothing all day," Mr. Blackstone told us. "Go home and do nothing. You will be exhausted."

"I know it's discouraging," said my mother on the way home.

"Not for me," I protested, but I felt myself begin to worry afresh about the next trial date.

Later that evening, Jim got back from New York. His face

looked drawn and tired. "How did it go?" was his first remark.

"Postponed. There was no judge to hear us. What about you?"

"Well. Have you had dinner? I'm starved."

"Jimmy!"

"I want to tell you about it but —"

"Jimmy, please," said my mother beseechingly. "Tell us the news."

"Well, I've been talking. I talked Monday, Tuesday, and Wednesday. I practically went to the president. The result is, I start with Cartwright in New York in a week."

"Jimmy!" My mother hugged and kissed him. I hugged and kissed him. Lucy flung her arms around his knees and clamored for a kiss too. "What a relief, Jim. No wonder you look tired," I said.

"You'd better believe it. It was only my whole life."

"Tell us all about it," said my mother.

"Tell me! Tell me!" urged Lucy, climbing up his knee to sit on his lap. I produced a bottle of champagne I had bought and saved for a special occasion. Jim deserved all the lucky breaks he got. He worked for his good luck. For many years all he had was rotten breaks.

The next day, Angie Morton, a friend I had met at a lunch, called me. She was a consultant. She had an airy manner and dressed to match it. Layers of scarves and skirts floated around her like a cloud.

"Elizabeth, Angie here. Remember me?" She had a soft, sultry voice that floated like her chiffon scarves. "My consulting work keeps me so busy, but I have a request from a dear friend. Does the name Roger Peters ring a bell, dear? He met you years ago at some function and fell madly in love. He was crushed when you married and was thrilled when I told him at a little soiree I gave last week that you were free. This man worships the ground you tread on. Now he's a dear, sensitive soul, but he would be charmed if you would come to a little dinner he is giving." I hesitated. Men worshiping the ground I walked on was lovely, but it sounded too good to be true. There had to be a catch.

"I'd love to come, but should I know him? I don't remember the name."

"He didn't think you'd remember."

"Is he very very old?" I wondered if he might be senile and confined to a wheelchair in a nursing home, but then he wouldn't be able to give dinner parties.

"No, no, no," cooed Angie. "Older than you by a fair bit, but handsome and very distinguished. What day?"

We settled on a Friday. Lucy had heard the doubt in my voice and looked at me anxiously when I hung up.

"Mummy? Okay?"

"Lucy, it's okay." I picked her up. "Mummy is going to a party."

"Party? Me party too!" She scrambled down and rummaged in her toy drawer for a colored paper hat that Jim had given her. When the phone rang again, it was Rob. His voice was far from anxious. It was firm, resonant, and smug. Erica Morgan had just been born after an easy, four-hour labor.

"She what?" I protested. "Janice was in labor for only four hours? It's not fair. When can we see her?" Erica was born at a hospital that had very limited visiting hours for new mothers. We set out after dinner. Jim carried Lucy from the parking lot. Mother and I dealt with the presents. My mother's face had taken on a tight, set look. Jim glanced at her.

"Worried?"

"Naturally."

"About Dad?"

"Of course."

"Maybe he won't be here," I said hopefully.

Jim cast me a look of scorn. "Of course Dad will be there." I tucked my arm around my mother. It would all be superficially friendly, which made it no less painful. We got off the elevator and headed down the corridor to Janice's room. Rob and Janice were there with the heavenly glow that envelopes a new parent. We crowded around Janice's bed to ask about the baby. My father was there, as we expected. I looked at Janice. She was quite unaware of anyone except Rob, who was gazing proudly at her. My mother was asking about her labor when a nurse came in. "Oh!" — the nurse gave a disapproving squeak and shuddered at the sight of Lucy. "No children allowed. Get her out of here immediately. Out to the end of the hall. And the babies are in view in the nursery now."

"Lucy, let's go see your cousin," said Jim. He took her out of my arms. "Come with Uncle Jimmy." Laughing and happy, she trotted beside him.

"I'll take her," I said. I came out into the hall after them. Jim tried to shoo me away.

"I want to see Baby Erica," I protested.

"Baby Erica?" asked Lucy.

"We're all coming," said my mother. "Erica is the star turn." All seven of us trooped down the hall.

The nursery had a plate-glass window with the curtain pulled aside.

"Bassinet six," said Janice. "I do think she's awfully sweet." Erica was a smaller baby than Lucy had been. She lay on her back in a blanket, pretty and peaceful, asleep with a gentle smile. We held Lucy up so she could see her.

"Babies. Babies. Babies!" said Lucy with delight. "Baby Ericas."

"One Baby Erica," explained Jim. "See. That one." He pointed.

"Hello, Baby Erica," said Lucy. "Pretty."

Janice beamed. A compliment from a child is a true compliment and Erica was truly pretty. Unlike most newborn babies, including Lucy, she did not look like Winston Churchill or George Schultz. I was glad for Rob and Janice and glad for

Lucy too. She was thrilled. She stayed glued to the window, talking to the world about "my Baby Erica."

"Do you have someone to look after her?" Jim asked Rob.

"Not yet." A fleeting look of worry crossed Janice's face.

"We'll find someone," said Rob. "No problem, sweetie." We walked Janice back to her room.

"The first one you hire won't work out, whatever happens," I told Janice. "They never do; you simply have to accept that. Sooner or later it falls into place." I remembered my hysteria two years before when I hadn't had someone to look after Lucy. I had made so many mistakes.

"Elizabeth, if we are left in the lurch," began Janice.

"Of course you can leave her with us. If it's okay with Mrs. Taylor, it's fine with me. We'd be happy to help."

She smiled her thanks and under Rob's anxious eye climbed back into bed with the triumph of the new mother. I hadn't realized how important Erica would be to Lucy. She talked about her all week and from then on scarcely a week went by without a visit to "my Baby Erica." Lucy had much insecurity to cope with. In Erica, who could neither walk, talk, nor drink from a cup, Lucy had found the only human she could feel infinitely superior to and protective of.

Lucy enjoyed helping me dress for the dinner party with Roger Peters and Angie Morton. She had come to understand that I sometimes went out in the evening. I tried to arrange my social life so that I went out when Lucy was away. It didn't always work. If my mother or Mrs. Taylor was not free to baby-sit, I didn't go out. Lucy was too afraid of being abandoned for me to leave her with anyone else. Tonight, it was my mother who would baby-sit. Lucy was sure I would forget my shoes.

"Shoes, Mummy," she said while I put in my curlers. Lucy tried to fit a left tennis shoe onto my right foot.

"Shoe, Mummy," and she lugged out my riding boots. Then she settled in for the ritual.

"Dipstick, Mummy, peese." I gave her a dab of lipstick.

"Pfoom, Mummy, peese." I gave her a squirt of cologne. "Power for my nose, Mummy, peese." I dabbed the powder. "More, peese, Mummy, peese."

"That's all," I said after the last dab. I kissed her good-bye. Her sticky fingers left a mark on my left shoulder. All my dresses had marks on the left shoulder from her affectionate clutch. I left in search of Roger Peters's house. I was invited for seven. I arrived at seven-fifteen. His was a weathered brick mansion in the heart of millionaire country. I had a happy fantasy of being married to this man of colossal wealth who worshiped the ground I walked on. I marched up the walk, which was lined with fragrant, old boxwoods clipped into squares, and rang the bell. A butler let me in. He led me up the carpeted stairway to a large drawing room. The rug was pale yellow and spotless. The long draperies and valances were pale green. Ornate mirrors covered some of the walls. Antique bookshelves lined the rest. The room was empty.

"A drink, madam?" asked the butler, standing by a drinks tray.

"Please. Do you have white wine?"

He nodded graciously and opened a bottle. The wine was presented with a small linen napkin on a silver tray.

"Mr. Peters is late. He will be down in a moment," the butler informed me and left the room. I sipped the wine. It was very good. I put it down. Where was the rest of the alleged dinner party? I was obviously expected. I would have to leave if this turned out to be a dinner alone with the elusive Mr. Peters. I strolled to the bookcase to inspect the contents. A title caught my eye. His books were peculiar to an extreme degree. I began to remember this man. How could I forget him? He had introduced himself at a fundraiser, brought me a drink, told me succinctly about his business and family, and, seriously, asked me to marry him. I had turned him down. After my disastrous marriage ended, I had often wondered if I had been wrong. This was my chance to find out.

The doorbell rang again. A moment later, Angie Morton floated in on a wave of pink chiffon, followed by the butler and her escort. Then came Mr. Peters. He was as I remembered him — handsome, intelligent, gallant, and oozing wealth. I knew why I had turned him down. I had been right. My memory assaulted me like a battering ram. This man lived for himself. I knew why he had been interested in me. He collected women. He had never had a surgeon in his menagerie. I was an interesting mutant.

"So kind of you to come, Dr. Morgan. May I call you Elizabeth?" He kissed my hand and, letting it go, gazed deep into my eyes. I felt, despite his gallantry, that he despised me.

"Yes, you may."

Angie and her chiffon settled like a cloud of butterflies on the sofa next to me. Her perfect complexion and the graceful shape of her face made her lovely. The heavy, carefully modulated voice and the ever-active, expressive eyes were distracting. I couldn't decide if she was a successful actress playing a rich woman or a rich woman playing a successful actress.

"Darling, so good to see you." She kissed me. "Elizabeth is so busy. So good of her to come. I've been busy too. Roger, dear, you'll be interested. You know all about houses. I'm buying another house, dear. Costa del Sol. Isn't that marvelous! I spent all day on the transatlantic phone. Gigi, you know, is managing it all for me. What would I do without her?"

"Ah yes. I met her at Ascot last year," said Roger Peters. "We were with the Royal party. Beautiful ears. I remember her ears. And the largest hat I've ever seen."

Their conversation flowed on like a river, wending its way across titles and gold prices and the problem of the fifth house and the latest Sotheby's auction. I felt gauche. I expected to feel gauche. These were not my kind of people. I smiled. I said "Oh really?" and "How interesting" when Angie or Roger turned to me for approval. After fifteen minutes, I began to wonder. Were they trying to impress me? Impossible. I was not important enough to try to impress. Were they trying to impress each other? Doubtful. Or did they just enjoy talking like this? I didn't care. I was intensely bored. I could have been home with Lucy. I could have been with friends. I had had to turn down another date because of this. Their talk turned to salmon fishing on Scottish estates and the virtues of the Rolls-Royce. I said "marvelous" and "fabulous." I felt phony. My face muscles ached. I tried to relax. I would be polite, have dinner, and leave. I would be polite. My mother had taught me to be polite. They were rich and they could behave like this. I would be polite and leave.

"So, did you by chance glance over my books?" Mr. Peters asked me. "I have some very rare first editions."

"You most certainly do," I said emphatically. "Could anyone miss them?" It was true. He displayed the books so people would notice. Still, I sounded a rude, jarring note. I reminded myself to be polite. There was a tiny pause.

"Oh, darling. Everyone knows about those," said Angie.

Mr. Peters shrugged. "One of my various collections. I'm sure you don't remember me, Elizabeth, do you? I have the clearest memory of where I met you. I cherish it."

"I remember you extremely well," I said with a little laugh. "You bought me a glass of wine and asked me to marry you." Angie Morton's bright, expressive smile froze on her face. Her escort gazed at me. Roger Peters took a deep breath and a little sip of wine. "It was a very good party," I said desperately.

How could I say such things? I floundered, blushing, trying to say something to extricate myself. My babbling was interrupted. Angie's escort spoke, for the first time that evening, saving me.

After my faux pas, I expected Roger Peters to ignore me completely. It had the reverse effect. He gazed at me and spoke only to me. Clearly, he had thought he had found in me an unusual parrot, only to discover that I was a great auk — less attractive perhaps, but rarer and worthy of collection. I listened to him discourse on investments, golf, China, and President Mitterand.

"Dinner is served," announced the butler. We were led into a formal dining room. Roger seated me and sat down next to me. "I hope you don't mind," he began. "I have returned from Tibet. Dinner tonight is Tibetan." I lived over a Chinese restaurant for two years. After that, I didn't care for steamed food and rice. As I sat down, it seemed that all the food around me was steamed and ricy. I ate my food and listened to him discourse on his travels. I was a perfect listener. To atone for my earlier rudeness, I ate all my rice like a good girl.

⇒ *eleven*

W E'RE GOING to miss you, Jim," said my mother, coming through the door with a tray of cookies.

"Oh, Mother!" we said joyfully, like schoolchildren. It was almost midnight. Lucy was asleep. Jim was packing. He would be leaving for New York in the morning.

"Elizabeth!" He tossed me four cans of shoe polish. "Anywhere you find a spot." He cheerfully shoved a recalcitrant rain parka into a suitcase crammed with paperback books. His approach to packing resembled mine. He straightened up. "Time for a break." We settled down to the cookies.

"I hope things go all right for you in New York," said my mother with a smile and a tinge of anxiety. "After all, you are my only eldest son." It was a family joke.

Jimmy patted her head. "I'll be fine, but if I can't work the dishwasher, I promise I'll bring all my dirty dishes home to you." He stood up and stretched. "Back to work. I'd like to be on the road by six and beat the traffic." I glanced at my mother. Staying up late made her wilt.

"I'm staying to help," she announced.

"Sure," said Jim, "and I'm going to bed to let you do all the work. You can either go to bed, Mother, or I'll carry you."

She hugged us and, laughing, let us shoo her to bed.

"I wish I could be here for the big day of the trial, kid," Jim said later. "Not that there is much I can do to help." He was packing his work clothes now — suits, ties, and white shirts.

He wouldn't let me touch them. They were precious. He folded each one precisely. There was a squawk over the intercom. Lucy had woken up.

"Juice," she said loudly in a sleepy voice. "Cookie. Nice cookie." There was a rustle of pillows, a thump, and silence. I went to her room to check her. She was fast asleep, with a little smile, dreaming, no doubt, of cookies. I watched her sleep in the moonlight. Without Jimmy, I would still have been with Ms. Jones. I knew that Lucy needed me. Now that I had Mr. Blackstone to protect me, I couldn't possibly lose custody. Or could I? I wasn't an unfit mother. The idea rankled, but I knew my ex. Mr. Blackstone didn't. My ex was a very, very clever, a very, very determined man. In his way, he was a genius. I forced myself to face the truth. Mr. Blackstone, with all his talent, might still not be able to handle him. Truth is fragile. I had always tended to be naive. If the judge believed me, I would keep Lucy. If not — I shivered at the thought and went back to help Jim pack.

He tossed me some shoes. "Having Mr. Blackstone really helped, didn't it?" he said in satisfaction. "You were jangled. You were getting Mother jangled. Lucy was getting jangled watching the two of you and I was getting jangled watching the three of you. Now I feel I can go to New York with peace of mind. You've got a Protector."

"It will be hard for you at first in New York. Let us help you, too." I had mother and Lucy with me and the three of us had a growing circle of friends. Jim was going to be completely on his own and under pressure to produce results, fast, for his firm.

At two his car was packed. He was gone in the morning before anyone else was awake.

"Uncle Dinny?" asked Lucy at breakfast.

"Uncle Jimmy is in New York," I explained to her. I showed her New York on a map. I pointed to Jim's new address.

"Dere's Uncle Dinny," she said happily, hitting Central Park with her cereal spoon.

Jim called at eleven. He had arrived. A new era in his life had begun.

The coming trial haunted me. It cast a shadow on my life. I felt hexed. The week approached. Then the day. I was to meet with Mr. Blackstone the day before the trial. Once again, he would go over every question and every answer. On the way to his office, I felt an oppression I couldn't bear. I felt trapped. I needed a peace of mind that no one could give me. On an impulse, I turned off the highway and drove to our church.

The church was cool and dark and quiet. I knelt down, but I couldn't pray. I didn't know what to pray for. Was it wrong for me to fight to keep my child? Did life have to be like this, ugly and quarrelsome? What was life, anyhow? I felt like driftwood. I prayed for help for myself, for Lucy, for her father, for all of us. A trapdoor in the middle of the aisle was pushed up. A workman climbed out.

"They say this place is haunted," he said with an uncertain guffaw. He peered down at someone in the cellar. "How much cable do we need?" He listened, turned, and tramped down the aisle. He didn't see me at first. Then he jumped, murmured an apology, and hurried by. He didn't distract me. Life had made no sense when I went in to pray. It still made no sense, but I felt more peaceful. I had done my best. I had done what I thought was right. It was all I could do. I prepared myself to face the worst. I drove to Mr. Blackstone's office.

"Ready?" He sat me down and spread out his papers. "Preparing for trial is like dress rehearsal for a show that may be canceled. We may go tomorrow, or we may not be heard for months. There simply aren't enough judges. We have to assume we will go. We'll do exactly what we did last time. It won't take as long."

At four, the court clerk called. "How does it look?" Mr. Blackstone asked eagerly. His face fell. "We are the second case up," he explained to me, hanging up the phone. "That means we're on call. It's easier on you than last time. You wait here in my office until the court calls us down. Unless something unexpected happens, I don't think we'll be heard. There's only one judge free, and two trials before ours." It wasn't what I had prayed for. I had prayed for nothing tangible. Still, it was a reprieve. If I was destined to lose Lucy, I had this much more time with her. Her life and mine were beyond my control. I couldn't think about losing her.

"All set?" Mr. Blackstone asked me the morning of the trial when we arrived at his office. My mother, loyal as ever, had come along. Lucy and Mrs. Taylor, Carol and Mrs. Lane had gone to the zoo. "What are you reading?" Mr. Blackstone asked. He inspected my clutch of books with a smile. "Dickens? That's progress. Your mother and I will educate you yet." He escorted us to a spare office and left us to ourselves. I sat down to read. My beeper went off. I called Beverly at the office.

"The ER needs to talk with you, Elizabeth. I have a few questions and a few calls for you." I took notes. I made my calls. My practice posed a problem. It kept growing. Like a tree, a practice either grew or died. I had to let it grow. I had the mortgage. I had Lucy's expenses. I had legal bills. It was hard to take an hour off. I didn't mind working the weekends when Lucy was away. The weekends with her were precious. My mornings and evenings with her were precious too. Solo practice and being a single, self-supporting mother seemed to be like oil and water. They didn't mix. Two years before, I had thought I could manage. I had managed, swaying perpetually between what I owed my patients and what I owed my child. For two years, I had controlled it, but there seemed to be no more elastic in the system. My practice soaked up time like a sponge and the older Lucy grew, the more she needed me. After my last phone call, I sat gazing out of the window.

"Elizabeth," said my mother. I turned to face her.

"Mother, I know what you are going to say."

"You know, my dear, but you don't know. You have struggled very hard to get where you are. There are rewards in private practice. You help people and in return you have status and money."

"I've needed that money," I said defensively. "Mr. Blackstone isn't for free."

"Of course not, but if you continue along this frenetic path, in twenty years —" She stopped.

I was afraid of what I might become in the years ahead — successful but tough, too busy for life because I insisted on being that way. We had grown up rather poor. I had always wanted success. I had worked to be what I was. But now hadn't I proved myself, to myself? Didn't I need a new route in life, perhaps less ambitious, but more content? I would do that for Lucy. But what if I lost custody? The thought flitted across my mind like a ghost. I knew the answer. The loss of my child would change me forever. I couldn't predict what it would do.

"Your residency burned up a lot of your health, Elizabeth," my mother went on. "Your marriage and this lawsuit are taking more. You're not indestructible. And what happens to Lucy if you get sick? What if you die of a heart attack like so many overworked doctors? What if you're in a car accident, coming back from an emergency at two AM? Who raises Lucy then? How can you make friends leading the life you lead? There is no time."

I gritted my teeth. The problem made me feel irritable. I had never faced it matter-of-factly.

"So what are my options, Mother? Part-time practice won't work. It won't pay my expenses. I could take an academic job." Even as I said it, I knew it was impractical. Surgical professors have to move as new opportunities arise. Lucy, my mother, and

I all needed stability. We would never get it if I were in a job in Chicago this year and in San Francisco the next. Besides, feuds between professors tend to make academic life bitter and quarrelsome.

"I could give it all up and become a lawyer," I went on. "I'm getting lots of on-the-job training."

"Do you have the money to do it?"

"I could go to night school."

"And not see Lucy for three years? I thought you wanted more time with her, not less."

I sighed. She was right. Besides, I liked being a doctor. I didn't want to be a lawyer.

My mother spoke next. "Now is not the time, but in the long run you need to change your life."

"It means giving up a lot," I said. Perhaps I had become a poor example for Lucy. I didn't want her to live the way I lived now, but how was she to know if I didn't show her?

My mother shrugged. "At your age, your father and I had almost nothing, not even a house. Did it hurt you to grow up poor?"

"It was good for me."

"You've got plenty, now," said my mother.

I agreed. I could cut my practice, or I could find a salaried job. It took me two seconds more to see the obvious: most of all, I needed less emergency call. I couldn't think of anyone offhand who would take my ER call. Still, some surgeons thrive on emergency work. I took out the on-call roster from my purse and started at the top. The first call was brief. I hung up, feeling dazed.

"No luck?" asked my mother.

"He'd love to take it. He'll start next month. And honestly, Mother, it's easier than I say it is. All I have to do is to take half a day off, the way lots of doctors do. I don't have to work this hard." My most urgent problem — not having enough time —

melted like snow in the sun. Less work meant less money, but it meant more time to be with Lucy. As long as I paid my bills, I would be satisfied.

Later, Mr. Blackstone looked in on us. "I'm sorry you've had to waste another day."

"It hasn't been wasted." I smiled. "We've been planning my future."

"Good. We're not going to get our trial heard today, obviously. That gets us into the summer." He took out his calendar. We agreed on the next date for the trial. It was three months away. I turned to my mother. "Now you can go to England to see Aunt Nicky."

She gave a little start. "So I can. I was going to wait until after the trial."

"Go next week," I suggested.

"When was your last vacation, Elizabeth?" demanded Mr. Blackstone.

"Two years ago."

"Are you taking one this year?"

"No, I don't think I can afford it." It was an automatic response. Of course I could take time off.

"I want you to take a vacation," said Mr. Blackstone. "Not healthy to work all the time. Your daughter needs you. Take a week at least. I'll be disappointed if you don't." He walked us to the elevator, a good man as well as a good lawyer.

We got home to find Cynthia Danvers on the patio with Mrs. Taylor and Lucy. Cynthia was letting Lucy take her by the hand. "Pimming pool," she was telling Cynthia, urging her into the inflatable plastic swimming pool I had bought her. "My pimming pool. Get in! Taer, get in." Lucy then saw me and ran over triumphantly. "Mummy! Get in! Get in! Peese, Mummy!" She knew her victim. To her delight, I took off my shoes and waded in.

"See what children do to you, Cynthia?" I protested.

"Sit down, Mummy!" I had reached my limit. Clothes were too expensive. I gathered her up in my arms and we all wandered indoors.

"I didn't really come to play," explained Cynthia, tossing back her mane of blond curls. Lucy studied her and tried to do the same. "The club's giving a reception this Sunday for all members. Can you come?" She turned to my mother. "Would you come?" I was grateful to her for including my mother. I did have nice friends. Lucy would be away and I was busy Saturday but not Sunday. I accepted. My mother, pleased to be asked, couldn't come. She was having lunch with some friends.

The club reception was held in a beautiful old home, not far from, but even more exclusive than, Roger Peters's. French windows from the vast dining room led out onto a formal lawn and garden. We were a cheerful group of women, some alone, some with husbands and dates. I had decided to come alone. I didn't know many men who would feel happy as part of a women's club. I made new friends that afternoon. I saw friends from previous meetings. We sipped wine and ate strawberries as the sun sank slowly in the west. Cynthia, a practiced hostess, saw that everyone was introduced to everyone else. One of her guests was an athletic, sunburned, outdoorsy man.

"So you're a doctor, are you?" he began genially. "I'm in oil and gas."

"Have another strawberry," I suggested.

"If you'll join me." He seemed a very nice man — witty, amusing, and fun. He was also kind and had impeccable manners. I liked him. He seemed to like me. After a while, we were leaning against the wall, eating more strawberries and joking, content to let the rest of the party float by us.

"Hi!" A friendly older club member joined us. She looked a pleasant extrovert. I wished she would go away. In a moment, she had told us about how her daughter was to be the school valedictorian. We congratulated her.

"So!" She turned to me briefly. "Enough of me and mine. Do you have any children?"

"Yes." The very nice man I had been talking to looked surprised and dismayed. Politely, leaving us to talk of our children, he drifted away into the crowd. For one mad moment, I wanted to grab his arm and say, "Just wait. I am divorced. I have one child! And she's darling!" but he was gone. I minded more than I should have for an acquaintance of ten minutes.

I called Cynthia later to congratulate her on her reception. "Elizabeth? I am so glad you called. My godmother is giving a charity ball," Cynthia explained breathlessly. "She wants me to make up a singles table. In two days! It is this Friday. Can you come?" I could. The ball started late. Lucy would be asleep by the time I left. Cynthia and I went together since we lived so close. It began as an unpromising evening. We arrived in the pouring rain. I met her other guests as we shed raincoats and dripped water in the foyer. There were eight women. Six men had arrived.

"Henry and John are coming, they said," announced Cynthia as we idled our way into the ballroom and down a buffet line overflowing with smoked salmon and raspberries.

"We hope not," replied one of the other men gallantly. John arrived once we sat down. The men went in search of drinks and the band began to play. I felt transported to a romantic era, when the men were rich and handsome, the women pampered and lovely. I was having fun.

"Henry! Over here!" called out Cynthia, waving a napkin over her head at a lone man in the entrance to the ballroom. He was the last to arrive. I was talking to a man in banking when Cynthia interrupted us, tapping her ring on a glass.

"We're all here now. Has everyone met? Henry, you know Philippe, you know Susan and Andy. This is Elizabeth . . ." Cynthia went smoothly around the table. The ballroom was dark. When Henry was introduced to me, his eyes flickered as though I puzzled him. He was trying to place me. I tried to place him. He was the outdoorsy man from the reception.

"What is that song?" said Cynthia, tapping her foot to the music when we sat down again.

" 'Sweet Little Sixteen.' Chuck Berry," I responded promptly. Everyone laughed. In school I had lived for rock and roll.

"You don't jitterbug, do you?" asked Henry incredulously, turning to me.

"Do I jitterbug? Did I wear bobby socks and crinolines?" We all stood up and shook ourselves out into couples to dance. I hadn't done the jitterbug for years, but what you learn at ten, you learn forever. I had a lot more practice that evening. The ball ended at midnight. Cynthia and I rolled home, footsore and rain-soaked. "My feet!" She pulled off her shoes in the car. "Agony, but wasn't it glorious?" She stretched like a cat. "If Henry were to ask me for your number, would you mind if I gave it to him?"

"No, I wouldn't mind."

"I thought not," she chuckled in the dark.

Lucy was asleep in my mother's room when I got home. She slept there if I went out late. That way she would not wake up and find herself alone. I picked her up quietly and tiptoed downstairs with her to my room. Her head rolled against my shoulder. I put her down on her bed in my room and went to bed.

"Mummy?" Lucy woke up suddenly. There was a little quiver in her voice that meant she was afraid.

"Mummy's here. Go to sleep, Lucy." She gave a little, happy chuckle and fell asleep.

That weekend started my emergency call for the month. My first call came at two AM the next night.

"Elizabeth? This is Jed Baron in the ER. I have got a kid who ran into a plate-glass window. He smashed his ankle and cut all the extensor tendons in his hand. I have to take him to the OR tonight for his ankle. Can you come in to do his hand?" The tendons could wait — a day, two days, even five. But there was no reason to put the injured boy to sleep twice for surgery when Jed Baron's operation and mine could be done at one time.

"Sure. See you soon." Lucy stirred in her sleep. She would wake up crying if I left her alone. I looked at the clock. My eyes had grown accustomed to the dark. With an effort, I got out of my bed. My body didn't like it. It felt weary, everywhere.

"This is insane," I started to say to myself as I dressed. "This is insane. What you could do, single, you can't do now. When mother is in England, what then? Take Lucy to Rob and Janice in the middle of the night?" I had lived like this for years and I hadn't seen that it couldn't work, in the long run. Then I remembered. I had done something about it. This was my last full stint in the ER. I smiled. Lucy whimpered again. I picked her up, all warm in her pink quilt.

"Mummy has to go to work, dear. You're going to sleep with Grandmother again. Okay?" She made a little sound, put her head on my shoulder, and was asleep again before we got upstairs to my mother's room.

An hour and a half later, under the bright lights of the OR, I tried to sort out a jumble of tendons. Seven years earlier, just out of residency, I had quaked when I saw such injuries. Experience does a lot. It wasn't routine for my patient, but it was for me. The tourniquet went up. That stopped the hemorrhage from the wrist. He had cut no arteries but he was a muscular boy. The cut veins poured blood out like water from a faucet. I mopped the blood and clots away from the wound. The scrub nurse held hooks in the skin, pulling the skin aside so I could see into the depths.

"I have to count aloud or I'll get confused," I explained to Jed, who was operating on the ankle. "Does it bother you?"

"Count away. I'm just irrigating the joint," he replied.

"Tunnel one is intact. Tunnel two —" I inspected the tendons in their fibrous envelopes in the wrist. "Cut. Tunnel three — cut. Tunnel four — cut. . . ." There were eight cut tendons. I had to find sixteen cut ends. Methodically I put a suture through each cut tendon in the hand. That was the easy part. Then I found its matching end. That was harder. The ends here had pulled back into the arm. I worked slowly. I was tired and it was difficult to concentrate. Talking aloud made me concentrate. I worked steadily across the wrist until all the tendons were identified and sutures placed loosely. Then, I double-checked that I had sutured the right tendon ends together. I had made no mistakes. I tied down the sutures. I checked the tendons again. I sewed up the skin. I put on the cast. Jed Baron was finishing his work on the ankle at the same time. I breathed a sigh of relief. The end was in sight. I would soon be home.

The intercom buzzed. "Dr. Morgan, they need you in the ER." I groaned, but it was only to be expected. At seven, when finally I got home, my mother and Lucy were getting up. I had to sleep. I was worn out. It meant missing my time with Lucy, but perhaps for the last time.

"We'll go and see Erica while you sleep," said my mother. "You go to bed. You're tired."

Lucy came over and took my hand. "Go to bed, Mummy. Mummy tired." Importantly she tried to lead me upstairs, just the way that every night I walked her up to bed. "Tuck in," she commanded me as I lay down. "I kiss you night night." She kissed me and closed the door. She was my delight. My marriage and every moment of trouble since was worth having her.

"I'm going to England very happy," said my mother that night. "You and Jim and Rob are all doing so well. As for your father . . ." she didn't finish her sentence.

"All is quiet on the western front. It's the best to hope for, Mother." She nodded. She had decided to go to England on standby. The vagaries of the trial date had prevented her from being able to reserve ahead at a discount. The flight left in the evening in the middle of the week. Lucy and I took her to the airport after I got home from work.

"Lucy, kiss Grandmother good-bye. Grandmother is going to England, in an airplane." Lucy ran to the airport window.

"Mummy, look! Nairplane!" A plane had landed and passengers were disembarking the old-fashioned way. They walked down steps from the plane door to the ground. "Grandmother and Nicky in Ningland in nairplane," Lucy informed a surprised Chinese boy standing next to her, also studying the airplane. She ran back to me. "Mummy, I want nairplane too." Laughing, I picked her up. The standbys were about to be called, but Pan Am was full. There was no standby seating. Frantically we ran to the far end of the airport. The British Airways flight had room. Two minutes before takeoff, we waved my mother onto the plane.

I took Mr. Blackstone's advice and took a week off to be with Lucy. We went to the zoo and she came home trying to be a gorilla. We splashed in the pool. I set up a playroom for her in the basement. I took her shopping. Young as she was, we were close to each other and we had fun the whole time.

"Mummy?" Lucy asked one Thursday morning out of the blue. "Grandmother in Ningland? Grandmother go 'way?"

"She'll be back, dear."

"Uncle Dinny in Ningland?"

"No. Uncle Jimmy is in New York."

"Uncle Dinny go 'way?"

"Yes. But he will come to visit us."

She seemed puzzled. "Baby Erica go 'way?"

"No."

"Uncle Wob go 'way?"

"No."

"Aunt Dance go 'way?"

"No."

She sat thinking. She looked at me sideways through her hair. "Mummy go 'way?"

"No, Mummy stays here."

"Me go 'way?"

"No. You'll stay here. You go away to visit Daddy but you come home here. Always." I hope, I added to myself . . . if Mr. Blackstone succeeds . . . if a judge lets you. She cheered up and we went down to breakfast. I called my mother in England and let Lucy talk to her. It reassured her, but I knew she was still upset. She thought everyone was leaving her. She felt abandoned. I didn't know how to help her.

Jim called me the next day. "When are you coming to see me?" was his first question.

"Next weekend, when Lucy is away."

"Bring her and come this weekend."

"I'd love to, but can you survive a two-year-old in a one-bedroom apartment for two days?"

"Sure thing."

"Then get ready, Jim. We're coming." Lucy was thrilled even though she didn't understand.

"I'm a nairport," she told the cabman on Saturday morning when we left for the airport to see Jim.

"Uncle Dinny is Noo Yerk," she told the ticket agent for the flight. She clapped her hands with joy when "families with small children" were called and we went on ahead of everyone else.

"You know she has to sit in her seat with a seat belt for take-off and landing," the busy attendant told me when we were seated. Lucy smiled endearingly from my lap. The plane loaded. The doors shut. The engines roared. Lucy sat on my lap and then stood up in her seat, taking it all in with big eyes. When the plane moved, I put her in her seat and fastened the belt. She tugged at it.

"Take off, Mummy."

"No, Lucy. Remember, I told you . . ." My words were drowned in her outraged screams. I had heard children scream on airplanes before. I wanted to strangle every one of them. Why couldn't a reasonable child be trained properly? I didn't know why, but mine wasn't any better than the rest. It wasn't the cabin pressure. Lucy stopped screaming the moment the plane was in the air and I could unfasten her seat belt.

"Hi!" Lucy said, turning to greet the Oriental women sitting next to us. Lucy was treated to the cold and fishy glare of an outraged adult. Lucy had her revenge. She screamed all the way down during the landing. I staggered off the plane, limp. The scream of a child has been studied scientifically. It has the decibel volume of a jackhammer, at two feet.

"Was she the one that screamed?" inquired a chubby, dowdy matron in ill-fitting pants beside us in the taxi line. I cringed.

"I'm afraid so. She didn't like the seat belt."

The matronly lady nodded. "But you kept it on all the same. Some mothers wouldn't. Good for you." Her turn came. She rolled comfortably away in her cab. It was the nicest thing anyone could have said to me. I tried to be a good mother. After Lucy's screaming I felt I had failed. Lucy looked up at me after the lady had gone and smiled sheepishly. She understood.

"We're going to see Uncle Jimmy soon," I told Lucy when we arrived at his apartment. Lucy explored the elevator buttons and turned on the elevator alarm twice on our way up.

When Jim, beaming, whisked the door open, Lucy stepped back and stared at him. "Uncle Dinny in Noo Yerk in nairplane," she said slowly, trying to figure this all out. She walked up and took his hand. "Me Noo Yerk too." She had a lovely time.

"You know, she really is cute," said Jim the next morning as we stood on the curb trying to flag down a cab for our trip home.

"Me cute," said Lucy proudly. I picked her up and kissed her.

"Want me to come down for the trial?" Jim asked. "Moral support?"

"No." I kissed him good-bye. "It will all be horrible. I don't want anyone there."

The new trial date approached at last. My mother came back from England in plenty of time. She was rested and full of energy. I felt mine ebb as the trial date approached. Mr. Blackstone and I sat in his office the afternoon before the trial. We went over once again what I was to say. At the end he nodded, satisfied, and smiled at me, kindly.

"I hope, regardless of the judge, to keep the scope of this fairly restricted. You're a fit mother. Lucy is flourishing. I'd like to keep this brief, and civilized." His phone rang. It was the clerk of the court.

"Good." Mr. Blackstone hung up the phone. "We're on! We'll be assigned a judge tomorrow at nine-thirty. Can you and your mother meet me in the cafeteria at the courthouse at eight-thirty?"

"I'll be there," I said. "I'm going to try to persuade my mother not to come. It will worry her."

"Don't waste your breath," said Mr. Blackstone, escorting me to the door. "She strikes me as a fairly devoted mother herself."

The next day at nine-thirty in the assignment room, Mr. Blackstone, my mother, and I sat in a vast, crowded room filled with rows of bolted-down metal chairs and we waited. Mr. Blackstone was well known. One of the many lawyers who greeted him stayed around to chat.

"Ill prepared as usual?" He pointed to the stack of boxes on a cart that Mr. Blackstone had at his side. Those boxes contained the records of my life, since Lucy was born. "Your client is the mother?" The lawyer nodded at me amiably.

Mr. Blackstone inclined his head. "Yes."

"So you're hoping for anyone except Old Jeff, eh?" The other attorney turned to me. "Judge Jeff went through a divorce trial himself."

"We'll take anyone who gives us a fair hearing," said Mr. Blackstone noncommittally. At that moment our case was called. Mr. Blackstone strode to the desk, talked to the clerk, and returned, as calm as ever.

"Courtroom G. Judge Jeff," he told us. We followed him. The other attorney looked after us, shaking his head.

My mother looked at Mr. Blackstone anxiously. "Do you mean that a judge who has had a divorce is allowed to judge a divorce?"

Mr. Blackstone nodded at her in reply.

"But how can that be?" persisted my mother. "He couldn't be impartial. How is that allowed?"

Mr. Blackstone didn't reply. He strode on intently, like a Viking into the fray. He and I had arranged that my mother was not to be called as a witness. I didn't want her involved. She would hate it. Mr. Blackstone had agreed.

"Can I stay here to listen?" she asked when we entered the courtroom. "Yes, you won't be a witness so you can stay," said Mr. Blackstone. I wanted her to go. She took a seat at the back. I looked around the dim courtroom. To my surprise, other people had come to listen to the trial. I recognized them, ghosts of my ex's past. I walked with Mr. Blackstone to the table in front. My ex and his lawyer arrived, whispering busily to each other. There was a loud knock on the judges' door. My heart began to pound.

"All rise for the judge."

There were preliminary matters for the judge to settle before he got to us. We waited. Then, after a brief recess, the judge took up our case. There was an immediate decision to be made. My ex had requested that the trial be closed to the public and the record sealed. The judge would decide whether or not to grant this request. I didn't know if I wanted it open or not. A closed trial would protect Lucy from any publicity, but publicity seemed unlikely and it would not matter to her now. On the other hand, if my ex wanted the trial sealed, he must have a reason. So from a tactical point of view, an open trial would help me.

Mr. Blackstone stood up and explained his view on a sealed trial to the judge. My ex's lawyer, looking more sharklike than ever, stood up in turn. The judge, a forbidding mountain of black robes, ominous, silent, and brooding, listened impassively. When the lawyers were done, the judge looked slowly around the courtroom. "In this jurisdiction," he intoned, "if one, only one, of the two parties of a custody trial requests that the trial be sealed, then the law says that the trial must be sealed."

Mr. Blackstone leaned toward me. "We made our point, but the judge is correct. That is what the law says," he murmured in my ear.

The judge surveyed the courtroom. "Everyone will now leave except the plaintiff, the defendant, and the two parties' lawyers."

In a way it was for the best. My mother would not be able to watch me be put on trial as an unfit mother. There was a general shuffling. People rose to their feet. The judge called another recess. The bailiff ushered everyone from the courtroom. I walked my mother to the courtroom door. She was distraught. "Elizabeth! That judge. I can see it in his face. I don't like his face." I began to feel afraid. My mother had been a psychologist. Personality had been her profession for thirty years. If she thought the judge was wrong for me, what lay ahead? I could imagine Lucy staring at me in shock as I handed her over to her father, to live with him. She had a loving home with me — but a judge could do what he saw fit to do. And with the trial sealed, I would be forbidden even to discuss it.

I heard the bailiff turn the lock in the courtroom door. I rejoined Mr. Blackstone at the front.

He turned to me. "You realize that you cannot talk about

the trial even to your mother. It would be a technical violation of the judge's order." I nodded. The power of the order was such that if I ever told specifically what went on during the two weeks of the trial, I would be held in contempt of court and I might lose custody of Lucy even if I won the case. To this day, only those who were present know what it was like. For two weeks, in that dark, sealed courtroom, I was forced to submit to psychological torture. Only if the records are unsealed can anyone else really understand what it was like.

The trial began with my testimony. I reminded myself, over and over, that I was a respectable, working mother. I supported my child. I loved her. I did everything I could for her. I had no dark secrets in my past.

My father had been in the OSS during World War II. He had trained spies and he had developed techniques of interrogation to weed out the fit and the unfit spy. "Lock them in a room. Keep up the pressure," he used to say with a grin. "Everyone cracks, sooner or later." The trial for Lucy's custody went on day after day, week after week, dragging me back in time to my marriage. I had worked so hard and so long to put those memories behind me, and to build a new life for myself and a loving home for Lucy. I knew women who had lost custody simply because they worked. If a working woman projects the wrong image — hard or cold, aggressive or emotional, too busy or too timid or simply too ambitious, she may alienate a judge. A working woman may be offensive to a judge's idea of a mother and she may lose custody because of that. I wondered what image I created. I was a doctor. That put me at a disadvantage. Women doctors have a tough image. I was a surgeon. That was even worse. The image of a surgeon is brusque and masculine. I wasn't like that. I was kind and gentle and loving, but my career lacked a motherly image. Would I lose her for that?

My father is right. Everyone cracks. Under the pressure of the trial, I could feel my personality being torn apart. As the other side built its case, day after day after day, I felt battered and bruised and disgusted, as though their distorted image was becoming the real me. The judge looked down at me coldly. After a week, I could no longer look up at him. I dropped my head like a penitent. I felt doomed.

One evening, I turned to Mr. Blackstone at the end of my ex's testimony. "The judge has made up his mind," I said. "He can't wait to take Lucy away from me."

Mr. Blackstone nodded, imperturbably. "I will need your help, Elizabeth. We need to decide what rebuttal witnesses to call." He was asking me to do the impossible. My ex, the man I had loved, had destroyed me in the course of the trial. During my delivery of Lucy, I had learned my limits for physical torment. My ex, in court, had taught me my limits for psychological torment. I had cracked.

I drove home. Mrs. Taylor was feeding Lucy dinner. She looked up. "How's it going?" she asked.

I opened my mouth. I couldn't talk. I turned my head away from Lucy so she wouldn't see me cry. "I'm going to lose her." Mrs. Taylor put her arm around me. I rested my head on her shoulder, tears running down my face.

"Pray for me, Mrs. Taylor."

"Life is hard," she said. She, too, had suffered. "You must accept life."

"I know." I wiped my tears away. Could I accept a society that wrested a baby from its loving mother? Lucy climbed into my lap, wanting me to hold her. She knew something was wrong. I called Jim. If anyone could help us now, he could.

"How's it going, kid?" I heard his television in the background. It was a football night.

"I'm losing her, Jim," I said in a tight voice.

"Oh yeah?" He put down the phone. I heard the television click off. "Listen, want me to come and testify?"

"Would it help?" I asked dully.

"I'll call Blackstone. He's an ace. Give me his number," Jim ordered.

An hour later, Mr. Blackstone called me back. "Your brother will fly down tomorrow. I want to talk to your mother. Is she in?"

She happened to come home just then and spoke with him. The color drained from her face. "Of course I'll testify. Just tell me what to say."

I heard Mr. Blackstone rumble, "The truth."

The next day, Jim flew down from New York and waited with my mother outside the courtroom while I walked in with Mr. Blackstone. My ex's testimony concluded that morning. When Mr. Blackstone rose to cross-examine him, I began to cry, silently, just as I had the night before, silently. I had been reviled. I had been degraded until there was nothing left. I hoped for nothing but for the end to come. My mother and Jim were called in to testify. I was aware of them but I was in another world. Mr. Blackstone recalled me to the witness stand. He asked me a question. I got hold of myself. I opened my mouth to reply. To my horror, I didn't answer. I screamed and buried my face in my hands. My stumbling reply was incoherent. The opposing attorney rose and cross-examined me. When, physically, I couldn't answer anymore, the judge told me to step down. "Simple and civilized" had been Mr. Blackstone's goal. It had been anything but that. At last it was over and the judge recessed to consider his verdict. He returned, and began to talk. In a daze I heard him award me custody of Lucy. Mr. Blackstone clutched my arm in triumph. I covered my face with my hands, crying out loud. I felt grateful and I felt bitter. What civilization was this that so reviled a woman and then graciously condescended to give her what was rightfully hers — her child. Mr. Blackstone led me out of the courtroom and turned me over to my mother and to Jim, who were waiting in the hall.

"We won," he said. "I know what it was like for me. I can't

imagine what it was like for her. Be good to her," he told them. "She's had a rough time." My mother put her arm around me.

"We heard a scream out here," said Jim grimly. "Was that you?"

I nodded. My ex and his lawyer came up behind us. Jim shifted himself to shield me from them. "Of course she kept custody," he boomed out in his rich, confident voice. "What did I tell you? This was the biggest waste of time and money I ever heard of."

It was two hours before I could stop crying. I went to church that weekend. I had to leave because I started to cry and I couldn't stop. It was days before I could sleep. Just as motherhood had changed me, so had this. I had been the victim of a brutal psychological assault, condoned by the legal system but shown, by the verdict, to be without merit. Giving me Lucy, whose rightful place was with me, was no cure for the scars left by the courtroom. I was afraid I had been destroyed, afraid that the system had given her to me after letting me be scarred, battered, broken, and rendered unfit to be a mother.

⮑ *epilogue*

I WAS WRONG. The mythical phoenix rises from the ashes of its dead self. This had never made sense to me. Six months after the trial, I understood. For the first two months, I was in a state of shock. I had nightmares. I woke up shaking, drenched in sweat, in the middle of the night. I had to touch Lucy to be sure she was alive. If something reminded me of the trial, I had to cover my face with my hands and squeeze my eyes shut to force down the ugly memories. I was exhausted. I couldn't laugh. I knew I had been permanently changed.

Still, in three months I could feel my mind healing. Almost overnight, I recovered. I bounced with an energy that amazed me. At the end of an operation, I felt disappointed. I wanted more. I cleaned the house. I fixed the car. I swam. I rode. I dated. I laughed. Nothing, not even teaching Sunday school, could wear me out. My looks changed, physically. The wrinkles around my lips smoothed out. The circles under my eyes faded. My hair gleamed. The only thing that could tire me was Lucy, when she pleaded, "Dance with Muvver." She would lead me, running forty times around the living room. She made me jump, clap, fall down, play ring-around-the-rosy, and give her a ride on my back. By the end, I would be collapsed on the couch. Lucy would be ready to start again.

And Lucy — what about her? Mothers have to be strong. I had hoped that once the trial was over, she too would improve, but she seemed more unhappy, more fretful. I wondered if Mrs.

Taylor, who preferred babies and was bored as Lucy got older, was part of the problem. Mrs. Taylor left for another job and by a stroke of luck, Janice told me about Mrs. Rogers — a jolly, gifted, middle-aged mother of four daughters. I decided, at the same time, that Lucy needed more of me, as much as I could possibly give her. I shortened my working day. If I had to go out, she came with me. With rare exceptions, if she couldn't come with me, I didn't go. My friends got used to it. They didn't mind as much as I expected. Lucy was a sweetheart. No matter what her problems, as long as she had me and her grubby pink quilt along, she was content.

I decided that she and I needed help together and I set out on a search for a psychiatrist for her. Dr. Oakes had been nice but had little to offer. I didn't return to him. I saw one. He was condescending and didn't believe what I told him. I saw another, but my ex objected to him. I saw a third and a fourth, neither of them right for Lucy. I finally settled on the fifth psychiatrist I interviewed. At the end of the first appointment with me, he not only seemed to understand, but he seemed to understand Lucy's problems even more than I could. He had had a lot of experience with disturbed, young children. His office was set up for children. It was a jolly place and he was a genial teddy bear of a man. Lucy and I could trust him. Lucy liked him. "He's not your friend, Muvver. He's my friend," she announced after her first session with him. She had a lot to tell him. It all seemed to help, little by little. I knew she was getting better the night she appeared, screeching with laughter, "in my ballet, Muvver" — a costume that consisted of my shorts, a black skating skirt, and red leotard pulled around her waist, pink leg-warmers, and my brown heels. It was the first time in almost two years that she was hilariously happy.

Her Sunday-school teacher told me she was "coming out of her shell." So did her preschool teacher. She still has a long way to go. It is a pity, all the same. Lucy was meant to be a jolly, normal, secure little girl. I am utterly convinced that when a little child is taken from its loving mother, even for visitation, it may lose its natural protector and its security. Men are all very well, but nature didn't make men for rearing little children. Mothers are known to be worriers — but a hen clucking over its chicks is clucking for a purpose — protection — and its chicks need to hear the clucking to feel safe. The American courts by their insensitivity to the obvious are capable of doing terrible harm with the best intentions.

What the law did to my child is not right. The law has no special interest in Lucy or any child. I told judge after judge of Lucy's problems. My testimony was discounted because I was her mother. In this country the rights of minorities and of women, of the handicapped and of criminals are recognized, but children have no rights, because they have no vote. A mother, assuming she is not unfit by mental or physical handicaps, should be allowed the vote for her little child. As mothers we deserve guidelines. We need panels of social workers, teachers, psychiatrists, to advise parents and the courts as to what visitation at what age is safe and what may harm. Above all, it is time the judges, mostly men, are made to realize that a loving mother does not want a fight. She wants what is best for her child. And what would have happened to Lucy and to me if I hadn't had the good luck of my career and of my family? Many women marry the wrong man. Custody battles are increasingly common. My ex is clever, determined, and had money to spend in his effort to prove me unfit. I wasn't unfit — far from it — but what if I hadn't been able to afford the legal fees? I could have sent Lucy through college and medical school on the money I spent to keep custody. If I hadn't had that money? Most women don't. If I hadn't had Jim to advise me? Most women don't. If I hadn't had Mr. Blackstone? Most women don't. During the trial I met a legal secretary, a woman too young and too charming to look as sad as she did.

"Are you going to Mr. Blackstone?" she asked wistfully.

"Yes. He's excellent. Do you need a lawyer?" I asked.

"No. It's all over now."

I waited.

"I have the most lovely little four-year-old daughter," she continued. "My heart breaks for her. The judge gave custody to her father. A lot of judges don't like women. My husband had a super lawyer. He had the money. They made me look like dirt. And on my salary, what kind of a lawyer could I afford? If you can't afford the top, you don't have a prayer!"

I held out my hand to her. "I am so sorry."

"You're lucky," she said, without bitterness, "but I'm not finished yet. I don't know what I'll do, but I'm not letting my child be raised by the man who broke my jaw."

Most women are good. Most men are good, but many like to fight. By and large, women don't like fighting. The legal system, if it is to be just, should not, as it does now, permit a man to work off his aggression on the mother of his children. Divorce is sad. But a father who seeks to destroy the mother may harm the child.

National guidelines on child support (based on the parents' incomes) and on visitation (based on the children's ages) are desperately needed. Even with such guidelines, children will still be victims. We believe in the ideal of justice for all, but "justice" depends on money and luck. The American mother and her children will continue to suffer.